# STORIES FROM SCOTTSVILLE

## Tales of a Small Virginia Town

Ruth W. Klippstein

This book is dedicated to Barry Grove (1942-2019), one time mayor of Scottsville, member of the Scottsville Museum Board, and devoted citizen of the town. It was his inspiration that led to the production of this book.

# Table of Contents

# Table of Contents

# Prologue

This book is made up of a collection of articles written for the *Scottsville Monthly* newspaper between 2003 and 2017 by Ruth Klippstein. Thoroughly researched and skillfully written, they were eagerly received by local readers. After she ceased writing them, the idea arose that they should be preserved in some way.

Ruth Welch Klippstein was born in New York City and grew up in the suburban community of Valhalla, NY. In 1979 she came to Scottsville with her family at the end of a long trek around the country looking for a permanent home. They found one at Springtree Community near Scottsville, where she and her husband, Tom, still live. She became active in the Scottsville community, serving on the Arts Council and the Architectural Review Board. She also worked part-time at the Scottsville Library, where for years she beat the drum for the weekly children's story hour and arranged artistic displays, illustrating the library's many offerings. She graduated from Vassar College with a major in literature, and earned a Master's degree in library service from Columbia University.

The impetus for the book came from the late Jesse B. Grove III, professionally a lawyer but privately a "history buff." He looked forward each month to reading Ruth's articles as they appeared. Barry grew up in Fairfax VA, but spent his summers with his grandmother, Agnes Beal, in Scottsville. She ran a grocery on Valley Street, and Barry was pressed into service delivering groceries around town. Although he went on to practice law in California, he frequently returned to Scottsville to visit his parents, Jacqueline Beal and Jesse Grove, Jr., and eventually retired here with his wife, Leanne. He began this project which has been continued and completed by

1

his widow. Our only regret is that he could not have lived to see the book published.

Ruth Klippstein would like to acknowledge the generosity of the many people in the Scottsville area that she interviewed for these articles. She is in debt to their profound local knowledge and willingness to talk. Our thanks also to Kristin Freshwater for awesome technical assistance in converting faded newspaper pages into a real book.

# 1.

# Hermitage Farm's Living History

*John Walter and Anne (Fontaine) Nicholas with their daughters and friends, 1915.*

When the Piedmont was first being settled by whites, and Albemarle was huge Goochland County, the Court House Road ran north and south through the land encircled by the Horseshoe Bend. Taking that road today, now paved as Route 20, several miles south of Scottsville, brings you to the private lane leading to The Hermitage Farm.

This old property is bounded on the north by the Snowden lands, and on the east by the James, and includes the high ridge overlooking the river, extensive woods, still-rich farming lands in the bottom, and a possibly c. 1776 frame house set far into the property. This hidden Jeffersonian dwelling, once home to descendants of the prominent Nicholas family, has been a site of the developing social and political history of Virginia up until the present.

Richard L. Nicholas, originally of Scottsville, living now in Charlottesville, researched deeds and other legal documents, as well as his family's memories for his 2002 monograph, "Land Ownership in the Horseshoe Bend of Northern Buckingham County and Southern Albemarle County and the History of the Nicholas Family in That Area." While that sounds like a big bite of history, it doesn't include the original story and unfolding fortunes of the first Nicholas to come to Virginia, for which we can turn to a 1973 UVa history dissertation by Victor Dennis Golladay, "The Nicholas Family of Virginia, 1722-1820."

"They really were scoundrels at the start," current Hermitage owner Judy Brown says of Dr. George Nicholas, indicating information from Golladay's paper that chronicles Nicholas's 1722 death sentence in London for one instance of forgery and counterfeiting, commuted by the king after pleadings from Nicholas's father, to life-time banishment and transportation to the colony. Nicholas was able to parlay his family's background, Cambridge education, a "slight medical training"—no degree—into a new status in his new home. He set up as a doctor in Williamsburg, took care of the governor's family, and quickly, though with threats and objections from her family, married a rich widow, the eldest daughter, Elizabeth, of Robert "King" Carter. Nicholas had to work patiently and adroitly to overcome negative perceptions of his background, abilities, lack of money and land, but he had, as Golladay characterizes it, "a streak of brass in his personality" and won over most detractors. "Quite a stunning coup," says Golladay.

Nicholas set out to acquire land in 1729, the only way to cement wealth and position, and to rise in church and state politics. He did it as many others did, purchasing cheap property others had title to but did not improve, as required, by clearing and settling. Nicholas got land north of the James, and eventually owned more than 4,000 acres of southern Albemarle and an extra 1,600 acres on the south side of the James; this was to be the inheritance of his three sons. The father died young, in 1734; his wealth had been seriously depleted by losses in developing iron mines and foundries. The land was divided and eldest son, John, took the 1,600 acres in Buckingham, to the west of the Horseshoe Bend.

It was in 1832 that the family, spreading out (George, grandson of Dr. George had nine children), bought the land and house called Hermitage. The move was made by Nancy (Ann) Scott Nicholas, widow of George Nicholas, the grandson; he had lived at the family's Seven Islands property. She went with her six children to the existing house there, and the Nicholas family continued to live, Richard Nicholas writes, "in this vicinity for another 135 years, before the family land would be sold."—It went, in part, to Dr. L. R. Stinson in 1940, who sold the house and surrounding acreage in 1955 to James Gardner; in 1959 John Hartmann bought it; and in 1977 James and Judy Brown, of Ohio, purchased the home and 278 acres. (This information greatly simplifies the extensive work done by Richard Nicholas, available at the Albemarle Charlottesville Historical Society.)

The date and builder of the house at Hermitage farm is of "considerable uncertainty," Richard Nicholas writes; "tradition and presence of alleged chimney markers suggest that the house was built in 1776." The deductions Nicholas makes from existing land records and family lore is that it's possible the house, on land then owned by Hardin Perkins, was built by him, likely in 1776; it is recorded that he lived and died, probably around 1795, in that place. There's also the possibility that this is not correct—it is a deduction.

Like other older houses in our area, and grand homes built up and down the major rivers, there are several faces to the Hermitage. A contemporary guest arrives at what looks like a front façade, porticoed, with a circular drive and boxwoods. But that makes the opposite face, overlooking the river, the back, and the current family there often considers that the front yard. The shorter south facade, facing the old road going down to the James, was probably the original front doors. It is accented with a small porch and brick walks.

It's quiet here on a warm autumn afternoon, the river passing green and calm beyond the leased farm fields and by the trees; only a blue jay objects to our presence, and later a mockingbird needs to assert his primacy over the grass. Judy Brown and I enjoy the shade of the long porch she and Jim added to the east side of the house as she tells the recent stories of the Hermitage.

The Browns, of Toledo, Ohio, were looking for a place to settle in their retirement that would become a gathering place for their growing family: five far-flung children, ready to start families of their own. They imagined building a rustic cabin on the banks of some body of water, but "we ended up here."

Not rustic, but the Hermitage was considerably ruined, "a mess," Judy says, untenanted for several years, termites in one wall, standing water on the basement's dirt floor when it rained. They were fortunate to engage Floyd Johnson, a Scottsville architect and early proponent of historical restoration, to design the rehabilitation of the Hermitage, a ten-year project, carefully planned to keep the Browns out of debt as the work proceeded. Johnson, Judy says, "knew exactly what to do." Her husband was "really happy with Floyd," and enjoyed his dictatorial pronouncement, "It's going to be a long haul—but you may not do anything I don't approve or we're done!" The Browns didn't.

The first year was consumed by digging around the house and waterproofing it; the second was dedicated to the basement. The family would come for a month in both spring and fall, and especially loved gathering for Thanksgiving. The house, as it returned to a habitable state, was rented out for three years—with the proviso that the renters had to welcome workmen and vacate for Thanksgiving. It took fifteen years to bring the Hermitage to its current beautiful, finished state.

By then, there were 13 grandchildren. A spring-fed pond was dug so they could swim closer to the house, as well as in the river. A ping pong table went in the barn, a pool table in an outbuilding on the front—or is it back—lawn. Two outbuildings, the original purpose unknown but considered to have to do with slaves on the property, were lovingly converted into cozy bunks.

The Browns, while still working in Ohio, bought an old Appomattox tobacco curing shed from a man who found old log structures, bought and carefully deconstructed them, and sold them for a new life elsewhere. The Browns' main carpenter, Eric Starks, of McCormick Construction, did all the work: spent a year gathering appropriate stones on the property for the foundation; re-stacked and chinked the logs; added lovely wood floor and ceiling, and natural-shaped branches for banisters and curtain rods. Along the way, what they thought was a one-story building became two, and now uses water from the pond for the toilet and washing, and has electricity; heat comes from a wood stove. The old unit used to make smoke to cure the tobacco leaves is now under the sink. It's been a special retreat for the owners, tucked into the woods with "windows" cut through the tree line to the river; Judy will camp there with one grandson this Thanksgiving.

The Thanksgiving traditions grow with the family. Sometimes there's been a home-grown turkey; the meal is on Friday, allowing everyone time to travel to Virginia. There's always a family poker game. Last year they had a pie contest, splitting the grandkids into teams and letting each, secretly and feverishly, produce a pie. At the taste-off, one was declared the winner. "I think it was the one with pears," Judy says. If you want something special to eat, she adds, you make it. Her son Scott often "devils his sisters" by adding raisins and nuts to traditional bread stuffing. They're horrified; he has to whip up his own batch and a regular batch. The kitchen, Judy points out, has been enlarged twice to accommodate everyone; one addition, projecting from the house, necessitated—according to Floyd a porch over the rest of that façade, to keep things balanced.

Scott and all the children, who love the Hermitage, Judy says, will continue to have an impact on the old house and property. Scott extended and fenced the lawn facing the river and planted a maple and willow oak that have become graceful and large. Another son asked for a hot tub. Floyd Johnson said, "OK, but it has to be Jeffersonian," so a white octagon with Chinese wood work surrounds it, giving the look of a gazebo. Scott has also brought Tim Kaine to the Hermitage on numerous occasions; they and a group of three others at Harvard Law School became "blood brothers" and often gather there. The Secret Service had to inspect everything before Kaine's arrival when he was a U.S. Senator, Judy says.

We no longer get to Scottsville by riding horses up the Court House Road and taking the ferry across the river, but our social and political lives, our sense of connection to, and love for the land still grows along the James, and is preserved in its old houses.

*Originally published November 2016*

# 2.

# Encountering Spirits of the Past

Ah, good, my dears; you are the strong ones; the brave, willing to come again and listen to an antiquarian's tales. Quickly, close the door against the fretful wind; hear that rain thrown against the window panes. Put your feet up by the fire and we'll talk. You're not frightened, are you? Of course, it is quite near the night when the souls of the dead revisit their homes, but we'll placate the wandering spirits and evil imps, and enjoy a story. Well, of course, it's all true.

You remember I have told you recently of the old sounds that barely linger, mere whispers, in our frantic, modern atmosphere, sounds that used to make Scottsville feel safe and children secure in their trundle beds: the old steam train coming around the Horseshoe Bend, and later, twilight games of hide and seek by the depot, someone calling "all-ee, all-ee in free." The lamplighter clattering by, bringing a warm glow to the evening streets; the rustle of water on the weeds and rocks by the ferry landing; cows on the hill, impatiently waiting to be called in for the evening milking at Valmont.

But behind every sound of comfort and cheer, you must be aware, as well as I am, of the loss and despair of some torment or tragedy. Sad sounds, ominous sounds, sounds still echoing. In 1832, Peter Field Jefferson's eldest boy drowned while trying to cross the James in a canoe. Distracted Mr. Pereira, his bank business lost, leaping from the third floor balcony of the Travellers' Rest Hotel; the midnight murder of Richard Harrison, night telegrapher at the depot, in 1913. They've never solved that, you know. I'm sure that is an unquiet spirit.

There were cholera epidemics around Scottsville in 1832 and 1849, small pox in 1855 lasting into 1856. There have been floods and fires, farm accidents and poisonings. Where are the ghosts tonight of those workers who were paid ten cents an hour to run Emmett Thomas' tomato cannery on Drivers' Hill; the black community complete with restaurants and other services right downtown; and—so long ago--but I know you can hear them tonight, if you're very quiet—Yankee soldiers, the 18th Massachusetts Infantry, camped up and down the Hardware River, east of town, at Henry Kidd's mills, looking for food and any spoils of war left in their marauding path? One soldier was seen carrying away lace veils from a plantation house, another soldier wrote in a letter. The swampy country, rather than enemy bullets, claimed many a one, never to return home to the North.

Even longer ago, the lost courthouse of early Albemarle County, somewhere west of our growing community along the river, vanished, so that not even our early magistrates' ghosts—Scott, Fry, Cabell, Peter Jefferson—can find a trace of where they meted out the law to our early miscreants. And the sounds along the old, often sunken, roads, like the Old Stage Road, over Green Mountain from Scottsville to Charlottesville: a dark and hidden passage. Before it carried the imported materials to build the university, and wheat and other grains for market—ruts can still be seen in the rock on the bankside, made by those heavy wagons with their wooden wheels -- before this, you know, it was an Indian trail, used by those silent people who are no more in Scottsville, but who left their burial mounds in the area.

Are they quiet tonight? Now hush yourselves and settle down—poke the fire gently, please. I'll tell you something about the spirits that have been seen, or heard, or sensed right around us, in our dear old river town.

Mr. and Mrs. Lafayette Harris and their three daughters ran a millinery shop on Valley Street. The building is still the Harris Building, though the business is A. Scott Ward Realty. Starting in 1846, they sold bonnets, dress goods and shoes, even groceries.

The Harris girls worked hard to help, especially after their father died. But they grew up, as girls do; one married, and one, the youngest, fell in love with a man who came from Charlottesville, John Jones. You remember I told you about him: in happier times, he rode his bicycle, the sort with the high front wheel, down to Scottsville—the first to ever do so. That was in 1883. John Jones and Nannie Harris became engaged to marry, though John had to go away to find a job and save money for their life together. He never returned. He never wrote, and it's only by chance I learned he ended up in California managing an orange grove. Nannie, poor girl, soon died.

Those who should know, who live in the rooms above the old store, where Nanny and Lafayette and all the family lived, say they've heard footfalls on the steep back stairs; a man's perhaps, and a girl's, revisiting their home. Their presence has been felt in the rooms. The new people are very clear about this; the spirits are there.

And out on Albevanna Springs Road, east of town and into Fluvanna County—that's old land too, you know, old homes and waterways, old haunts and vanished settlements—Captain John B. Anderson once owned about a thousand acres near the Hardware River. His great-great granddaughter, Eileen Brackin, now of Newport News, and gatherer of her family's history and heritage, told me the following story. I believe it; you will, too.

Anderson, his grandson-in-law Thomas Cleveland Sadler wrote, "was very rough spoken and might scare you to death if you did not know him....," but he was a hard-working, honest man. He died in 1911. Eventually his house was purchased by the Talbot family, who began to renovate it closer to its original form. One day, as Eileen tells it, the young daughter was missing for a while. When located, she told her mother, "I've been down in the cellar talking to my new friend." "What did you talk about? What did he look like? What was his name?," Shelia Talbot inquired. "He had a long beard, and his name is Anderson. He built our house, and he said he was glad we were fixing it up."

Another day, the girl told Sheila she was outside playing with her "other mother." "I'm your only mother," Sheila responded, and her daughter described the woman as having dark skin, and said they were playing on a pile of lumber left from taking down slave quarters on the property. Eileen said Captain Anderson owned about 24 slaves, and she remembers the wood pile herself. One of the women, called Mammy, saved Eileen's great-aunt by wet nursing her.

And down along the James, in that almost-vanished town of Howardsville, the old house named Llanarth—"an emissary from another time," they call it, has recently had a new sighting of the benign spirit who in life never wanted to leave there. Hidden in the woods now, the house was purchased by a son of the owner in 1871; George Walker Gilmer, CSA veteran, was a successful farmer, inventor, and father of eight children. But we speak now of the daughter Edmonia Gilmer, known at the latter end of her long life as Miss Monney. She lived happily at her ancestral place, though before she reached her final age of 105, her family took her off to a nursing home. "She was dragged kicking and screaming," the current owner of Llanarth, Kathryne Finn, was told; she said she wanted to die there. Miss Monney, Kathryne feels sure, is drawn to the house, drawn to Kathryne's cats; she has felt her presence over the years in the house, but mainly in the room Kathryne and her cats usually inhabit. It's a sensation of strangeness—others have felt it, too, and doors that were closed stand open, and open doors shut mysteriously.

But do not think all this is long ago, my young ones; no, just recently, a helper in the house, making a bed upstairs, saw the figure of a white-haired woman in the mirror. "Oh, what's Kathryne doing upstairs?" this hard-working, down-to-earth woman thought while smoothing out the sheets. She mentioned it to Kathryne later. "No," said Kathryne, "I was not upstairs. Miss Monney is a presence," she said, "but her good heart makes her a benevolent one."

Now listen to the clock strike; it's very late and you must be going if you do not want to meet spirits in the streets and alleys tonight. Remember, they will all be about for the Museum's *Twilight Tours through History*, October 22, 6-8, and October 23, 5-7; the walking tours take an hour and leave the Museum every twenty minutes. Buy a ticket at the Scottsville Museum for the night you choose, or get one online. Etta Harris, who shot at her beau will be there; an Irish washerwomen from the canal boat days, a Civil War soldier; and, most famous and dire of all, the Moon ghost.

Do be careful.

*Originally published October 2016*

# 3.

# The Bottled Goods of Scottsville's Past

I have returned to talk to two of the important keepers of Scottsville memories, whose efforts to build and consolidate the historical record of our town have helped so much. Jack Hamner, who lives in the area, was born in Scottsville, became a collector of arrowheads early, then buried metal pieces and other material artifacts that give weight and texture to our stories. Keith Van Allen is in Richmond, caring for his 100-year old mother, Mollie, daughter of Scottsville-born architect and inventor, and designer of Victory Hall, D. Wiley Anderson.

*Milk bottles from Snowden Dairy*

Jack Hamner has a long history of collecting glass bottles of Scottsville-based products. Some of these bottles he found under the old Tavern on Main Street when he lived in that historic, and then drafty, structure years ago. His collection was somewhat depleted upon the birth of his first child, when his wife Ann suggested either the bottles went or she would. He's kept a few. Jack says, "For a small town, Scottsville has produced an impressive array of bottling companies. While many of the bottles themselves were likely produced elsewhere, at least half a dozen (including variations), boast "Scottsville, Virginia" embossed on them. There were also numerous bottles with paper labels put on by local apothecaries, drug stores, spring water bottlers, and perhaps others.

"The earliest known embossed Scottsville bottles," Jack continues, "were designed to contain horse liniment, although this Little's White Oil was purported to benefit man as well as beast. This patent formula, invented by C.E. Little of New York State, was produced as early as 1837 and "although the elixir itself would remain virtually unchanged, the bottles underwent many transformations, from free-blown to machine-made with cork closures to screw top," Jack says. The Little brothers, C.E. and T.W., on a selling trip through the South, were impressed by Scottsville's potential as a transportation hub and moved here in 1842; they became involved in many businesses, running a grocery, a wool carding factory, and a broom factory. "Bottles of Little's White Oil and their contents probably had the longest life span of any Scottsville product," Jack says, being sold throughout 23 states, "making an impressive run from the mid- 1800s to possibly the 1940s or '50s. All bottle variations were either aqua or clear flint glass and were embossed 'Little's White Oil, Scottsville, Virginia.'"

An old pamphlet Jack owns extols the virtues of this mysterious concoction for ring worm, sprains and rheumatism, as well as any horse ailment. According to this advertisement, the oil was "prepared and sold by W. D. Hart, of this place." The testimonial of John S. Martin in 1848 (brother of U.S. Senator Thomas Staples Martin and, at this time, owner of Cliffside) says that after a 200-mile trip on his "very much galled horse," the liniment healed the animal quickly. People from other states wrote about its "almost miraculous" qualities—possibly a reason for its remarkable longevity, Jack thinks. "Had not the automobile overtaken the horse as the vehicle of choice, we might perhaps still be rubbing Little's White Oil on our horses as well as ourselves!"

The next container to appear, Jack says, was a clear or sun-colored amethyst strap-sided whiskey bottle embossed "Scottsville Dispensary, Scottsville, Va." This bottle came in half-pints, pints, and (rarely) quarts. There are at least two lettering variations as well as one plain example with a paper label which reads "Gibson Pure Rye Whiskey"— (and another called "Old Jasper," as seen in the Scottsville Museum) by "Scottsville Dispensary, Scottsville, Va." Although absolute dates of production of this whiskey are not known, Jack's educated guess would be from the late 1800s up until the time of Prohibition. The original dispensary building was a large brick structure on the site of the present day Scottsville Police Department building, the former Silver Grill. The brick structure was bought by Dr. Percy Harris and the bricks re-used to construct his residence, still sitting on a rise above a rock wall between Dorrier Park and the Scottsville School Apartments.

With the arrival of the twentieth century in Scottsville came the advent of no fewer than four new bottled products, Jack says— milk from two dairies, spring water, and a cola drink. "Although exact dates are once again hard to establish, all four of these new companies probably came into being more or less simultaneously around the second decade of this new century."

Valmont Dairy was a large farm just northwest of Scottsville; its rolling green hills overlook the James River. It boasted a large herd of golden Guernsey cows, whose milk was bottled on site and delivered throughout the community by a fleet of trucks driven by local men. Valmont was by far the most widely promoted dairy of the Scottsville area. Jack has collected many advertisements, calendars, giveaways, and photographs; these can still be found at sales on occasion. The dairy changed hands many times; it was owned by William Moon, Peyton Harrison, the Gantt family, and finally, Dr. R. L. Stinson.

Valmont bottles came in half-pints, pints and quarts, and a few lettering variations, although these, Jack says, were limited in nature. One interesting side note is that Scottsville was incorrectly spelled "Scottesville" on a precious few half-pint bottles. Evidently this mistake was soon corrected, as Jack has only one example with this error.

The other, but much less known dairy with the embossed Scottsville name, Jack says, was Snowden Dairy, just across the James River in Buckingham County. Bottles have been found in pints and quarts, but are quite scarce. Just as scarce is concrete data concerning this quaint dairy. Worth noting while discussing local dairies is the herd at Fair View Farm on the east side of Route 20, north of town. It was operated by Jack Manahan's father. Milk produced there was sold in bulk to Monticello Dairy of Charlottesville, who marketed it under their franchise.

Another example in the twentieth century lineup of Scottsville bottles is a soft drink, "Christo Cola—The Nation's Joy Drink." "Scottsville, Va." is embossed on the bottom of the bottle. Jack says, "I have never tasted it, but my best guess would be that it is much like Coke or Pepsi." Christo Cola was bottled by Dr. Harris, who lived in the West Main Street home constructed of Scottsville Dispensary brick.

Before Dr. Harris bottled the drink in recycled bottles, the glass had to be thoroughly cleaned. "That task was awarded to my father," Jack says, "who was a young but enterprising boy in about 1911. Dr. Harris would prepare a huge vat, fill it with water and heaven knows what else, and sink the used bottles down into it. My father's job, paid at something like a penny a bottle, was to remove all old chewing gum, flies, ants, straws, cigarette butts, bees, small mice, and whatever else may have found its way into these bottles. He then washed them with soap and water, rinsed, and maybe even sterilized them (but I doubt it!). They were then ready to be refilled, although where this happened I don't know. Neither do I know any more about this business; I own just a single Scottsville Christo Cola bottle."

Jack tells us that "just southeast of Scottsville, on Albevanna Spring Road, there stands a wonderful spring which produced an extraordinary water that not only tasted great but many believed possessed amazing curative powers. The water, called Ponce de Leon, was bottled and sold in large aqua glass bottles, in wooden crates, as well as paper-labelled quarts, but no embossed examples are known to exist. Savvy marketing strategies were employed by this company, as evidenced by extensive pamphlets, fliers, and even

William Burgess stereo postcards," one of which shows the elite young of Scottsville in turn-of-the-century clothing, enjoying a summer outing to the spring.

One advertisement lists the water's benefits for complexion, stomach, and kidneys. Testimonials include B.L. Dillard's, a Scottsville doctor, who said he recommends it to patients for bladder and kidney troubles; one "can see no reason," he writes, "why the Albevanna Springs should not become very popular as a health resort." In 1934, Dr. Percy Harris of Scottsville also gave an endorsement for the water, which contains measurable calcium, iron, magnesium, potassium, silica and other elements.

Keith Van Allen has coordinated much of the Anderson family history, gathering memories from the extensive and ebullient clan. Their quick wit and playfulness are evident in the stories, as well as strong ties to each other. Mollie Anderson, at 100, Keith says, "is always talking about the spring; and we all do. It's so central to the soul of the family."

"Mollie remembers the pond and picnic table by it, Papa Anderson [her father D. Wiley, 1864-1940] fishing for frogs which Mama would cook for him." The family had lively reunions over the years at the Albevanna Springs house, Keith says, where D. Wiley Anderson had developed the spring, built a bottling house by the road, and was selling Albevanna spring water in Charlottesville and Richmond as early as 1911. Thomas Staples Martin once took some, a Congressional Record notes, to distribute at the Senate.

American springs' rise to fame followed the practice of the well-to-do in Europe "taking the waters." A family in Maine started bottling the water that became known as Poland Springs in 1845; Saratoga Springs in New York was selling seven million bottles a year by 1856. Popularity was fueled by new glass-making techniques in the early nineteenth century that made the bottles more practical and affordable. Ponce de Leon water was analyzed as having .01 ppm of lithium. Natural lithia springs are rare in Virginia, though one, Wildwood, was developed north of Palmyra in the early twentieth century, when that area was reached by the Virginia Airline Railroad. Lithium bicarbonate was elsewhere added to water to bottle.

Lithium's "neuropathic abilities" came into prominence after medical studies in the mid-twentieth century.

D. Wiley Anderson could bank on the good taste of his spring water. Scottsvillians came to the place on a weekly basis to get it. D. Wiley, Keith says, built a special rack for his truck to carry the bottles further afield, and eventually sold Ponce de Leon water in North Carolina, Ohio, and New York up until the mid- 1930s.

The architect and inventor had bigger schemes, too, and in September, 1920, ran an ad in a commercial periodical, "Doorways," for his property: "'Albevanna Ponce de Leon Spring,' eight room dwelling, 200 acres of land, beautifully situated near Scottsville, Virginia.... Spring contains wonderful healing and other therapeutic properties, now ready for development. Just the place for a Hotel-Sanitarium; or the most exquisite home for a party of wealth desiring a health location...with exclusiveness; numerous streams and picturesque surroundings. Nothing else like it to be found. Price $50,000."

But when no "party of wealth" stepped forward, Anderson, in 1923, was drawing up his own plans for "the Albevanna Hotel....and Pleasure Resort." This ambitious scheme was never achieved, but has left memories and a few tangible reminders in the form of glass bottles. As Jack sums it up, "Horse liniment, whiskey, water, milk, cola, all bottled, marketed, and sold right in and around the small town of Scottsville. I know of no other towns the size of ours that can claim such a variety of bottled goods with their own hometown logo embossed on them. As we peer into these long retired Scottsville vessels one final time, we can't help but see the reflection of a diverse and proud past, and, we can hope, a bright future."

*Originally published September 2016*

## 4.

# Memories of the Town of Warren and the Whitted Family

The town of Warren, as envisioned by Wilson Cary Nicholas—"the wealthiest person in Albemarle County in 1800," according to K. Edward Lay's *Architecture of Jefferson Country* with "more than 7,700 acres of land, 97 slaves, and 58 horses," more than anyone else in the county—was to be a town of great importance and a major transportation terminus. Nicholas' grandfather first patented the land along the James, about five miles up-river from Scottsville, in 1729; it thrived through the shipping of wheat on river and canal.

As the town grew, it added a tavern, gristmill, distillery, and blacksmith shop. A friend of Thomas Jefferson's and governor of Virginia from 1814-1816, Nicholas fought hard for the supremacy of Warren, but the government's 1817 decision to route Rockfish Turnpike to Scottsville, with its wheat and tobacco warehouses and tolls, was the end of the battle and culmination of the "bitter feud" between the Scott family and Nicholas, according to John Hammond Moore's *Albemarle, Jefferson's County, 1727-1976.*

Memories still cluster around Warren, with its one main road leading between the homes, old and new, across the railroad tracks, and down through woods beside Ballinger's Creek to the James, once the site of the Warren ferry. A generation ago there was at least one other major landmark still extant, the Whitted store and post office just west of the tracks.

Clarence Whitted and his wife Mary "Willie" Gardner Whitted ran C.A. Whitted and Company, her grandfather William Jones' general store. Jones had come from Buckingham County and bought out William Staton in the 1880s, Willie said in a June, 1984, unnamed newspaper interview from the Charlottesville-Albemarle Historical Society. Staton was one of a long line of Warren store keepers and post- masters, as was Whitted after him. The post office, which had originally operated in a different store east of the tracks, was established around April, 1796. After 166 years, it was closed in September of 1962, and made a rural branch of the Scottsville post office. Clarence served from 1940 until he died in the winter of 1961; Willie was clerk and assistant post master, though she never became post master.

Bob Spencer remembers Clarence and Willie as "very staunch, prominent members of the Scottsville Baptist Church." Clarence, he says, was superintendent of the Sunday school; he also was a teacher of the men's Bible class and chair of the board of deacons, as well as a Mason. The Whitteds had three daughters, Margaret, Patricia, and

Clare-Marie. Margaret Whitted Burruss, who lives in Charlottesville, recently said that her parents instilled in them strong moral values, and the weekly trip to Sunday school was eagerly anticipated.

Willie was lively, full of stories about growing up in the early twentieth century in Warren, when she and her brother would deliver groceries for their father by horse and buggy. Their elementary schooling took place at nearby Pierson Scott's house, now burned, with their aunt Nelly Gardner as teacher. "A sleigh used to come in the winter and take us to school at Donegal Farm [originally called Oakland, built for his daughter by Wilson Cary Nicholas]—two horses with bells on," she remembers in the 1984 interview. "We put heavy lap robes over us, and heated bricks and irons wrapped in old woolen things to warm our feet. The winters were so bad then that the snow would drift over the fences. People would...burn the outhouses to keep warm." Willie finished her schooling at Scottsville High School, then taught first, second, and third grades in Howardsville.

Willie's father once owned the ferry at Warren. It had been established in colonial times, and Willie said the stones used to build Nicholas' tavern were ferried across the river from Buckingham. "My father built the boat. It was a flat boat that carried three cars; Mr. Gardner hired a ferryman for $100 a month." The toll then was 25 cents for vehicles, 5 cents for pedestrians. "Mrs. Whitted said no toll was charged if you were coming across to the store" her father ran [*Daily Progress*, February 23, 1968]. The state took over the ferry in 1935. In 1967, according to this same article by Allen Hale, it carried 1,262 cars, 612 pickups, 71 trucks, and 226 pedestrians. The flood from Hurricane Camille probably destroyed the ferry, though the line high across the river, used by the ferrymen to help direct the current in pushing the boat, is still in place.

Floods were a recurring menace in Warren, a fact of life each spring. Willie and Clarence's house, so close to the river and along two creeks, was often under water up to the first floor. One year, Margaret says, the dam on the Ballinger Creek mill pond broke, and the rush of the flood caught up lumber and railroad ties her father stored and sold, further threatening the house. "That one was ankle-deep on the first floor," Margaret says, and her father, who'd been away at the time, had to be restrained from trying to cross the flood to get to his family. One year Willie lost all her chickens, which had been setting on eggs, and the girls waded into the flood to try to save them. After she sold her house, Willie built a small brick home on higher ground.

*W.E. Burgess postcard, early 20th c.*

The railroad supplied its own dangers. The depot had been built on the east side, uphill of the tracks, and was over the old James River and Kanawha Canal. In 1913, Boyce Loving reported in a September 28, 1962, *Daily Progress* article on the closing of Whitted's store, 20 loaded coal cars derailed in front of the building. Willie was twelve years old and said "something told me just before to get back." Coal began pouring through the door; she got a small injury to her knee, and two men in the store "found themselves standing in coal up to their waists."

In 1934 two engines collided head on near the store and

depot. All but two cars of the trains derailed. Those were standing on the tracks directly in front of the store. Margaret vividly recalls the accident, the "terrible noise" in the night, the awful awareness that, except for providence, those two cars would have tipped over and torn down the house. Edna Anderson, who grew up nearby on half of Governor Nicholas' Mt. Warren property, recalls an incident when Mrs. Gardner, Willie's mother who lived with them, was sitting in the afternoon shade on the front porch when a rail car tipped off the tracks and coal rushed down the hill and broke one of her knees. "Everyone was picking up coal for quite a while!"

In the 1940s and '50s the Whitted store was, according to Edna Anderson, "a gathering place. Warren was a real community then—everyone looked out for everyone else." She thinks the store was a "tremendous help" to the surrounding area—railroad workers, rural folks who could drive there for groceries, and "One-Egg Tony," a man whose habit it was to bring in an egg from his hens' nests to trade for a piece of candy. Other people traded their groceries for produce and farm products. "It was a typical country store—someone in a chair leaning back against the counter, pot-bellied stove, busy but not hyperactive," remembers Anne Moore Foster.

Margaret characterizes Warren as a small hamlet, quiet and a safe place to grow up. "Let's go 'way back back," she says, starting her stories. "People depended on and helped one another." She worked in the store when she was old enough, and recalls the cold-water soda bottle dispenser, and the pleasure in the community when the Whitteds got a freezer and could sell ice cream and popsicles—"quite a treat!" Besides playing with other children, their only entertainment was going to the movies in Scottsville. One special time she and three friends rode horses to town and tied them up outside during the show.

The Whitteds grew what they ate, and Willie loved to fish. Margaret recalls that in the evenings she would bait hooks with pieces of Ivory soap and tie the lines to a nearby bush. In the mornings she'd haul in the lines to gather "a whole mess of catfish." They bought clothing from catalogs, and Margaret says she "thought it would be very nice to go to Charlottesville and not go to the dentist." Margaret went to Mary Washington College, majoring in business, and helped later with the books for the store. She taught school in Charlottesville and married a man she met there; her wedding was at Donegal, as Pierson Scott and Clarence Whitted had kept up their special friendship.

Clarence Whitted, who usually had a cigar in his mouth, according to Tom Stargell, would frighten and delight youngsters with his trick of pushing out his complete set of false teeth at them. He carried "a little bit of everything," Edna Anderson says: "shoes, work pants, red union suits." Marshall Burruss, Margaret Whitted's son, recalls the "glass-fronted case with old-time candies like Mary Janes. Grandfather would set me up on his knees and I'd point to what I wanted—and he'd say, 'No, you can only have one.'" In various outbuildings Clarence sold seed and other farm needs.

Willie "enjoyed people, enjoyed life," according to Margaret. She was a "good story teller and had lots to tell." Margaret recalls her as active in the community, trying "to put Warren on the map." Later in life, driving her car, people couldn't see her behind the wheel, due to her short stature. "If you don't see anyone, get out of the way," they'd say; "It's Miss Willie."

Edna and her sister Paige would spend playtime with Tricia Whitted, and Edna fondly remembers walking the two miles to the store on Saturdays, sometimes staying overnight. Mrs. Gardner, Willie's mother who lived with them, and lived to be over 100, would read them bedtime stories until one by one the girls fell asleep.

Anne Moore Foster, who also says Warren "was a good place to grow up in," calls the post office/store "the cultural hub of Warren." She remembers being there while her parents got mail and bought what they needed; she walked around the porches to find a secret place where a hammock was strung between two big trees. "I'd think I was in heaven," she says, especially when her father treated her to a small grape drink, her favorite. Her parents bought groceries there, including she thinks, fresh meat at a butcher counter, until, like so many, they learned the ease of going to Charlottesville. Anne says the Whitteds had a gas pump along the road to the river— Whitted grandson Marshall Burruss says it was Esso gas; and Clarence had a small office between the store and residence part of the house. Willie would host home demonstration meetings there for the neighborhood women.

Anne Moore Foster's brother Bill worked at the depot, and she recalls him having a pole with a string across the end to which he'd attach notices for the train man to grab as the train made its way through Warren. Gene Harding thinks the mail would be moved the same way, in a bag on a forked stick, with the trainman throwing off the incoming mail in sacks. The depot, store, and the neighbors were all on the same party line, Anne says, increasing the sense of neighborhood—and knowing what everyone was up to.

Willlie sold the Whitted place at auction in 1962 to a large family. It was for sale again in 1979 when Tom and Marianne Ramsden (she is the former Scottsville branch library head) were "yearning for a big, old and rambling house with some acreage where we could live off the land and our own labor and where the kids could grow up. We went to take a look. It was huge (14 rooms), it was old (1870 or thereabouts), it was rambling (with extensions tacked on here and there with no discernible plan)." That first look, Marianne says, was "thwarted by the loud racket of a train barreling by blowing its horn. 'Was it coming inside?'—Sure sounded like it, but we shouldn't have been so surprised with the tracks 10 feet from the house. We shook our heads. No way would we buy that house. "After mentally listing all the great assets, we changed our minds. Three sheds, six fertile acres, two streams, four porches, seven doors leading to as many outside locations. One very important advantage was the huge workshop. The price was ridiculously low and we had the cash for it. That was good, as no bank would ever finance it; there was no heat, no air conditioning, power outlets were few, a rudimentary bathroom with an iffy septic system, and possibly a leaky roof. No insulation...but the place won us over. We called it 'The Old House.' It's the only place we've lived we ever gave a name. Sometimes we say: 'That house was magical.'

"After months of cleaning, repairing, painting, and turning the power on, we moved in. Building the memories began. The parties we had—such a big house and a large contingent of friends had to be paired. Loud music and wild dancing were not bothering neighbors—they were quite a distance away. Often guests spent the night and told harrowing tales about trains trying to come into their room. Sometimes a very long train simply gave up and stopped in front of the house, effectively blocking the crossing. Sometimes for hours. Usually it didn't matter—the kids counted cars, read the logos, put bets on when it would start up with the familiar clatter and banging. Now and then it did matter, especially when guests really wanted to go home and we, the hosts, really, really wanted them gone. Or right before the kids stepped off the school bus. The one forbidden activity was to crawl under the train.

"The decks and porches served us well at all times. The back deck overlooked one of the tree-lined creeks where, as the evening went on, we saw the lightning bugs dance to the music. The front porch was a great place to sit in the ubiquitous rocking chairs and watch whatever or whoever passed by. Neighbors stopped to chat, cars drove slowly by often with inner tubes stacked high. Once a very sunburnt couple came straggling up from the river. They had misjudged the distance from Howardsville to Scottsville, misjudged how low water levels could make the trip seem eternal, and had left their sunscreen at home. We gave them shelter, water, aloe lotion, and a ride to their car.

"Regularly on a Sunday morning a group of fishermen stopped by to ask for a ride upriver where they would slowly float down to Warren. We received fish, offers for free dry cleaning by a Charlottesville business man, and money, which we refused for a few weeks, but then accepted when we realized how often our Sunday mornings would interrupt sleep and recuperation from Saturday's revelry. Tom named the two resident black snakes George and Martha. They lived in the basement, but came upstairs now and then just to scare the **** out of Marianne by resting curled up on a stack of towels. Another black snake wrapped itself around Tom's waist as he evicted it from the hen house.

"We kept goats: Annie, Holly, and Lars—the yellow slit-eyed menace. Tom and son David did all the milking, with Deya (at age three) helping out now and then. Marianne processed the milk, sometimes into yogurt, cottage cheese or soft chevre rolled in herbs or cracked pepper. Lars was her sworn enemy and would narrow his eyes and charge at her, horns lowered, at any opportunity. That and escaping the fenced area with the skill of Houdini were his reasons for existing; having been castrated shortly after birth he did the ladies no good. His days ended tragically on the railroad tracks.

"The floods were, at this point, only interesting and exciting. We'd put a cinder block at the water level on the road and move it up until finally the water began to recede. Then came the 1985 'Election Day' flood that didn't recede for days and days. We moved what we could upstairs, sent our daughter to friends, and thought we could sleep in the sofa bed downstairs. However, when we could hear gurgling water from the basement we left through the one door not blocked by water. After that flood some of the magic left.

"After eight years of magical living we sold The Old House, but we still call it a magical place. There we grew our own food, tapped maple trees for syrup, kept bees, chickens, and goats, and watched the children grow. We talk about it and often find it in our dreams. We remember all the good parts."

The Whitted place became a rental property, and without the love and attention of a permanent resident family, deteriorated and finally burned down. Two years ago one could still wander around the foundations; now everything is vines, trees, and poison ivy. As Marshall Burruss says, "It was so long ago." But Warren and the James River roll on, leaving their mark on our time and place.

*Originally published August 2016*

# 5.

# Exploring the History of
# the Rock House

Large land holdings of wealthy families expanding west from the Tidewater characterize the early white settlement of southern Albemarle County and Scottsville. As with Edward Scott of Goochland County, who patented 550 acres in 1732 along Totier Creek, north of the James River—then identified as the Fluvanna in the Patent Books—these owners probably never visited their rolling green acres, instead sending overseers and slaves to create the farms that would secure their property. The second and third generations bought more land and came to stay.

These early families, including Thomas Meriwether's and John Lewis' in our area, strengthened their economic power with positions of importance in the early church and local government. Around Scottsville, St. Anne's Parish was the "sole religious unit" when the vestry first met in 1742, according to John H. Moore's *Albemarle, Jefferson's Country*. All members were representatives of "the landed gentry."

Within St. Anne's Parish, to the west of town, large farms developed in the eighteenth century which still show remnants today—though no real memory of their early time exists. When we're lucky, we can find their names on old maps and deeds. So it is with Allendale and Mountain View, Valmont and Scottlands, and the small home called the Rock House on Langhorne Rd.

The old property boundaries have changed so often it is difficult to trace them in the county's deed books, when those are available to see. The Rock House has been owned by Nancy and Harry Koenig since 1986; Nancy kindly offered her time to explain what she knows of it and the surrounding land. Nancy thinks the site of the original Allendale house was on a small rise just west of the Koenig's barn. Sheep they kept for years "used to turn up brick after brick," she says. Their own house clearly sports its date on the riser of the top step under the porch: May 1930. The house is made of rock, not dressed or cut stone. Nancy shows a matching pile of rocks she's planning to use for a garden wall. Nearby Rock Castle Creek, flowing into the Totier, suggests the rock-filled nature of the surrounding region. Frank A. Massie's 1907 map of southern Albemarle County labels it "Mesozoic Area," with the rock called Rock Castle Conglomerate. Closer to the river, the prevailing characteristic is Jurassic Brownstone and Red Sandstone.

The names of the house's builders are not yet discovered, but it was probably they who incised their initials in a wooden lintel over the rear door, now leading from the enclosed porch to the main house: "1930, S + J + H," with a stylishly carved hand, finger pointing to the writing, shirt sleeve neatly cuffed. "It might have been brothers. They loved this place," Nancy says, and "must have had so much fun" making it.

The architectural style is Craftsman, the "dominant style for smaller houses built throughout the country during the period of around 1905 until the early 1920s," according to Virginia and Lee McAlester in *Field Guide to American Houses*. Developed in southern California, the Craftsman style spread by pattern books and popular magazines. "Few were built after 1930." The rock house's gable-peaked, deeply sloping roof creates wide porches typical of the style. Heavy columns underpin the front porch facing north to Green Mountain. Their lower sections are rock, upper are brick, and while the McAlesters say such combinations of materials are frequent in Craftsman columns, Nancy has been told by a student of architecture they are unique for this area. The *Field Guide* states that "probably 90 percent of American houses use a wooden structural system," though European immigrants brought with them "intimate knowledge of masonry techniques" from vernacular architecture in England, France, and the Netherlands.

The unshaped rock of this house is mortared thickly with concrete. There are two side chimneys and a front gable for the upper story. The house originally had four rooms on the first floor, two on the second. The original living room floor boards are the narrow-cut style of the Depression. Various walls have been removed to alter the downstairs configuration.

Another significant change in the house was the decision, in the late 1950s or early '60s, to paint the exterior white. Mary Frances McCormick, who has always lived at nearby Hillside farm, says her "Daddy and Granddaddy were hired to do the job, and hated it each time they painted over a rock." (Due to the difficulties of following the particular property the Rock House is on through the many deeds, I can only say it is possible the owner at this time was DeBrew [also styled DeBruce] Willis and his wife Grace Bates Spangler. Owners before them were likely Lindsay Pitts and his wife Hester McFarlane Pitts. There seems to have been some speculating, with quick turnarounds of the property at this time.) Another neighbor, Johnny

Layne, says no one ever liked that paint job. But Sam Spangler, an owner of the house in the mid-1980s, notes "it must have been very good paint because it was 60 years ago."

We do know that Koenigs bought the Rock House from Doris and Allen Cobb; the deed says they were from Fredericksburg. B.L. Powell, a neighbor of 41 years, recalls that Cobb had known "a lot about the house," and was responsible for some of the interior remodeling, including, as Nancy Koenig points out, the added insulation that results in the deep window recesses.

The Allmans then built a house behind it, later lived in by Boog and Estelle Heath, that has since burned. Norma was in college at the time, not living at home, but remembers it as "a lovely home, seemingly family-built" in a "beautiful setting. Because it was rock, in summer it was very comfortable, especially the back screened porch, with tall trees all around." The magnificent white oaks, an ash and mulberry are main features of the place now.

Sam Spangler remembers what his family always identified as a "squirrel painted on the east side of the house about three feet off the ground." The Koenigs have added metal cellar doors there, but black lines are still visible that may be a squirrel, a tree, perhaps a dog. Stare at the rock and the paint long enough and you'll see a variety of designs.

Other animals were firmly identified with the house. When the Koenigs moved in and Nancy was first shopping at the IGA, she told the clerk she lived at the Rock House. "Oh," the clerk said, "you know, we call that the Snake House." In short order, Nancy found two black snakes entangled on the kitchen floor, another in a cupboard; and Harry had one drop just behind him from a tree near the barn. "But we have no copperheads," Nancy notes, "and not many mice."

Without extensive history for the Rock House or Allendale, looking at the old deeds and plats highlights some of Scottsville's more general story. We see the names Pitts and Dorrier, who owned nearby Valmont in 1891, which had been part of Edward, and later Daniel, Scott's patents on the hills above town. David Pitts was a Confederate veteran, later a member of the Virginia General Assembly; William Dorrier built, in 1912, the Dorrier Building for his general merchandise store—it is now James River Tavern. John O. Lewis owned nearby land; his home, taken over by Sheridan's troops in March, 1865, was Cliffside. Mt. View farm was owned circa 1900 by Captain John L. Pitts, once a James River and Kanawha Canal boat captain and then C&O contractor; and later by his son Lindsay Pitts. Thomas S. Martin of Scottsville, a county supervisor and later U.S. Senator, is named in several deeds as trustee, as is John N. Moon. And the Scotts' many acres surrounded the place; John Scott, c.1725-1798, owned as many as 5,133 acres here, says Richard Nicholas in his monograph "John Scott I and his Family of Scottlands." Charles A. Scott, 1777-1843, was an early neighbor of this property. Boundary markers, described in the plats as "Three Birches, the dead Beech, Chestnut tree, a Pine stump, a pile of rock, and other markers," including "the ford on the Scottsville Road," are long gone. We're fortunate for what remains.

*The front porch and steps with date of house.*

*Originally published July 2016*

# 6.

# Scottsville's Confederates:
# The Failed Migration to Venezuala

On September 13, 1865, Venezuela, in the names of Alvares de Lugo and Florencio Ribas, joined the history of Scottsville, in the name of Dr. Henry M. Price. The Venezuelans were granting Price extensive rights to colonize "all the unoccupied land which lies south of the 8th degree of northern latitude on the river Orinoco" (about 240,000 square miles) and to give him and his future colonists various rights to minerals, to build factories and rail roads, to import and export. Dr. Price of Scottsville accepted the grant in February of 1866 and the Venezuelan government offered him $10,000 to "use in aiding the first immigrants that arrive...."

"Dr. Price's sole object," Florencio Ribas wrote, "in seeking and obtaining this grant was to provide a home for those in the South, whom he had foresight enough to see, could not remain in their old homes under the vulgar domination of their heartless victors; and for the poor Confederate soldiers and their widows and orphans."

"If it is not inconvenient to you I advise you to join. The climate is generally healthy." Scottsville and Venezuela: the connection is still hazy, fraught with hyperbole, propaganda, and problems, hope and despair. Alfred and Kathryn Hanna, in their 1960 "Confederate Exiles in Venezuela," note that while Southerners went to Cuba after the war, to Argentina, Brazil, and Peru, it is the Venezuela project that is characterized as "both unsuccessful and tragic." And we are still trying to learn all about Dr. Henry Manore Price.

Gary Kidd and his wife Joyce, of Stafford, Virginia, have been researching the Price Grant for years. Price was Kidd's great-grand-father, a man they've learned to revere and whose reputation they try to protect. The Kidds are hoping, in their retirement, to write a book about Price's life and project. Price's birth place and date are given differently by various sources. One U.S. Census lists 1823 as his birthdate; other places say 1821. When Price applied for a Confederate pension in 1903 he listed his birthplace as Bryman Fullersburg County, Virginia. The Kidds say he was born in Boydton, "down in Mecklenburg County" or perhaps Petersburg. Price's father is listed in the 1880 Census as an Englishmen; the Kidds have learned he was a major in Wellington's forces at Waterloo and then immigrated to Mecklenburg, married, and later moved to Charlottesville, where his tailor shop is part of the historical tour around the courthouse.

Henry Manore (his mother always called him by his middle name, to distinguish him from Henry his father) gave his address as Cunningham, Fluvanna County, during the 1880 Census and he had married Francis E. Price in 1849. He is described as a physician. In the previous census, 1870, his home was Columbia, with a Scottsville post office address. He and Francis had three children, two of whom lived into adulthood. By 1900, Price is living in Madison, Tennessee.

It is not yet certain where Price received his training. His obituary says he was educated and later taught at Randolph Macon, according to Gary Kidd. No place he might have received his M.D. has records of his attendance; the Kidds have learned of a "Medical School close to Charlottesville that only operated for a few years prior to the Civil War" that taught eclectic medicine, the discipline Price followed. Price was editor in his early twenties of the periodical "The Southern Medical Reformer," and was a lecturer for a group called the Scientific and Eclectic Institute in Petersburg, where he is listed in 1847 as Professor of Materia Medica, Therapeutics and Pharmacy.

In February, 1857, Price gave an extended oratory on the steps of the Nicholas Court House, Virginia, later printed as "An Address on the Destiny of the United States." On the occasion of Washington's birthday and meant to extol the country and its Constitution, the speech is full of the rhetoric of the time, orotund and almost endless. In it, Price shows keen awareness of the important qualities of the

Union, and the danger that can be done to it by "a sect of fanatics in libeling one section of the Union."

He seems to suggest a greater United States with a broad hegemony over both Canada and Central and South America, including Cuba, Jamaica, Haiti, and Brazil. "Then, what a destiny looms up before us in the dim, shadowy outline of the future!" leading to a time when "Anglo-Saxon shall be the dialect of the whole earth [and] the Anglo-Americans may decide the destinies of the world in some terrible and hard fought battle on the plains of Palestine...." Here we read his first ideas for populating southern provinces such as Brazil.

Price joined the Confederacy early in the war, and in 1862 transferred from Company K of the 44th Virginia Infantry to Company G, 19th Battalion, Virginia Artillery. After the war he wrote a description, correcting misinformation about the Rich Mountain battle in which he'd fought. And either he worked before the war to groom sympathetic Venezuelan diplomats, or unusually quickly after it, to promote so soon his new idea for a Southern colony in Venezuela.

When Price applied to the Venezuelan government they were still suffering from their Federal War of 1859-69 "in which hundreds of thousands lost their lives." They seemed happy to give away empty land in the eastern part of their country. Price envisioned planters recreating their successes from home in the Grant, but without slavery. He would give land to Confederates, sell it to others. Price asked Great Britain to support his plans in exchange for a monopoly on the cotton they were to produce. "Not surprisingly," says a British online source, "his request met a firm refusal."

There had been publicity about Latin American lands in the United States in the 1840s and '50s. The Hannas write that the French had courted Southerners to help them make a stronger presence in Mexico. After that colonization ended with Maximilian's execution in 1867, settlers looked to Yucatan, British Honduras, and further south. "The transforming force was the state of complete desperation that came over the South following the surrender at Appomattox."

Virginia Moore writes in *Scottsville on the James*, "Four years of war followed by five of virtual dictatorship—the town was exhausted. Price and four other men, including John A. Doll and Jacob H. Briggs of Scottsville, C. Hornsey of Fluvanna, and others from Georgia, New Orleans, St. Louis, and London, formed a joint stock company, "American, English, and Venezuelan Trading and Commercial Company," in Scottsville, December 17, 1867. Their charter stated their purpose to carry passengers and freight in steam and sailing vessels to Venezuela to settle the Price Grant. Jacob Briggs, a supervisor of locks for the James River and Kanawha Canal Co. before the war and respected businessman afterward, was secretary of the company. Doll, a minister who helped found Union Baptist Church for blacks in 1865, was on the board of directors with Price. The Kidds think that "it may be a clue as to how [Price] had the social or political connections that enabled him to obtain the grant: during his childhood in Charlottesville he and his family were neighbors with Simon Bolivar's nephew, who was sent to school at the University of Virginia by his uncle, the great South American Liberator."

The company sends "several groups to Venezuela between 1866 and 1868," according to Judith Ewell, "Venezuela and the U.S.; from Monroe's Hemisphere to Petroleum's Empire," noting that Venezuela needed laborers and new settlers, but had no money or organization to support them. Price himself went out in April of 1867. It would be pleasant to think he found conditions as alluring as those described by Margaret Amanda Pattison in her "The Emigrant's Vade-Mecum or Guide to the 'Price Grant' in Venezuelan Guyana," written in 1865 (reprinted in 1940 by the California State Library) to inform and engage settlers. Besides a description of legal rights given by Venezuela, including immediate citizenship upon arrival, it tells of the richness of the soil and waters, abundance of fruit, coffee, sugar, and tobacco. The healthful climate is extolled. Ads for the land appeared in various newspapers and editorials were written about this "Garden of Eden."

Price wrote letters home to Francis—Fanny—his wife, during the six-weeks' passage from Wilmington, NC. He's eager to publicize the effort, prove its worth to Southerners, and wants to have his Scottsville friends Doll and Briggs take the next ship to Venezuela. There are "ups and downs" on the voyage, but they arrive safely;

Price is impressed by the "beautiful sight...of flowers and evergreen trees" and grey parrots along the river banks. "I advise all our friends in Virginia and North Carolina to select this point," he writes after arriving up-river at the site of the settlement. The view of mountains reminds him of the Blue Ridge "as seen from Scottsville." "Tobacco, wheat, barley, rice, sugar, cotton, tropical fruits, grapes, peaches, almonds, and plums all grown well here....All should bring garden seed, Egyptian spring wheat for seed, also barley for seed." In another letter of 1867 he says, "I feel, my dear wife, you and my dear children will be happy here."

There were, of course, some problems. Potential settlers went off to mine gold instead; some stayed in the port city to learn skills or join local girls. Few British people, despite the "Vade-Mecum," were induced to try the isolation of the Price Grant. Charles Dickens put it in his sights in his 1869-70 *All the Year Round*, a weekly journal, saying ironically that "of all the places in the world for the emigrant, Venezuelan Guyana is the very best; and further, that in the whole of Venezuela there is not such another eligible situation as Dr. Price's grant....Everything grows in Venezuela...." Later he reported that immigrants were "almost destitute, [sent to] an unhealthy, uncleared, and undrained locality." The place, he continued "was merely a dense, uncleared, tropical forest, liable in many places to be overflowed by the river...and it was the chosen home of fever and dysentery." There had been deaths already.

Price, according to "Confederate Exiles in Venezuela," despite his beautiful locale, presided over an early exodus of settlers, "afraid of revolutions, malaria, huge snakes, overpowering heat" they imagined to come. Conflict broke out among the Confederates and a new Venezuelan government over the terms of the grant, and in late 1867 Price left. The Kidds write that he "returned to the U.S. by way of New York in the hold of a cargo ship loaded with raw cattle hides.... He arrived at New York deathly ill in August 1867, suffering with malaria and cholera." He was aided by the Sisters of Charity and was able to return to Fluvanna by December.

The Kidds have found that Price had a real estate business near Palmyra, and that he "was also running a vineyard near Scottsville in Fluvanna County in the late 1860s". A daughter was born in 1870; she died before the 1880 Census. Price lived at a farm property his mother had purchased for him in 1863 at the junction of Rolling Road and Kidd Dairy Road, in nearby Fluvanna. He taught school at Antioch and was the Antioch postmaster. The Kidds, in talking to their many cousins, learned that he may also have "attempted to become a preacher at Antioch Baptist Church but was disqualified when he was discovered drinking spiked eggnog punch and dancing during a Christmas party."

The last ship of immigrants that arrived on the Orinoco in 1869 were told the grant no longer existed, revoked due to non-fulfillment of its conditions. Price did not give up easily, however. He spent years petitioning anyone in the U.S. government he thought might help him redress the insult and injury against him. He could not, according to the Hannas, "comprehend that the issue" was dead. In dusty State Department files there may still exist the memo in which the Secretary demanded an underling make "some answer to keep him quiet." Finally, in June 1901, the Acting Secretary David Hill was able to do what others had not, to stop the Price correspondence; "This decision is final," he wrote. Price was crushed. A courageous, forward-thinking personality, Gary Kidd thinks, a "very interesting and complex man," Price moved to Tennessee and died in 1907. "If anything," the Kidds say, "he was just naïve."

*Originally published May 2016*

# 7.

# How the
# Herndon House Endured

The small house at 347 East Main Street, now painted grey and prettily set off by a white picket fence and two cherry trees in the front yard, has recently changed hands. The Herndon House has been a fixture of the Scottsville real estate market lately, but its construction—estimated between 1790 and 1840 in printed sources—dates back to the earliest days of the town.

Debi Dotson, who sold the house for owners Christopher and

Deborah Shook in 2004, and again in December, says this building "went from hand-to-hand in nineteenth century Scottsville," having been owned in its early life by Jonathan Pitts, whose imposing c. 1831 brick house (regrettably razed in 1955) was further west, now the site of East Main garage.

The first Herndon mentioned in relation to the structure in county records—which go no further back—is Robert, who was living in the house on February 28, 1883, when Luther and Lillie Pitts, and Richard, Mary, and James Tutwiler conveyed it to him. By 1926, when the house and its two lots was owned by Laura Herndon and her current husband Charles Stieren, Robert Herndon had been dead "for several years."

John S. Martin, Senator Thomas Staples Martin's brother and owner of other Scottsville property (including Cliffview, now the home of George and Lucinda Wheeler,) bought the house; the deed is notarized by S.R. Gault. Martin sold it in 1931 for $3000 to Sallie Marsh; and Mrs. Marsh willed it to her nephew Harold Parr and his wife Ruby. With the introduction of these names, some people in Scottsville begin to remember who lived in the Herndon House, or at least to recognize the place. It hasn't loomed large in Scottsville history.

Pat Pitts and Bill Mason, reliable keepers of our local stories, concur that there must have been no children there, or they'd certainly remember more; 96-year old Margaret Duncan agrees. Bill Mason's parents lived across the street; he says Sallie Marsh and other women on that end of Main were friends of his mother's. Hunter Woody, who with his wife Eula still lives across the street, does not recall any particular stories of the house or of its inhabitants. Marshall Johnson remembers nothing to add.

The Parrs, whether they lived at Herndon House or not--before moving to Chester on James River Road--sold it in 1976 to the Duffs. The price was up to $27,000 then, its floodplain location still vulnerable to the two big hurricanes and more to come.

In 1977 the Duffs sold the house to Halsey Scott, who in 1980 sold it to Karen and Andy Johnson. The Johnsons would renovate it and hold on to what Andy calls "a really neat little house," working and raising their daughter, until 1991. (The house changed hands in 1993, 1998, 2004, and December, 2015.)

Andy Johnson was then restoration specialist and later architecture conservator at Monticello. Expanding into his work there, he undertook a major, time-consuming renovation of the Herndon house. The back porch became a new kitchen, with the addition stretching across the entire rear façade; they exposed the original cornice on the roof—"which is really fancy," Andy notes; and uncovered the ornate dentil wood work on an interior wall. Bob Self, who later became architecture conservator at Monticello and at this time, owned a furniture restoration shop in Scottsville, helped to extend this the full length of the current room. Mac Derry and Peter Marks worked on the carpentry, Richard Scharer on the masonry, and Joe Madison was part of the crew. Earlier work Derry executed in Scottsville included repointing the brick of Haden Anderson's Jackson Street home.

The group of men were friends, all young and skillful, as well as lively. One day, returning from his job, Andy found "one god-awful pink brick" placed by Scharer in the repaired chimney. It would late be covered by the flashing, and was there just to tease him, a construction joke.

Mac Derry remembers that when the new kitchen was beautifully completed, Andy looked around and said he would "fly speck the ceiling with sepia paint." Karen, his wife, "gave him this look like, 'idiot.'" Andy claims no recall of this sequence of events.

There are two exterior chimneys on the ends of the Herndon house—standing several inches away from the structure, as they were usually made in the early nineteenth century--and a metal steeply-pitched gable roof. Andy found an "incredible fireplace" in one of the two front rooms, highly decorated with a surround in a sunburst pattern made of little pieces of wood; it did not match the fireplace of the other room.

The interior doors of the house had all been cut in half when the Johnsons moved in. Andy put in new ones, and grained them in the "fancy painting" style he was beginning to use at Monticello. When writing about the house in 2002, Rosalind Warfiled-Brown noted in

*The Hook* that "the place's plain charm" is enhanced by Andy's "beautiful work and artistry," including an "interesting painted pattern on the dining area floor."

Historic information on the Herndon House is scant. Ed Lay, former dean of UVA's School of Architecture, writes about it in *Architecture of Jefferson's Country*: "the ubiquitous single-cell, one-story frame house persisted well into the nineteenth century. The Herndon house, a one-story dwelling in Scottsville, began as a single-cell frame house. Its features include double-ramped brick chimneys, beaded siding, and nine-over-six sash windows." The 1976 registration form for Scottsville's Historic District, which includes this structure, says "the earliest buildings in the district contain very few stylistic elements; the character of these buildings is based mostly on their form." The Department of Historic Resources in Richmond details a partial-width front porch, "supported by posts, and a four-light transom," distinguishing it from its neighbor to the west, the Fore House, or Colonial Cottage.

The first Herndons came early to America from England, and some of the brothers migrated south to Virginia. The Scottsville Museum owns a Scottsville business ledger from 1889-1893 that lists five different men with this last name trading locally; Albert and Benjamin Herndon are buried in the Scottsville cemetery; Anna Herndon is pictured in an 1892 Scottsville School photograph. I asked some of the area's Herndons if they knew of a connection to the old house. Leroy Herndon said, "Not all Herndons here are kin to the original Herndon—there were others." Leroy's sisters, Lillian Hamshar and Etta Collins, are equally equivocal. Lillian says "Chances are great [the house was owned by] one of our ancestors. There are many around who were, and we think we're all connected, but it's so far back we don't have proof."

Some printed sources suggest the house is small enough to have been designed originally as an office for the canal company. It was well-sited for that, close to the canal, the warehouse, gauge dock and turning basin. Warfield-Brown opines in *The Hook*, "it does seem a shame that modern adaptation, possibly including carving up the space [into offices] may be on tap for an appealing old place that has endured so much."

I can find nothing to corroborate the idea that the building was an office for the canal company. Whether it was constructed in 1790 or 1820, the canal then was just an idea in its infancy, and the James River Company, chartered in 1785, was trying to make the river itself navigable, especially around Richmond. This was expensive and basically a failure; the state took control in 1820 and resumed work. In 1835 the James River and Kanawha Canal Company was instituted to forward the effort. That decade saw much activity, with work being pushed towards Scottsville but lots of disagreements with landowners along the route--similar to the natural gas pipeline controversy today—and trouble with salaries and hierarchy. In 1836 the Lockkeeper's House, at Lock 7 in Goochland (much more substantial than the Herndon House and still inhabited as a private home) was built, indicating big hopes and lots of effort.

During the last months of the Civil War, when Union forces under Philip Sheridan entered Scottsville, the useful infrastructure of the Confederacy was their prime target. Chief Engineer of the James River and Kanawha Canal Company, Edward Lorraine, reported detailed destruction of bridges, dams, locks, and, in town, the "Company's shop burnt with all tools, forage...timber...as well as 200 pounds of beef and a barrel of flour." Richard Nicholas studied tax assements before and after the war to evaluate collateral damage—homes burned by being too near actual targets, and discovered that Lots 22 and 10, site of the Herndon House, were three lots east of any burning.

"Four Decades of Social Change, Scottsville, Virginia, 1820-1860," a UVA dissertation by Karl Hess in 1973, notes that "in 1820, there were only two merchants' stores, a warehouse, a ferry...and several modest homes" in Scottsville. Development occurred in the next generation, as families consolidated and population grew; the Staunton and James River Turnpike opened; and the canal began collecting tolls. It seems easy to imagine that one of those modest homes was the Herndon House. Jack Larkin, in *Where We Live, the American Home from 1775 to 1840*, says that "the South had a higher proportion of very small houses than New England." And this house was certainly large enough for many a family.

The charm of this little structure (real estate agent Debi Dotson notes the "utterly amazing floors," original newel posts, windows) was not easily won. Six months after Andy Johnson finished his restoration and took a family vacation, the November, 1985, hurricane roared in. Friend and house-keeper Gloria Scharer unlocked the house, moved what she could to the top floor. I was there that November 12, Wellington-booted and bandana'd, helping shove water and muck out the front door with mops. Andy recalls that when they arrived home, the family found, in the middle of their wet, mud-coated new house, a cabbage sitting ten steps up the interior stairway.

Herndon House continues to look better and better, and help tie together visual improvements from East Main to north on Valley. As it evolves, we can echo *The Hook*, "Any use that keeps the house vital and alive will be fine with us."

*The kitchen addition, from the south.*

*Originally published April 2016*

# 8.

# A Peek at a Patch of Scottsville History

Brock Cleveland, of Cleveland Tree Service, cut down the tall, dense holly tree in front of Thacker Brothers Funeral Home Friday, September 25, "root and everything!" Bill Mason reported; "one of the prettiest things in town," Ted Childress responded when he heard the news; Gene Harding concurred. Denise Davis said, "That tree was big. And now there was no other choice." Bradley Howdyshell, current owner of Thacker Brothers, with his wife, Yvonne, says his insurance company pushed the decision.

American hollies, *Ilex opaca*, are native to this region, often growing as an understory in forests, but 70 or more feet tall in the open. Their lifespan averages 100 years, Virginia Tech writes in its website, with a maximum of 150, but UNC lists a 200-year old holly on campus. This tree, Bill Mason judges from one on his own property, could have been planted in the early 1900s.

One result of the tree's absence is an unimpeded view of the white frame house, 650 Valley Street, that was in the shade of the holly. The house, now the offices of the funeral home, is part of Scottsville's Historic District and therefore on the National Register of Historic Places. A two-story building of three bays in an L plan, two bays covered with a one-story front porch, it has a hipped, shingled roof with two cross gables facing the street. On the original nomination form for inclusion in the National Register of Historic Places, July, 1976, the building is described as "early 20th century," in the Georgian Revival style. In the 2003 updated form, which adds the town's boundary increase, it is called a 1920 dwelling in Queen Anne style, converted to commercial use. Georgian Revival style features uniform rectangular buildings, while Queen Anne is distinguished by its asymmetrical facades, partial porches, and other irregular shapes. These inconsistencies aside, the house is often called the Clements House.

Pat Pitts remembers Mr. Ollie Clements, a "nice old gentleman"; his full name was Edward Oliver Clements, 1868-1952. Late in his life, Denise Davis says, he married Miss Mary Jones, Civil War veteran Zach Jones's daughter. That family lived on Bird Street, west of the current library site. Miss Mary is recalled by Marie Lane, whose Combs family lived at the nearby northwest end of Warren Street, as a "dear, sweet lady," white-haired, who sat rocking in a rocking chair on Mr. Ollie's porch when they were dating and always smiled when Marie went past. Marie, as a girl, thought the late marriage "romantic and sweet" and enjoyed seeing the couple rocking on the porch together. (There are pictures on the Scottsville Museum website.) Denise Davis, who now owns one of the Clements' rocking chairs and put in a new seat, uncovering old horsehair and a vintage English newspaper, says that Mr. Ollie died not long after he and Miss Mary wed; Mary eventually went to the Hermitage Road Home in Richmond. She sold the Scottsville property to A. Raymon and Homer Thacker in 1963; she died in December, 1967. Mary, besides working with the youth programs at the Scottsville Methodist Church, was a founding member and later secretary of the Scottsville chapter of the United Daughters of the Confederacy. The Thackers' funeral business formally began in 1931 in a small converted service station near the Methodist Church on Main Street. They moved uptown in the mid-1960s, and in the November 21, 1962, *Scottsville Sun* there is a photo and report of a building "on Thacker property" being razed to make way for a new, concrete block chapel, the building so closely next-door to the Clements House they are attached by a short hall. Ted Childress remembers that the Rittenhouse Brothers did the demolition. That destroyed building is recalled by Pat Pitts as a garage where he played as a boy on the second floor, with Raymon Thacker's sons Arthur and Sonny. Pat says the upstairs "was filled with Willie Burgess postcards—hundreds of them." Raymon and Burgess had originally been business partners. Jack Hamner, whose family lived across the street, remembers the place as abandoned when he played there, "up to my knees in Burgess postcards," he ruefully says, as they are now sought-after and collected photographic records of early 20th century Scottsville.

While time has tended to conflate the two buildings, Martha Alice Newcomer is very clear about them. Her family, the Golladays, lived north of Ollie Clements, the first house up Warren Street. She was born and raised there until she was in seventh grade. Growing up, Martha played outside with neighboring children all day long. One of her few rules was not to go south of the alley beside the former ABC store on weekdays; she could on Sunday. Neighborhood mothers, most of them home all day, knew who was supposed to be where, and when; Martha remembers "Mama" Combs, Marie Lane's mother, yelling across Valley to her to get out of the creek. That creek, which joins Mink Creek further down, is carried under Valley Street in a culvert; Martha says she could walk from across the street from her own house to the Clements house, under the street, in the culvert, entered from a small concrete bridge on the banks. There was lots of playing on top of the streets, too. Baxter Allison Pitts remembers roller skating on the sidewalks here, as does Ida Clements Patterson, who lived on nearby Moore's Hill and is "no relation" to Mr. Ollie; she says they would "jump over cracks" in their skates, or walk along the railroad tracks in a gang of kids.

Martha Newcomer recalls that Miss Mary, her Sunday school teacher, "sometimes liked children, sometimes didn't; we never knew, and had to be careful." She says the structure south of the Clements House was an unpainted, two-story wooden shed, perhaps a garage, with an outside staircase to the second floor; she too remembers that floor being covered in post cards. Martha says that "when I was little, Miss Mary would sometimes" (accent on the sometimes) "let us sit at the top of the stairs" as a treat.

Ida Clements Patterson recalls Miss Mary as a "sweet person" too, and it's her recollection that the structure taken down was the Gibbs house: "but it's been many long years back." Bill Mason remembers that Mr. Gibbs was a butcher in Scottsville; he thinks the Gibbs place was to the north of the Clements. This is borne out in deeds at the County clerk's office; that house was once owned by T.E. Clements. The property moved through various members of the Clements family. It was originally comprised of Lots 191 and 192 on the 1873 Moon map of Scottsville, called Lots 1 and 2 by Peter White on his earlier map. Back before the deeds I can trace in the Albemarle County clerk's records, the property was owned by D.A. Clements—I presume the David Anderson Clements buried in the Scottsville cemetery; he left it to his children Maggie and D.O. Clements. In 2007, when D.O. was living in Glouster County, Maggie in Scottsville, they sold it to T. Emmett Clements. One other deed, July, 1938, moves the property from Elieza Clements Ball and her husband William to E. O. Clements. Here, as in the prior deed, the property is described as "a part of that land...formerly known as the 'old tan yard'...."

Mayor Thacker has described the old tan yard pits in what I believe to be the north part of the lots. Tanning was an important industry of the colonies and early United States, starting at Jamestown. Its necessity and economic benefits must have overpowered the bad smells and polluted water it produced. Not much is recorded of our own tan yard, and the sole reference I find here in Scottsville is from the 1937 booklet produced by the senior class of Scottsville

High School, "Historical Sketches of the Town of Scottsville." In the section on "Old Time Industries," they say of the tannery, "the proprietor of this organization was Mr. D. O. Clements....This was operated as late as 1880 (perhaps longer). It was conducted in a low frame building and vats in an open space almost a block in extent."

Bob Spencer recalls seeing Raymon and Homer's parents when they lived in the house at 650 Valley Street. He says Raymon's first wife and their children lived there, too. We know, from the Scottsville Museum website, that in 1920, Scottsville High School principal William Day Smith and his wife Parke Harris Smith lived there. Eventually, Parke's parents, Charles and Helen Harris, who established Fairview, now High Meadows, joined them; after her husband's death in 1930, Helen moved to Charlottesville.

*Funeral home lawn after removal of holly.*

Prior to this, the building had been, the Scottsville Museum website states, Betty Harrison's boarding house. She served a good lunch, and Parke's brother, Charles Jr., a Scottsville baseball team member who also played in the Scottsville band and clerked for his father at their clothing store on Valley Street, was a friend of Betty's son, Richard, and often ate there. Charles fell in love with his friend's sister, Alexina Harrison, and in 1912 they married. They went on to build their own house on the extensive grounds of Fairview/High Meadows. These narratives do not account for the changing dimensions of the Clements property, dates of the building of structures or their uses, but record what we remember.

There's a small street, an alley, between Page and Harrison streets, called Clements. Virginia Moore, in *Scottsville on the James*, says it, with Blair and Lindsay streets, "honor local families." Though some structures, like the old holly tree, are inevitably lost, we save what we can.

*Originally published November 2015*

# 9.

# Virginia McGraw Still
# Leading Scottsville

*1945: Father and mother, Guy and Pearl, center back; sister Blanche to left, twin brother Dancy to right; front row, center, Virginia, flanked by twin sisters Grace (l) and Pauline (r). Family photo courtesy of Hollis Lumpkin.*

The internet, with its temptations for snarkiness, does not necessarily seem a fair place for Scottsville to be judged. But out-of-towners who've eaten at Lumpkin's Restaurant and posted reviews on the website Yelp all get it: "the locals, food and atmosphere were more than enough to make this a memorable experience"; "God Bless Mrs. Lumpkin and her family, she is wonderful, tells tons of stories and is still going strong....A cornerstone of the community and an old fashioned restaurant." "It makes me happy."

Virginia McGraw Lumpkin was born to a farming family in Buckingham County 91 years ago. The doctor who attended her mother at home was satisfied with the birth, ready to leave, when the midwife called him back for Virginia's twin brother, born a half-hour later. The family had two sets of twins, five girls and this one boy, Dancy. "I don't mind telling you—I haven't had an easy life," Virginia said on a recent sunny afternoon, resting at home on James River Road with her two well-loved cats and the heel slice of bread with jelly. Virginia's most recent difficult experience was a dangerous bout of pneumonia that kept her in the hospital for a month, but her warm, forthright attitude has been restored and she's glad to be home again.

Virginia grew up as another boy on the farm, her father choosing her his primary helper. She credits him with "making me ornery and tough," which turned out to be helpful in her life. Her mother, Pearl, emigrating from Scotland to oversee land she owned here, subsequently transferred the 600 acres ten miles from Dillwyn to Guy McGraw, the man she married. Virginia graduated from Buckingham High School at 18 with the assumption she'd get a job. A cousin then asked her to come to Scottsville to help nurse her mother, Virginia's aunt Lavinia Virginia, and she replied, "Sure, I'll come over." This was the beginning of her long career in Scottsville.

After cooking and caring for her aunt through the then-arduous process of cataract surgery, Virginia was surprised and gratified to be asked by Agnes Payne Beal—a relative of Livie's—to work in her grocery store on Valley Street. "It made me feel good," Virginia remembers, still thinking of herself as a young country girl without special skills; all she thought she'd be able to do was clean the place, but she knew she could help. A neighbor drove her to the store daily, and at first she cleaned and stocked the shelves. Little by little she began waiting on customers, getting what they wanted (this was the Scottsville grocery with a crate of live chickens on the front sidewalk) but not ringing them up. Finally she learned to use the cash register, and she continued to work at Beal's "for years and years."

*A drawing of the McGraws' family home in Buckingham. Photo Courtesy of Hollis Lumpkin.*

One of the many stories that stud Virginia's reminiscences and give her great pleasure involves a small African American boy who helped Agnes. One afternoon Virginia asked him to clean out the back room, and when he reported he had finished the job, Virginia inspected. She showed him what she meant by "clean out" and had him finish the job. Twice. When leaving work, the boy complained to Agnes Beal, "That's the meanest white woman ever crossed that bridge down there." Agnes laughed and gave him an extra dollar for his trouble.

Virginia's high standards and strong work ethic allowed her to continue to support herself and live happily in Scottsville. She felt friendly with everyone, though she was careful. One day Dr. Stinson asked Agnes if her assistant could take some time off; he then told Virginia that if she'd accompany him to Bruce's Drug Store for a Coke he'd give her $50. She declined on the strength of the bad reputation associated with Dr. Stinson due to his abortion practice. He was amazed and pleased with her decision: "You're the first woman to ever turn me down!"

Virginia left Agnes Beal's employ in 1950 when Agnes' own children were old enough to help her, and began working at the Traveler's Rest Hotel on the corner of Valley and Main, a huge, rambling structure that burned down in a 1976 arson fire. She had learned all about running the 19- room hotel with a dining room that sat 60, from checking in guests to cooking and orchestrating the meals. Now she had begun to think of getting married, and was looking only for a man who respected women, a "pleasant man with good manners towards women." (She knew what she didn't like. Another of her "my big mouth" stories involves George Omohundro, who ran the hardware store in the ground floor of the hotel; his wife kept the accounts. Once when Virginia made a mistake in bookkeeping she asked Mrs. Omohundro for help. "I never made a mistake in my life," she proudly announced. "Oh, yes, you did," Virginia answered, referencing Mr. Omohundro, who, Virginia says, "liked the women." Mrs. Omohundro took no offence.)

Nelson Lumpkin, from Danville, was one of the salesmen who sold supplies to the Traveler's Rest Hotel. Virginia found in him the respect she demanded and companionship she desired. They were married April 9, 1955, and he opened doors for her "for the rest of his life"; they had two children, Marlean and Hollis. The Lumpkins socialized with Arbutus and Mayor Raymon Thacker and the Co-hens, Rose and Milton, who ran The Hub, a Scottsville clothing store vital to the women in town. The Hub offered everyday clothing and Rose would make purchases in Baltimore for customers who ordered a special Sunday outfit or a wedding dress. Virginia, Nelson, and the other couples would attend dances at the Fireman's Hall—the Canal Warehouse—where the Scottsville Orchestra played Saturday nights. Virginia says she didn't dance, but would keep and pass out the private liquor people brought. Her husband liked to dance.

At the Traveler's Rest, railroad workers and salesmen—drum-mers—were the main clients, as well as the crew who installed the natural gas pipeline in nearby Fluvanna. Other Scottsville enterpris-es Virginia remembers from this time include the Pitts' grocery, the drug store, a liquor store, the Silver Grill restaurant, a dime store, furniture store, cleaners, three gas stations, and the movie house. Lee's Restaurant, on Valley Street, the spot now Amici's (the restaurant there has never closed; "it just goes hand to hand," Virginia observes) was run by "a really nice man," George Lee. In 1962 Lee was ready to turn over ownership of the restaurant. He came to the hotel, asked Virginia to accompany him to what he described as an auction of his place, and once there, handed her the keys to the business. She and Hollis paid him an amount he determined to be sufficient over time. While Virginia continued to manage the hotel, Hollis ran the restaurant.

A small story from the hotel days involves a pet flying squirrel Virginia kept, often in her blouse, but that sometimes got out and ran around the hotel. It was a favorite, and a great sadness when someone found it drowned in a toilet. The squirrel received a re-spectful burial behind the hotel.

Many of Virginia's warmest memories of this time center on her dear friend Edith Taggart, Scottsville's telephone operator. These stories have been often told and are collected on the Museum web-site. Edith had polio when she was eight and was left crippled. Her mother, Central before her, taught her to use the switchboard; Miss Edith became the voice, the eyes, and ears of the community, hold-ing Scottsville together as the pace of life sped up. But forty years later, when switchboard technology was replaced by dial phones, Miss Edith "was thrown over," Virginia says, by the phone company, with no sensitivity or consideration. Virginia asked her "sweet and smart" friend to live with them at the hotel, answering the phone and helping guests, as well as assisting Virginia with the two children. Edith stayed at Traveler's Rest the remainder of her life and is buried in Virginia's plot in the Scottsville cemetery. After Miss Edith's death, the bank notified Virginia of a $1000 account she had saved for Marlean's education; they were real family. Virginia does not forget the strength and importance of that friendship.

The Lumpkins stayed at the hotel until 1962, but as business dwindled, they moved to the apartment above Lee's Restaurant. They then bought almost an acre of land at the north edge of downtown Scottsville—all there was of town then—for their motel and restaurant. Virginia had inherited 75 acres of timber in Buckingham, and she cut it to raise money to build. She's "worked every day," she notes, being strict in raising her children after Nelson's death in 1980, and pleased she could send them to college, start them in their life's work. "I've enjoyed it."

Virginia muses on hers and Scottsville's twentieth century, the developments and changes. She credits the loss of the plant as well as the high school with damaging the essence of the town, but she also says that things are more positive and pleasant, "nice," in town now than mid-century. "Scottsville didn't have a very good name because of the drunks. There was a lot of moonshine in Scottsville when I came; a lot of drunks." She explains that

*Virginia, in an undated photo, in the restaurant kitchen, cooking. Photo courtesy of Hollis Lumpkin.*

you could see more drinking—or the effects of it—then than now. Men used to walk into town to drink on Saturdays. If they behaved, they were left alone. If not, the police took them home. She was told, when she took over Lee's Restaurant, to say nothing about the men drinking if "they didn't act bad."

Another fact of Scottsville life was segregation. Lee's had a "Colored Only" room at the rear with its own entrance. Virginia got respect from the men there, she says, if she had to tell them to turn down the music; she also helped with money to get home if needed, even food, and she felt they all had an understood relationship. One night a black soldier in uniform tried to encourage those in the back with a $100 bill to integrate the front room, but to a man, they declined. Life changed when the law changed.

Virginia Lumpkin looks forward with pride to watching Hollis's children grow, to keeping up with friends, maybe getting her iris and peonies weeded. She takes comfort in Hollis's loving attention to her, as well as his success with the restaurant: "His desserts could make you slap your mama down!" Virginia Lumpkin, the grand marshal of our Fourth of July parade in 2004, is still leading us all.

*Originally published October 2015*

# 10.

# "Dear Old Scottsville.
# Dear Old School."

In the late 1920s, the period Virginia Moore calls "New Century, New Hope" in her *Scottsville on the James, an Informal History*, the brand new Scottsville High School was as full of activity and growth as she describes, animating the entire town. The school's corner stone had been laid by the Scottsville Masons in 1924, and now the shrubs along the front walk had been planted and the tenor of the institution was blossoming.

We have a special look at this period in a scrapbook now a part of the Scottsville Museum. Its 17 pages are mostly filled, the 22"x11" heavy brown paper tied together with crumbling suede leather thongs and the cover printed with the lines Character Education, and Scottsville High School, with a pencil and watercolor drawing of the building between.

This undated scrapbook is stamped on page one with the designation "Joseph P. Blair Memorial Library of Local History," a project instituted by Blair's daughter Susie Blair, and kept, according to Bob Spencer, in the high school principal's office. Blair was not only Scottsville's dentist and a Town Council member, but our representative to the Albemarle School Board for 37 years, and chairman of it when he died in 1931. Miss Susie, herself a professor of drama at Hollins College, was active around Scottsville, and one of the early Museum committee members.

"Character Education" is still a current pedagogical practice, though it is not without its critics, who say it favors the formation of docile, well-behaved pupils rather than thinkers. In the Scottsville High School, with grades four through twelve, and the next-door primary school with the first three grades, the concept was apparently sponsored by "Charlottesville Banks...by giving $100 each year in prizes."

Two bank representatives whose 2x3" sepia-toned photographs appear on page one are H. R. Boswell, of Peoples National Bank, and C.T. O'Neil. (I date the scrap book not only by the just-planted shrubs along the front walk, but by the appearance, in the photographs of the men taken on the building's roof, of the 1927 Methodist steeple in the distance.) A 1925 Albemarle School Board publication, "Albemarle County Geography Supplement," states that "One of the most important factors in the promotion of progress in a county is its banks. Albemarle has six banks with total

*Students stand in front of Scottsville High School holding*
*all the required school materials in 1927.*

resources in 1923 of $12,338,578. Three of these banks are in Charlottesville and one is in each of the towns of Scottsville, Crozet, and Esmont."

Page one contains pictures of A.L. Bennett, Albemarle school superintendent, "Our Best Friend," Mrs. B.R. Dunnett; and Miss Marietta Powers, "Our everyday helper with everyday problems." Marietta was always called "Miss Met" in town, "a wonderful lady," according to Bob Spencer, a teacher also skilled at book mending and binding; her father, David Pinckney Powers, had been Albemarle County school superintendent and had founded a private school, Pine Grove Academy, on Rt. 20 north of town. Miss Met later ran the Scottsville library, a self-funded enterprise open Wednesday afternoons, until 1953, after which library services were provided by the Charlottesville book mobile.

Page two of the scrapbook shows the school building; "Grade Faculty and Principal"; a hand-written table of contents; and what I take to be a later paste-in, a picture of the school—hedge rising high—dated October, 1935. At the end of the book, besides pages of forms for "Scoring Character Education Points," grade one through 7, is a "Morality Code," written on letterhead stationery of William Day Smith, principal of the school. The handwriting, the beautiful, readable Palmer style, seems to be the same as the table of contents, leading me to think William Day Smith himself put together the scrap book.

"The children of today are the citizens of tomorrow," is his theme; "truthfulness, honesty, health, thrift, loyalty, courtesy and obedience to duty" are the benchmarks. Smith explains that children "were on their honor to report themselves" and the scores were kept on classroom black boards to encourage cooperation in good behavior, leading to high marks and the prize money.

The little photographs of the school, all taken outdoors and supplemented with cut-out printed pictures of classroom interiors, are small, somewhat blurry, and light-struck at the edges. We can see, however, what values were being stressed and how the students look. Boys in the various classes wore short pants, long pants or overalls, knickers with long socks. Shoes are high-topped or low, in leather. Shirts are long-sleeved, white, and occasionally worn with neckties. There are a few zippered jackets with elastic at the waist, some sport coats, and heavy sweaters. The girls are in knee- length dresses, usually featuring deep rounded collars, and knee socks or short socks with low leather shoes; there are a few large bows perched on the crown of the head, and long banana curls, but most of their hairdos are sensible short bobs with bangs. The teachers pictured, six women, are in boxy, low-waisted 1920s style outfits, with T-strap heeled shoes.

Since all shots are posed, there is no real record of general activity around the school. One boy mows the grass to the north of the building with a reel mower; several girls dress in their Red Cross aprons and caps; and there are calisthenics behind the school for Physical Education. Group activities include honor roll, 4H, and "Five Point" pupils—maybe part of the Character Education, Junior League, and a Bird Sanctuary, possibly sponsored by Audubon, comprised of one or two bird houses on high poles. School equipment that is brought outside to be photographed includes a first aid kit and a globe Bob Spencer recalls situated in the principal's office—"still there when I was going to school." Cut-out pre-printed pictures of pencil sharpeners, scales, a sand table, glass-fronted case filled with books ("in each room") supplement the photos; "two sanitary toilets" are noted with an appropriate illustration.

The primary school, on Bird at Page Street, predated the high school by almost a decade. It was built on a half-acre of the Belle Haven land, rising up the hill behind it, and formally deeded to the Scottsville School Board of Albemarle County by the Pitts family in 1918; the papers stipulate the purpose was "for a White Primary School." It is important to remember that all the teachers, administration, and students here were white only.

Photographs of this now-vanished building, burned in 1980 by a late-night lightning strike and now the site of the JMRL library, show students gathered around the short flight of front steps and under the four columns (now inside the Scottsville Library, in the kids' section) that hold up the portico. Flowers have been planted along the walkway that ends in a gate at Page Street, facing the home now owned by the Wheelers. In another shot, students at the rear foundation are shown "helping to keep buildings in repair."

More believable are the playground pictures, even the one of four girls staged for a toss-up with a basketball by the wooden backstop. Another shot shows a large open structure by the playground, the pavilion Bob Spencer says was always filled at recess by the students who didn't chose to run around. "Most of us just played," he says, but others would sit there and talk.

One of the most outstanding elements of this brief record of 1920s Scottsville High School, further reading shows, is the principal himself, William Day Smith. There is a short biography and appreciation of him on the Scottsville Museum website. He was born in Connecticut, educated at Amherst College in Massachusetts. Prior to his 1908 arrival in Scottsville he had been a school administrator. Here he took over the school on the hill, the one without indoor plumbing, and by 1913 made it the first state accredited high school in Virginia. He championed athletics and oversaw the teaching, as outlined by the Virginia School Laws of 1915, of reading, spelling, writing, arithmetic, grammar, geography, physiology, hygiene, civil government, US history, Virginia history, and drawing. "Provision shall be made," the Laws state, "for moral education in the public schools...extended throughout the entire course." He presided over the contested move of the high school to the west end of Main Street.

Smith was a Latin scholar, Phi Beta Kappa at his college, and a well-versed botanist with a specialty in ferns. He often took from his pocket some plant or stone or object found around Scottsville to use as the start of his daily convocation of the students. The son of a minister, he also used Bible readings to help impart what he called "true wisdom," and initiated the practice of having the students read their own chosen parts of the Bible and lead a prayer at the day's opening exercises. He also took pupils on nature hikes after school.

"Such a wonderful man," Bob Spencer recalls. The memories of most other Scottsville High School students extend back only to the fact that Smith wrote the high school song:

"Dear old Scottsville! Dear old School! Fond the memory of thy rule!

Now our hearts would hymn a message of good cheer! Fondest thoughts about thee cling.

While with voices glad we sing, Scottsville! Scottsville! Scottsville!

Ever praise to thee."

There are two more stanzas, ending, "Scottsville! Scottsville! Scottsville!/ Happy days with thee." Smith had written a similar-sounding ode for his Amherst college class, 1882; he stayed at the college for his Master's degree, 1884.

William Day Smith had married in 1888 and was widowed in 1907. In 1910 he married one of his Scottsville teachers, Annie Parker Harris, called Parke. They lived with their two children in a house at the north end of Valley Street, now gone, at the site of the funeral home. Even with his status as a "beloved teacher," Smith was not immune from student pranks. Raymon Thacker has told how one Halloween some kids "put a 20 penny spike under the weather boarding of the house, attached a long binder twine they had waxed ('they went to a lot of trouble') and from across Warren Street, at Charles Terrell's blacksmith shop, they scraped with a piece of metal along the taut line so that, at the house, it sounded as if the weather boarding were being ripped off. Smith burst from his home, could find nothing amiss, and returned, apparently to settle comfortably in his favorite chair. The boys created the noise again, with the same result, and teased the principal until one or the others of them tired of the game."

Smith retired in 1938. Alumni gave him a reception in the school's flower-filled auditorium, with Leslie Walton opening the festivities and George Omohundro, Jr. presenting Smith a check from the alumni. "Throughout the entire program," according to a booklet printed on the occasion of Smith's 90th birthday in 1949, "there was evidenced the love and respect in which Mr. Smith is held by the graduates and an appreciation of the high ideals, as a scholar and a Christian gentleman, he has exemplified by his life in the community." A William Day Smith Award was established at the high school for leadership.

In 1967 the high school was closed for sophomores, juniors,

and seniors, who after that date went to Albemarle High School. It remained a junior high until 1976, dried out and cleaned up after the deep floods of 1969 and 1972, and finally closed as a school in 1979. Losing the school, Gene Harding is quoted as saying in a 1995 *Daily Progress* article about its fourth reunion, was losing "the biggest part of our community."

Before that happened, when the character of Scottsville's future citizens was being formed there, and the distinctions of polypody ferns described, William Day Smith could look at his teachers and students, his buildings and grounds, and write, "We seek for willing hearts and hands to make our school life the best, and if we obtain anywhere near our goal the result is gratifying....Happy the school where teachers and students act justly, love mercy, and walk humbly."

*Miss Marietta Powers, our everyday helper with everyday problems.*

*Originally published August 2015*

# 11.

# Scottsville Continues Winning Streak

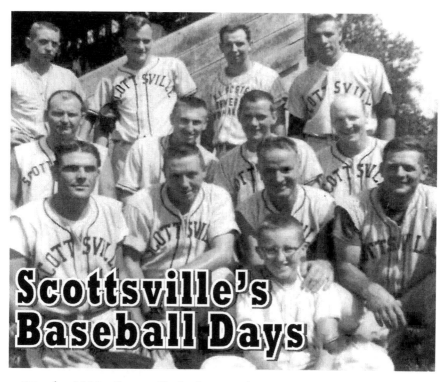

Scottsville's Baseball Days

In the 1950s, Scottsville had not only a town baseball team but a newspaper, J. Bernard McDearmon's *Scottsville Sun*, to report on the team's doings. As the Scottsville Museum inaugurates a summer project to digitally scan Bob Spencer's collection of the *Sun*, we can take a sneak preview of some of what will appear on the museum's website.

It was Thursday, June 11, 1953, when the *Sun* announced the baseball team's winning streak. They beat Alberene 5-2 at home, making them 6 and 0 for the season. "Austin Easton was heavy hitter...3 out of 4, one of which was a double," and Talmadge Tyler and Joe Brochu both got triples. The Scottsville team, the *Sun* reported, "will enter the State Tournament, in Charlottesville." Billy Goodwin was manager, Austin Easton the captain. Other names—last only—on the roster: Rittenhouse, Childress, Hamner, Moulton, Maupin, and Price.

June 28, the next week, Scottsville engaged in "a hurling duel" with Buckingham. Pitcher Simpson "bested Lefty Watts...as the local nine edged Buckingham, 2 to 1. Simpson gave up three hits, one a homer; Easton scored the winning run for Scottsville on a triple, coming home on an out."

June 25, 1954, the sad news was reported in the center column of the front page: "Scottsville Nine Loses First Game of the Season, 6 to 5." Playing in Shipman, Joe Brochu's home run wasn't enough to lift the Scottsville team to victory.

In early May 1953, the Scottsville team's schedule was announced for the Tri-County League. From May 10 through September 13, they would play teams from Alberene, Charlottesville Motors, Superior Stone, Buckingham, Shipman, and elsewhere. Local businesses advertising in the paper that summer include C.R. Dorrier's General Merchandise, Scottsville Flour Mill and the Jefferson Mills, Bruce-Dorrier Motor Company and Smith Chevrolet, Ripley's Cab ("Call 2341, Silver Grill, for prompt service") and Victory Theater, showing "Come Back, Little Sheba" and "Ivanhoe."

"The biggest thing that happened in Scottsville was the Sunday baseball game," Bill Mason remembers. "I was really into baseball," he says, and though he didn't play past high school, he was a bat boy for Scottsville when he was around 10 to 12 years old. Billy Pitts, who "was born downtown," would go every Sunday at 2 p.m. to watch. There was no gate, but a man with a cigar box would take your quarter. And maybe a hat would be passed during the game for fundraising.

The grandstand, six to eight feet high as he recalls, was

essentially just south of where the Farmers Market is now, with center field toward the rear wall of the former post office, left field where the basketball hoop is. Behind the seats was a creek—it's there still; foul balls would pop into the poison ivy and mud, and kids were paid to fetch them out, as "there weren't but so many baseballs," according to Tommy Stargell. Stargell recalls the stands as "a nice, sound structure"; others remember it as a bit more rickety. It sat two to three hundred, thinks Bobby Pollard. The stands were built by Red Rittenhouse, who ran a construction company, as well as managed the baseball team; Red also mowed the grass each Saturday.

Junior Tyler, one of the star players, says they would fill the grandstand for each Sunday game; fans also went to away games— Greene, Lovingston, Orange. "Greene and us had a hard time getting along," he recalls; "not the players, the fans." Some people would pull up in their cars to sit and watch. No one remembers the grandstand in place after the flood of 1969.

Bill Mason recalls concessions being sold by Leslie Harrison, who had a stand and offered hot dogs, hamburgers, and soft drinks cooled in wooden half barrels of ice. Harrison was "a real fixture." Food could have been bought at Lumpkin's restaurant or Dawson's stand as well. Sometimes, other men recalled, pies or cakes would be donated for sale. Marvin Ripley recalls that a fundraiser might have involved something like a special seed being baked into a cake that would win the person who bought it a prize.

While the Tri-County League shifted names and make-up over the years before "fading away," according to Ripley, in the 1960s, it benefitted from the strong baseball program at Scottsville High School. Until 1967, the school had fielded excellent teams ever since the middle of the 1920s, according to John Randolph Phillips in "Of Town and the River." "Baseball was coached," he writes, "by John Pitts, a baseball genius…. [The team was] remarkable for a small-town high school."

Dave Cattlett, who played third base for the school, says, "We beat everybody. It doesn't get any better that that!…I remember all of the players," he says, and lists the Fernybough family—nine boys— from Carter's Bridge; pitchers Arthur Thacker, Whitfield Bryant, and

Jackie Armstead; Billy Moon; and others. Thacker, a good friend of his who moved to California, was "an ace pitcher, with good control and a mixture of pitches." The other players on the team "didn't have to be but so good because of the pitching. We weren't necessarily the best in the world, but the best of the seven high schools in the area."

Some of the high school players were on, or later joined, the Scottsville team. Red Clements was catcher in high school in 1947; "I have played ball all my life," he says. Red was on the high school and town team at the same time. He had to play center field for Scottsville, as players weren't allowed to hold the same position on both teams. Red recalls that the town team's practice was fairly informal: "in the afternoons, someone would be there to play"; there was no special schedule. Local men would work as umpires. "Mr. Boatwright, SJ's daddy, was an excellent umpire. When he said strike, it was a strike!"

At 6'4"—when he was 18—Red was lead-off hitter. He recalls as one of his best memories a Fourth of July when a man from Richmond came in as their pitcher for a double-header and pitched the first game right handed, the second left-handed. "That's amazing."

Austin Easton recalled his Scottsville baseball days for the World

*The Scottsville Baseball Grandstand, 1914 Raymon Thacker Collection, Scottsville Museum.*

War II oral history project at the Scottsville Museum. He played baseball for the Army and came home to play for the town. "I played 17 years for Scottsville as a catcher. When I came home, I became a pitcher. Since I hit, I usually hit two home runs a game." Junior Tyler was a pitcher on the team for years and is often mentioned by the others recalling Scottsville baseball. He began young, when his hometown of Schuyler didn't have a high school, and stayed on the town team despite Schuyler having its own. Red Rittenhouse would often pick him up and drive him to the games. Junior says he never had arm trouble, never had to learn to pitch; "I just played baseball all my life."

Marvin Ripley, from Howardsville, played baseball for Scottsville High School, as well as for the town. He recalls, "Every community, just about, had a team. They practiced some, but they just played. This has disappeared now, except for kids. Back then, it was big time—uniforms and everything." The team groomed the dirt infield, laid out the bases and lines. Bill Mason tells about summer rain leaving puddles on the base paths; he recalls gasoline being poured on the water and set afire to evaporate the moisture.

Ripley points out that the game was segregated; he says black teams played in some towns, and Scottsville would go to watch if the games were nearby. Scottsville liked to play in Charlottesville, he remembers, because they would give a trophy at a tournament, drawing in 100 to 125 teams. In high school, he said, "you knew everybody—four or five on every team. We played as far away as Gladstone, Zion Crossroads, Buckingham. People always checked the rosters, talked about the players. Baseball was everything."

Among the men remembered on the town team are Chester Baker, Gordon Rutland, Wilbur Bryant, Charlie Roberts. Barbara Brochu recalled her father-in-law, Big Joe Brochu, a stand-out player, teaching his grandchildren to throw and catch. "We'd all play on the weekends. He tried to pass on his expertise. He was an inspiration to us all."

Remembered by everyone is Red Rittenhouse, the guiding force behind the town team. "Red was the main guy—he kept it going," said Junior Tyler. Billy Pitts puts it this way: "If it hadn't been for

Red, that thing wouldn't have lasted that long." He paid for some of the uniforms, cut the grass with his own tractor. A "real organizer," according to Bill Mason.

Red's son Keith, who played basketball, not baseball—though as a child he kept score for his father—says Red "was a really good baseball player." Keith chose four stories to tell about his father's character and impact on the game in Scottsville. He says Junior Tyler once hit a home run to center field, to where the post office would be built in 1965. Men standing out there declared that a time out had been called, so the run didn't count. Junior sat down, dejected and frustrated. Red, the manager, talked to him, "cajoled and reasoned with him." Got him to say he'd return to the game. He hit another home run.

Once, with Red catching in a close game, he was crouched over home plate, protecting it. The runner, one of two brothers on the opposing team, slid in with his spikes up and intentionally hit Red in the face. Red reacted, was going to go after the player, but Scottsville's Maynard Rice appeared, collared the runner as well as his brother and held them off the ground, one in each hand. "Red said, 'I got so tickled at Maynard that I couldn't be mad anymore.'"

Red was the second oldest of ten siblings. During the Depression, he left school to join the Civilian Conservation Corps, which had a baseball team in each camp. Playing one day, he "hit everything in sight," his son says. "Someone asked 'Who are you—what's your job?' 'I'm Red Rittenhouse, and I don't have one.' 'Now you do—you're batting cleanup!'" Only later in life did Red confess to homesickness in the CCC camp.

Red played into his 40s, Keith says. Once Scottsville met an opposing team with semi-pro players and a fast ball pitcher. Bottom of the ninth, bases loaded, Red at bat. He fouled balls off, and the count got to 3 and 2. Keith's grandfather, watching his son, heard opposing fans taunting Red: "Ah, the old man can't hit." "Turns out they were wrong," says Keith. The next foul went over Page Street beside the current playground. Then Red hit a line drive, and the ball landed beyond the road, on the sidewalk in front of the school--a grand slam home run. Keith said: "After the dust settled, grandfather looked over his shoulder and said, 'Oh, the old man can't hit, huh?' Very poignant."

Keith recalls the names of more of the players, some of them in the accompanying photograph from around 1957: Jim Godsey; Eugene McKamey of Woodridge; Homer Tyler; Ted Denby, a powerful left-hander; Ronny Lynch; Bill Mark; the Grummeck brothers from Antioch; and Cecil Shifflett.

There's even earlier baseball history recorded in the area. The women of the Algoma household, an estate near Howardsville and south of the James, kept a record of their summer activities from 1890-1893. Edited by Elizabeth Scott in 2003 and available to read in the Scottsville library, the book tells of the social life of the well-to-do. July 6, 1892, "the Howardsville boys played a baseball game with the Scottsville team, who won, 12-11." July 15, "The boys went down to Scottsville and played; they were beaten 15-13." The next year, June 23, 1893, "Grand game of baseball in Howardsville when the Howardsville team [finally] beat the Scottsville team." But July 7,

*The 1914 Scottsville Baseball Club, Raymond Thacker Collection, Scottsville Muse;um.*

"The boys went to Scottsville to play baseball. Scottsville 10, Howardsville 8. The Scottsville 'umpire' cheated!"

There were sometimes two teams in Scottsville, one fielded by the US Rubber Plant. In 1950-1953, the two teams would meet for donkey baseball, with predictable results. The point was hilarity and fundraising, often for the Lions, with the animals stealing the show. June 26, 1952, the *Sun* reports that 300 fans watched the Scottsville team beat the Rubber Plant 4-3, with "more falls than hits." "The big trouble...was the players' inability to remain on the back of their transportation." June 17, 1954, "side-splitting laughter" was recorded and $100 was raised for the Lions. The roster included Donald Carroll, Russell Moon, G.B. Cleveland, and Sam Spencer. Sometimes women played, with Shirley Dorrier once getting on base, if not staying on the donkey.

Considering the Scottsville town team and its opponents, Tommy Stargell says, "It was the closest thing you had then to professional ball. We loved it." Some of the players mentioned here were considered professional quality, but no one really wanted to leave home, play in Arkansas or some other distant minor league. Red Clements said, "Funny thing—Charlottesville had Triple A; that was the extent of being promoted." There was no point and no need to look to baseball then as a profession. Tommy Stargell says, "I maintain that's when baseball was real—played by people like ourselves and played better than now."

Why did town baseball end in Scottsville? Some of the men who considered this question said, like Junior Tyler, "The players got too old!" Marvin Ripley said that, after World War II and into the 1960s, "people got money and cars, and other things to do. Roads were paved, and everyone went looking for the party. Or girls. Or something faster than baseball; baseball was too slow."

In Ken Burns' documentary "Baseball," poet Donald Hall says, "Baseball, because of its continuity over the space of America and the time of America, is a place where memory gathers." And Scottsville is definitely a part of that place.

*Originally published July 2015*

# 12.

# Loving the Luv'n Oven

When the door opened at the new version of the Luv'n Oven last month, crowds gathered for the much-remembered chicken and French fries. The restaurant opened, but due to its popularity, the food ran out that first day.

The Luv'n Oven has been the kind of restaurant that helps define Scottsville. Not for its reviews, its ambiance, the way the food is plated surrounded by swirls of sauce, but just because it has satisfied, day after day, meal after meal, the needs of the community to gather, talk, and eat. Now that the Luv'n Oven has been reborn, it's time to remember its beginnings.

From our town's inception, Scottsville has been outlined by

Valley and Main Street, the river and the hills. South beyond the James is Buckingham, north beyond the hill, Albemarle. Floods came to the bowl between. Then, in 1972, there was one flood too many for the beleaguered merchants, and they began to cast their eyes to the hills. Mayor A. Raymon Thacker envisioned a gutted downtown, left as barren as Columbia or Howardsville by the raging waters; he saw the tax revenues and business license fees going to Albemarle.

The massive attack Raymon Thacker waged against the elements for years is often recounted. With great personal effort, he finally achieved the levee, in 1984, that keeps us safe from the waters, and his second effort, to add the land immediately north of town to Scottsville, finally bore fruit in 1993. None of it was easy, either politically or socially, with tempers and opinions running high, but finally Albemarle gave the mayor a "boundary adjustment"—not an annexation, as a birthday present. That was when he was only 84.

Businesses began moving uptown before the boundary adjustment was effected, and the bank led the way. The shopping center, or "Uptown Commercial Center," according to the town's Comprehensive Plan, was built during 1973-1974. This was when Frances Baker had her own plan: to open a new restaurant on the higher ground.

Frances Baker recently recalled her early days with her husband at the Luv'n Oven. She already ran the downtown Scottsville eatery The Village, where Amici's is now; and she had operated restaurants in Fork Union. In the 1972 flood, the James rose in The Village to the ceiling. "We go to Amici's to eat now," she says.

Frances, whose husband Chester Baker ran the Chevrolet dealership across from the shopping center on James River Road, negotiated with "a man in Farmville." His name is lost, but he had, according to Frances' daughter Terry Baker Bryan, "three or four locations." Chester Baker's intention was to buy the fried chicken recipe and use the name Luv'n Oven. "Two men from Farmville came in and helped us start up," Frances says.

"Being prepared is the secret. Have everything you need at your fingertips." Frances had three children in college, and when they were home, Friday evenings to Sunday afternoons, they worked in the restaurant," along with other young people. "I couldn't have done it without the kids," she says. Terry says the cooks cut up the whole chickens themselves: "Four or five or six cases of chicken a week. Two or three people would work across the table from each other with knives flying!"

Frances Baker came from a large Fluvanna family; her parents had 16 children. They all worked on the farm, Terry says, and the responsibility and effort made them appreciate what they had and how to value it. Terry managed the Luv'n Oven during her college years. "We worked hard, and it was a success."

Jason Woodson has a quick answer when asked about his memories of Luv'n Oven: "Good food at a good price, and you always saw good people." Jason, as a kid, particularly liked the arcade games—the pinball and video games, the first he had ever seen. He recalls the jukebox and the game with the steering wheel you manipulated, just as if you were driving, as pictures of the road flashed by in front of you.

Chub Walsh used to go to the Luv'n Oven "a couple of times a day, sometimes." He'd meet friends there, felt comfortable stretching out one cup of coffee, talking. It was a gathering place, "and I always enjoyed going in." Denise Davis recalls that her father, Ivery Davis, who ran the local cab company, "used to love those chicken livers and gizzards." Denise favored the fries, and would get a milkshake. The Luv'n Oven French fries are frequently mentioned. Students stopped in for an order after school, and parents were happy to buy them for their clamoring children. Barbara Brochu recalls that "when we first moved to Esmont, 35 years ago, my mother-in-law would drive us to get an ice cream cone" at Luv'n Oven. "It was always fun."

Marianne Ramsden, former branch head of the Scottsville Library, remembers taking her family to Luv'n Oven for her son's 10th birthday. "We ordered pizza, and evidently they had run out. We saw a server sprint over to the IGA, and in 15 minutes we had our birthday meal. They really went above and beyond." Marianne also says Luv'n Oven had "some of the best three-piece chicken meals ever—cooked to perfection." The video games were a draw for her Swedish nephew who, on a visit in the 1980s, spent all his American money on them. She herself favored the oldies selection on the jukebox. "My kids, as they got older, would stop at Luv'n Oven for baskets of fries after a summer tubing trip on the James— their idea of a healthy meal!"

Mark Stevens, who owns and operates Coleman's Outdoors downtown, went to Luv'n Oven for lunch. When asked what drew him, he quickly answers, "the fries and the chicken livers." He'd sometimes meet friends there for lunch. "Lots of guys had nowhere else to go and would meet there."

*Nip Chisolm and the lunch staff keep busy.*

Tom Woodson worked at the IGA when he was 17 years old and had left school. It was easy for him to walk to the Luv'n Oven for his lunch break; it had been started, after all, by his former school bus driver, he says, Frances Baker. There were fresh homemade cakes, all the food from scratch. Frances' mother, Northy—Granny—Haislip, made a special sweet potato pie that never stayed on the counter long enough to get cool. He recalls the various lunch specials—ham steak, pork chops, squash casserole, pinto beans with onions. "Good food, quick service," Tom comments. "Frances Baker was a good cook and a good lady. Her mother was an old-fashioned cook, too." Tom was especially fond of the breaded chicken baked the second day in barbeque sauce—"nice and warm, it was delicious." He taught his wife how to make it.

Frances Baker is Bobby Pollard's aunt. Bobby recalls that she "sold chicken by the barrel—what we'd call a bucket" and that the gizzard dinners were very popular. As a kid, though, he mostly remembers the pinball machines, "three of them on the right hand side." The profits from them, he said Frances once told him, paid most of the expenses of the restaurant. "Anything she sold after noon was profit," he remembers her explaining to him. Bobby recalls the many men who gathered there, whom he dubbed "the Scottsville Town Council": Carl Allen, Chub Walsh, Russell Boatwright, and others who came in to sit over coffee.

The work of running the Luv'n Oven took its toll, and Frances, with Terry, sold the restaurant to Frances' sister, Karlen Layne. Karlen ran the Luv'n Oven in 1988 and 1989, and she found that, profitable or not, "14 hours a day, seven days a week was rough." She decided they didn't need to work that hard, and again the place was sold.

Nip Chisholm had another successful run with the Luv'n Oven. Mark Stevens recalls that Nip always had a smile on his face, was always friendly and acknowledged each customer. The *Rural Virginian*, May 1995, ran a Luv'n Oven ad encouraging people to "Come in and see our newly remodeled dining area"; the Luv'n Oven then had catering available and a three-flavor soft-serve ice cream machine.

By 2007, the Luv'n Oven was under the new managership of Donna Spradlin and her sister Shirley Dudley. They had six employees and still produced the spicy deep-fried livers and gizzards, milkshakes, and meatloaf specials on Tuesdays.

Again, the work was found to be difficult, and despite the popularity of the restaurant, it was sold. A succession of owners tried a variety of themes and food in the space, and recently it has been shuttered. Once again, the Chisholms are running it. (As Bobby Pollard notes, "Jimmy's mother is Frances Baker's niece; "three different Haislips have had a hand in it.") Jimmy Chisholm out front, Nip standing by. "I'm right back where I started 40 years ago," he told customer Bill Mason. "It's good to see the family running it again," says Mark Stevens.

Frances Baker, "always remembering back," said she wouldn't give Jimmy any advice. But if she did, it would be, "Keep the food fresh, and don't be lazy." Come on in, grab a booth, a cup of coffee or a corndog, chicken on a bun, a piece of chocolate cake. Bring a friend. That's what Luv'n Oven is all about.

*Former owner Nip Chisholm oversees the lunch staff.*

*Originally published June 2015*

# 13.

# The Life and Times of Scottsville's Town Council

*This Scottsville Town Council, like others before and since, was made up of prominent local businessmen. Row One: Jacinto V. Pereira, Peter Foland, W.E. Moon; Row Two: Dr. Joseph P. Blair, Tom Heath, Jackson Beal, and Thomas A. Fox. . Photo courtesy of the Scottsville Museum.*

Seven men look at us directly, or at least at the photographer, William Burgess, around 1900 or shortly thereafter. Burgess, who lived from 1871-1935, was Scottsville's professional photographer, and with his studio Idylwood, on Drivers Hill east of downtown, documented much of the town's life, from individuals to events to panoramic views. Give a party, it was said, and Willie would show up with his big box camera, invited or not.

Here he caught the Town Council, including Mayor Peter Foland in the white beard, as they assume a formal pose in the studio with a general attitude of indulgent good humor on their faces. The Scottsville Museum shows a different version of the photograph, cropped at the knees of the men in the front row and captioned: "This Scottsville Town Council, like others before and since, was made up of prominent local businessmen: Row One (L to R): Jacinto V. Pereira, Peter Foland, W.E. Moon; Row Two (L to R): Dr. Joseph P. Blair, Tom Heath, Jackson Beal, Thomas A. Fox." The picture is dated both 1900 and circa 1909 in different places on the museum website.

What was the first decade of the twentieth century like in the Scottsville these men governed? The *Scottsville Courier*, published from 1877 to 1906, was continued by the *Scottsville Enterprise*, but a complete run of issues does not exist locally. Without newspapers, we can use Burgess' photographs to outline the time and place. Valley and Main Street were unpaved, though a concrete sidewalk had been built. Standing with your back to the current police station and the James River bridge, looking north, you would have seen—most imposingly—the gabled-roofed Traveler's Rest Hotel, a balcony at the second floor on Main Street, Sclater's Hardware Store in the eastern bay beneath. Next to the hotel, with its 60-seat dining room to feed locals and, indeed, travelers, and 19 rooms to lodge the drummers who came to show shop owners new lines of goods, was the wooden livery stables. The canal company stables that had been in this location during the Civil War were burned by Sheridan. S. Philips rebuilt them, and horses maintained their dominance on this corner until the roads were paved and people chose to own and drive automobiles. A filling station was established by the 1940s.

Valley Street had trees only on the east side. Electricity was not available early in the century; another Burgess photo shows a man lighting one of the carbide street lamps. The Carlton House, later Bruce's Drug Store, on the southwest corner of Valley and Main, was another Scottsville hotel at the time. Downstairs was Dickenson's Drug Store. Directly across West Main, the C.R. Dorrier General

Merchandise store was erected around 1912, offering everything from vegetables to overalls, seed and fertilizer, boots and shoes. This is now the James River Tavern.

At this vantage point, in 1900, the police station was not behind you, nor the Silver Grill that preceded it, but the two-story brick Brady Building. This was Scottsville's school from 1876 to 1906. Susie Blair, whose father Joseph is one of the pictured Town Council members, recalled the school "once upon a time": the painted-over front windows along the street, so students weren't distracted; high fences, dirt, gender-separated play yard in the rear, toward the river; the school bell. Heated with wood stoves, the youngest pupils were grouped together under the famously strict Miss Willie Hickok; across the hall the middle grades were presided over by one of Hickok's former students, Miss Ella Farrar. The older students were upstairs "in the principal's room, where everybody met in the morning to sing a hymn and say the Lord's Prayer." It's not clear that grades as high as 11 or 12 were offered; perhaps students who stayed on were taught what the teacher knew, but it wasn't until the new building on Schoolhouse Hill, above Victory Hall, became Virginia's first accredited high school in 1913 that Scottsville formally offered a four-year high school curriculum.

The population of Scottsville proper dropped from 1900-1910, Virginia Moore notes in *Scottsville on the James*, from 384 to 283. It had, in fact, declined since the 1850s, when many goods from the valley were transshipped not from Scottsville but from Charlottesville or Baltimore. There was a smallpox epidemic in 1900; the Great Migration that took so many Black people north to live and work was just beginning. But still there was plenty of entertainment and activity in Scottsville: music, skating on the river or ponds in winter, community-wide light operas and pageants, horse races, parties and dances at the big houses. The "grand Jollification," the c. 1905 celebration of CSA Major James C. Hill, included state politicos, plenty of speeches, and a parade through town.

The Council, perhaps facing the population decline, the odd mix of blacksmith shops and carriage works with automobiles, bought an ad in the April 11, 1909 *Richmond Times-Dispatch*: "Invest

Your Money," the ad suggested, "Make Your Home in Scottsville." The text listed the need for a furniture factory, wagon factory, barrel factory, manufacturer of shirts and overalls, creameries; it listed as enticing attributes "no city tax…pure water, paved sidewalks, good roads, two growing banks…beautiful homes and home sites."

While the town's plumbing "remained in a rather primitive state," Virginia Moore observes, many modern changes were beginning to take place. The telephone and telegraph were possibilities, railroads linked Scottsville north and south. President Theodore Roosevelt, his wife Edith, and often some of their children visited their nearby rustic retreat, Pine Knot, from 1905 to 1908, hiring Dick McDaniel from the Antioch neighborhood to cook for them and guide the president on hunts. McDaniel kept Roosevelt's dogs and stabled his horse in Scottsville.

Thomas Cleveland Sadler, born 1889 and living in the Antioch area northeast of town, remembered Dr. Stinson and his first automobile in Scottsville; the novelty of beginning to use oil lamps rather than candles; ice houses and smoking the hams after hog-killing; and delivering mail over dirt roads and across creeks. Sadler's grandfather died in 1903. "Two years before he died, President McKinley was shot. It was about a week before we heard about it. Sixty-two years later, President Kennedy was shot, and the whole world knew about it within the hour."

Susan Hill Dunn, born 1869, wrote her memories of growing up in Scottsville in 1934. She recalled entertaining on front porches, taking the train and muddy roads to visit friends in far-off Nelson County, and her 1896 wedding party, where everyone who ate the raw oysters offered on ice became ill. Scottsville "was the home of many men of ability and position," she says; "they form a circle, not in the least fashionable but intelligent and neighborly."

Records are not complete, but it wasn't until 1976 that Susie Blair and Cenie Moon were elected to Council, then Jacqueline Grove in 1984 and Lucinda Wheeler in 1988. Here the men of the Town Council are secure in gazing out at their world, more settled than ours, but nevertheless changing. Jacinto Pereira, in this grouping, presents a distinctive look.

Miranda Burnett, recent Civil War-era re-enactor, guide at Ash Lawn-Highland, and Scottsville Museum board member, considers it "very interesting that he seems most different in clothing and manner." A Richmond Times-Dispatch article of April 1909 says that Pereira came to the U.S. from his native England in 1877, travelled in the South, and settled in Scottsville. He is praised as "one of the best businessmen in town [and] one of the most reliable of the city fathers." Pereira established and ran the Fidelity Bank, on the west side of Valley Street, near the corner of Main, and built the Traveler's Rest Hotel in 1909.

The cut of Pereira's clothes is generally like that of the others, but the material of the coat and waistcoat is heavier. The velvet collar—like the collar on the popular Chesterfield coat—denotes an outdoor jacket, Miranda says. The waistcoat is possibly quilted. Alone among the men whose footwear we can see, Pereira wears tall leather gaiters, exactly like those shown, Miranda points out, in the 1908 Sears Catalog (now online)—"Russet English Riding Leggings, used largely throughout Great Britain by the best class of horseman." "Did he come in late and not change his outdoor jacket?" Miranda wonders. "The others are like, 'Dude, you're keeping us waiting!' His hair is mussed, he sticks out like a sore thumb." Is the mayor's body language, his slight lean away from Pereira, expressive?

The mayor, Peter Foland, wears the same type of suit, then called a lounge suit, in its single-breasted form, with the mandatory watch chain and fob. By this time, Miranda says, the rise of the railroads had led to the importance of "everything being on schedule. A watch was a statement: 'You can depend on me; I'm on time.'" Wristwatches were not much used by men until after World War I. Foland has a stiff collar, like the others (around $1.90 a dozen from Sears), but no cuffs, which Miranda finds significant. His black tie is possibly folded and tucked, rather than tied. His stiff shirtfront is held together with a stud. The linen shirtfronts, cuffs, and collars were all shown in the Sears Catalog, starting at nine cents each.

Foland's shoes are Oxford style. Like the other men in the front row, he sits on one of Burgess's ornate three-legged stools, his feet resting on the photographer's odd, almost grass-like rug. In the 1900 census, Foland's age is given as 55; his wife, Bettie's, 54; they married in 1867. Six of their eight children were alive in 1900. Foland had served with the Tennessee Volunteers in the Civil War. He gave his occupation as "ferryman" in the 1880 U.S. Census, and by 1900, he was listed as a salesman in Scottsville.

The third occupant of the front row is W.E. (Willie) Moon. Perusal of "Sketches of the Moon and Barclay Families," 1939, in the Scottsville Local History Corner, suggests he is not a Moon of the Moon Ghost family, along with Orianna and Lottie Moon, and he is not buried in the Scottsville Cemetery. W.E.'s birth year is 1868 or '69, in Fluvanna; he was the son of John Washington Moon. He was buried in 1942 at the Antioch Baptist Church. Willie married Cora, and they had six children. He told the U.S. Census in 1940 that he was a shopkeeper, owned his home, and went to school through eighth grade. The museum says he owned the Mercantile Store on East Main, one building east of Dr. Blair's dentistry office. Willie is the only town councilor in a striped suit jacket—maybe from his own store. He sports the only patterned tie as well, and in his cuffs, "dumbbell" rather than leverback style, cufflinks set with a stone of a sort shown by the 1908 Sears Catalog as very up-to-date.

Dr. Joseph P. Blair, top row left, was Scottsville's dentist. Born in 1864 or '65, he lived in a house he first rented, then owned, on Jackson Street, near his in-laws. His practice was in a long-gone frame building just to the east of the Brady Building, virtually on top of Mink Creek. There was a grocery on the ground floor (later a barbershop and shoe-shine place). His parents bought the Tipton House on Harrison Street after his father served in the Confederacy. Blair definitely graced the upper echelon of Scottsville society. He married Susie Powers, who lived at the Terrace on Jackson and in a hotel the Powers owned on Main Street. Susie Blair, their daughter, returned to Scottsville after teaching speech and drama at Hollins College and became a beloved Scottsville figure. Blair played baritone horn in the Scottsville town band. He was chairman of the Albemarle School Board for 37 years, the only chairman—when he died in 1931—they'd ever had. Blair's clothing is much like the others'. As does Jackson Beal, he has a pin just below the knot of his necktie, perhaps an organizational emblem.

Thomas S. Heath, one of the oldest of the town fathers, stands next to Blair, confident and alert. Like Fox, at the end of the row, he wears wire-rimmed glasses, shown in a wide variety of styles in Sears at around $1.90 each. (Sears also offered an eye chart for self-diagnosis.) His tie is the same white as his shirt, a formal approach to menswear in 1900, Miranda says. Born in either 1848 or 1849—the census figures vary—or 1848, according to his Scottsville Cemetery gravestone, Heath married Mary S. Heath in 1870 and had two children. He owned and operated the Heath Mill, making flour at a site now at the foot of the current bridge. Raymon Thacker said that the mill dates from 1920; Heath must have had other work as well. According to the Scottsville Museum website, the Heaths lived in the Tavern on Main Street.

Jackson Beal, third from the left in the back row, was born about 1846. He told the U.S. Census that he went through eighth grade, married Mary E. Bledsoe, and had a son, Jackson Beal, Jr. He owned his home on Harrison Street and was an insurance agent, as well as Scottsville's Justice of the Peace. The museum adds that his office was in the Beal Building on Valley Street and Bird. Mayor Barry Grove's great grandfather, Jackson Beal, was Scottsville's mayor from 1905 to 1930, and mentored Raymon Thacker.

Thomas Fox is said on the Scottsville Museum website to be "the first plumbing contractor in Scottsville and installed the first water and sewer system in town." He is not buried in the Scottsville Cemetery. Fox looks as if he could be wearing a handkerchief in his left breast pocket, a style then gaining popularity, but Miranda thinks it is more likely a folded paper note.

Miranda Burnett is beginning to plan for this year's late-October Twilight Tour, looking for new people to participate and new characters to portray. Her own combined interests in textile arts and history prove to be a fascinating way of "getting close to your ancestors, knowing what their life was like." She sews all her own clothes, and likes to wear 1940s styles. "This is accepted now as part of a person's interests and character but never was in the past.

You used to be shunned if you didn't wear what everyone else was wearing."

The period 1900-1910 was one of a changing system for fashion, affected greatly by ready-to-wear clothing for men. No longer was everything made by hand; at the end of the nineteenth century, men's trousers, jackets, coats, shirts, and undergarments could all be bought at a store or from a catalog. There tended to be a functional simplicity in men's clothing—fashions didn't change quickly—and now this was reinforced by uniform sizing and styling. The Scottsville Town Council were individuals, men who'd worked to help make their way, and they dressed, mostly alike, to show it.

*Originally published April 2015*

# 14.

# The Yankees Ride Into Scottsville

Buildings in place at the time the Yankees rode through Scottsville.
Photo Courtesy of the Scottsville Museum.

One fact both Northerners and Southerners could agree upon, in early March of 1865, was that "the roads [were] awful, and the weather exceeding bad," as Judy Egberd Watson of Charlottesville wrote to her daughter in Greensboro. With "no railroad communication now in any direction, and no mails from anywhere," she said she was sending this undated letter by a friend to Lynchburg for mailing (Mary Rawlings, "Sheridan's Raid Through Albemarle," *Magazine of Albemarle County History*, 1954).

Her news was not about troop numbers, the campaign in Waynesboro, or other matters military. She reported what she was seeing in Charlottesville as Sheridan's Army of the Shenandoah spread out "in various places—this writer invited a colonel to stay in her house [on Park Street] and use the stables." After receiving a polite acceptance and "an elegant [visiting] card," she gratifyingly found that no other soldiers disturbed her. She wrote that public property had been stolen, "but no buildings were burnt in town; even the Depot was spared, because its destruction by fire would have endangered private property." (While the university buildings and military hospitals were passed over, damage was in fact done to warehouses and factories, a tannery, and several railroad bridges. Dr. Orianna Moon of Viewmont, who would later open a hospital with her husband in Scottsville, was a surgeon at Charlottesville's General Hospital.)

*2nd US cavalry reenactment showing a 2010 exercise.*

Sheridan quartered himself at 522 Park Street, where "Miss Betsy Coles of the Enniscorthy family" was living; Merritt at 303 East High; Custer at The Farm, in the c. 1825 house there, in the southeast section of Charlottesville. The soldiers were scattered in the surrounding countryside, which consequently fared less well; "our country friends have suffered dreadfully. Corn meal, flour, hay, horses, and negroes were all in great demand." The Union came March 3rd; on Monday, the 6th, they marched south in three columns.

It was sixteen months since President Lincoln had spoken at the Gettysburg Cemetery, urging on the effort that had already killed so many: "It is right for us to be here dedicated to the great task remaining....That this nation, under God, shall have a new birth of freedom...." It was less than a month before the two armies would meet at Appomattox Court House and, acting on Lincoln's demand that "there be no hangings, there must be no bloody work, there must be none of that," Grant would decline Lee's symbolically proffered sword and later, when leaving the McLean house, tip his hat to the surrendered Southern leader.

In between these dates came mud, rain, and the raid in Scottsville. Sheridan divided his 3rd Cavalry into two large divisions, sending Major General Wesley Merritt and Brigadier General Thomas Devin directly south toward Scottsville, and Brevet General Custer with three divisions, Sheridan accompanying, southwest along the railroad and through North and South Garden almost to Amherst Court House. He sent a smaller troop toward Palmyra. The forces were to reunite after damaging as much useful infrastructure as possible March 8th at New Market (now Norwood) on the James River in nearby Nelson County.

Devin and Merritt, aged 43 and 31 respectively ("the war at this stage was mostly a young man's effort," with Sheridan and Custer aged 34 and 26 respectively, according to *Trices of Virginia* by Robert H. Trice, quoting Nicholas) went south along the unsurfaced road, generally paralleling what we know as Route 20. There is still not major development along this road linking Albemarle County's past and current courthouse towns. In places, except for power lines and machine-rolled hay, the land might look as it did through the pouring rain that early spring.

Scouts had given reports to Sheridan in Charlottesville; a map was not necessary. The shorter marches of this period of the campaign were in that way different from much of the war, when the absence of maps—North and South, commercial as well as military maps—led, as Richard Stephenson writes in *Virginia in Maps, Four Centuries of Settlement, Growth, and Development*, 2000, "to the spectacle of Northern—and Southern—generals fighting in their own country and not knowing where they were going or how to get there." Jedediah Hotchkiss, the Confederate's best topographical engineer and cartographer, a self-taught Staunton schoolteacher, produced his maps usually after drawing from horseback. Hotchkiss sketched the informal map, pictured here, in July 1865, emphasizing the relative ease of getting from Charlottesville to Scottsville and the James. "The Yankees marched in good order in spite of the heavy spring rains," writes Ervin L. Jordan, Jr. in *Charlottesville and the University of Virginia in the Civil War*, 1988.

Authoritative firsthand accounts of the following days in Scottsville are limited to U.S.—Northern—official records and reports, though family memories remain. We are fortunate that Richard L. Nicholas, who grew up "on a bluff looking at the James River in Buckingham"—directly across the river from Lock 22, where his ancestors at The Hermitage might have watched the marching and the burning in Scottsville unfold, and who went to Scottsville High School, has written the well-researched and useful *Sheridan's James River Campaign of 1865 Through Central Virginia*, 2012. (This book is available now at Baine's Books and Coffee and at the Scottsville Museum after it opens in April.)

Using the 1875 Green Peyton map of Albemarle, Nicholas shows a few properties on the way from Charlottesville to Scottsville: Hartman's Mill on Moore's Creek, a few places just under Southwest Mountain, and then T. Wingfield at Bellair, off to the right (or west) of the road. A large 1834 mill in that vicinity, Eolus, was not burned, due either to the heavy rain or to the successful intervention of a devoted miller. The men were moving toward the James River and Kanawha Canal, where there would be sufficient work to do. (K. Edward Lay, in *Architecture of Jefferson County*, 2000, notes that Union troops did burn the mill complex owned by William D. Meriwether at Moore's Creek near the Three Notch'd Road.)

Four miles north of Scottsville, at George W. Dillard's c. 1810 Glendower—Dillard also owned the 1847 Chester, on River Road in Scottsville, which soon became a Union encampment—the soldiers took two horses, according to Dillard, after having been given the contents of his smokehouse and mill. At the close of the war, Dillard tried to get reparations as a Union sympathizer, to no avail.

The Union troops arrived in Scottsville "the first time...from mid-afternoon on Monday, March 6." They would leave March 7th and return the 9th and 10th. The official reports, Nicholas says, give "very limited information on Scottsville....In fact, none of the reports specifically state that they spent a night in town." But the troops, bent on destruction, caused damage that Nicholas follows in the Land Tax

Assessments of Albemarle County for 1866; eleven lots in town had assessments lowered because of "injury by fire"—"a clear reference to destruction resulting from Sheridan's raid," Nicholas notes. The chief engineer of the James River Canal Co., Edward Lorraine, reported that besides two canal bridges, the company's shop, equipment, and stores such as beef and corn were all damaged; he says 26 houses were burned.

Can we not assume that the initial wave of Sheridan's men, under Devin and Merritt, marching down Valley Street, would first have seen the still imposing three-story brick mill and later tobacco warehouse and 20th century braid factory, now the James River Brewery, built around 1836? It would have been spared destruction for its use as a Confederate hospital, thereby leaving one of Scottsville's notable structures untouched for its future development. Just north of that building was (and is) the 1800 brick two-and-a-half story building with a wood frame structure, a summer kitchen and slave quarters in its rear, near Mink Creek, possibly from 1790, according to the National Register of Historic Places registration form for Scottsville's Historic District. Since the mill wasn't burned, neither was this large house, which is now for sale.

What else still exists in Scottsville that the invading soldiers would have seen and evaluated? Across and south on Route 20, the two-story brick townhouse from about 1832—to become Scottsville's apothecary in 1876 and much later the Sesame Seed natural food store—must have looked much as it does now. The Harris Building, c. 1840, housed Martha Harris's millinery and dry goods store and now Ward Realty. In the next block south, the Beal building, constructed from 1841 to 1850 as the Beal family's hardware and general merchandise store, showed both its stepped-back parapets, the south one now gone. The Griffin building, c. 1840, which "may have served as an inn during Scottsville's canal days," according to the 2010 Scottsville Museum's pamphlet entitled "Scottsville On the James, Town Guide and Walking Tour" (available at Baine's and at the museum), still has its upper windows in their original locations, while the treatment of the façade now suggests the presence of two buildings rather than one.

*The Hotchkiss map. Jedediah Hotchkiss, the confederate's best topographical engineer and cartographer produced his maps usually drawing from horseback. He shows the relative ease of getting from Charlottesville to Scottsville and the James River. Photo courtesy of the Library of Congress.*

West, up Bird Street, the 1832 Presbyterian Church, with an exterior staircase to its slave gallery, was in place, though the Episcopal Church further west wasn't constructed until 1875. Some of our important commercial buildings date from the turn of the 20th century, after what Virginia Moore calls "the agony of Reconstruction." Many of those from the heyday of the Scottsville economic boom, however, Moore's "Golden Era," were there then, as now: c. 1840 Eagle Hotel—later the Carlton House on the northwest corner of Valley and Main, long known as Bruce's Drug Store, now Balance Studio, was part of the Confederate hospital; an 1833 version of the

Scottsville Methodist Church on Main, burned down in 1976; the 1846 Disciples of Christ Church, now the Scottsville Museum, and the nextdoor Barclay House from 1800-1838. Further down Main Street, on the north side, the Doll family house was probably constructed in the first decade of the 19th century, according to the "Town Guide and Walking Tour." The Tavern had greeted visitors and businesspeople since around 1840. Across the street, one of the town's earliest structures, often called the Colonial Cottage and now called the Fore House, was built around 1780, architectural expert K. Edward Lay concludes. Next to it, the Herndon House from the early 19th century would have also witnessed the passage of the troops. It is believed that Devin found quarters on March 9th up Old Drivers Hill to the north.

Small domestic buildings such as these cottages and the Tompkins House, possibly constructed in 1780 on Jackson Street, with

*The 2nd US Cavalry reenactment begins the ride to Scottsvile. Photo by Robert London.*

its four corner chimneys, were not of interest to the Union soldiers unless they contained food. Near to them, however, the Canal Warehouse and canal turning basin must have been. Again, by good fortune, the warehouse was not damaged—until the next flood—and instead left to await its rebirth as Scottsville continued to develop. Canal boats, as Nicholas writes, and their stores were destroyed. The foodstuffs they had been loaded with were hunted down in private homes, and Elias Mahoney's houseboat was burned.

Returning to Harrison Street, the 1830 house we know as Old Hall was commandeered by General Merritt on the Union's return to Scottsville, on their way to Columbia. Custer housed himself on Warren Street at the 1835 Cliffside, with soldiers camped all over the lawns; that story was a centerpiece of the original Scottsville 1908 UDC women's narratives of their Civil War connections. Shadows, 470 Harrison, is "the only frame Greek Revival structure" in the downtown area, notes the "Town Guide." Built around 1825, it might well have housed a Union general but was spared. Homes further along were also marched past and not molested: 521 Harrison, built in the early 19th century and identified later as Dr. Reuben Lindsay's house; the Jefferies-Bruce House, c. 1838, owned after the war by a Confederate army sergeant, a doctor-druggist, whose family later sold the house to Thomas Ellison Bruce, of Bruce's Drug Store. The 1842-1844 Tipton House, further along Harrison, is also on a high English basement, in Greek Revival style. There was next another fine brick house, later razed by the Scottsville Baptist Church, and the church itself, first constructed in 1840. Finally, the Lewis House, now called Wynnewood, on Warren Street, was built in 1850 on the massive Lewis property; lower-ranking Union officers stayed there.

While much of the spring of 1865 was rainy and foggy, with the rivers too high to cross and the citizens in "despair and misery" (Jordan), some of the March days the Union were in Scottsville were, at least as recorded by Jedediah Hotchkiss in his journal, "fine" while frosty, or raining only at night. The day the 3,000 Union troops moved out of Scottsville toward Richmond, leaving us the legend of Sheridan's cufflinks, given to the little girl on the street who pointed, when asked by the General, in the correct direction—and, as the

Scottsville Museum site says, leaving economic destruction it would take forty years to recover from—that day, March 10th, was, according to Hotchkiss, "a fine day."

*Originally published February 2015*

# 15.

# William Walker House: A Piece of History Caught in Time

The early settlers of Albemarle, writes John Hammond Moore in *Albemarle, Jefferson's Country, 1727-1976*, were "fortunate [to have] the broad James almost at their doorsteps. And in time, rude pathways became roads cutting through the forest to various landing and ferry sites, some of them growing into little river towns of considerable importance, notably Howardsville, Warren, and Scottsville."

While Howardsville might no longer describe its position on the river as fortunate, with improvements, Scottsville does. Warren grew and flourished in the early nineteenth century, largely because of its place on the river, but was not, like Howardsville, overwhelmed by the James. Its demise came well before mid-century as planters took their grains and crops to Scottsville for shipment and merchants moved their businesses there to accommodate them.

Dr. George Nicholas held a large patent in huge Albemarle County, owning 2,600 acres by 1729 and establishing the settlement of Warren by 1735. Nearby Scottsville was established in 1745. The Nicholas family was rich in land, goods, and influence. Brothers George and Wilson Cary were Albemarle delegates to the 1788 Constitutional Convention, and Wilson Cary became Virginia's nineteenth governor in 1814.

Wilson Cary Nicholas built a plantation house on his grandfather's land, calling it Mt. Warren. The vision of a major settlement and transport center was enhanced by establishing a landing at the James and Ballinger Creek, a warehouse, and later a mill and tavern. It was here Thomas Jefferson stayed the night when journeying to his Poplar Forest estate. Establishing a ferry (finally destroyed by hurricanes Camille and Agnes) and later the Kanawha Canal seemed to cement Warren's importance. The state legislature formally established the town of Warren Ferry in 1795; there was a depot for wheat and for tobacco, as well as a distillery.

To this promising settlement came William Walker, a merchant who arrived in America from Donegal, Ireland in 1780 when he was ten years old. He married Elizabeth Jones and brought his wife to Warren in 1793; they probably first resided at his store near Ballinger Creek. He began speculating in real estate and bought the saw mill and distillery with two partners, Samuel Shelton and John Staples.

Walker also bought two lots from Nicholas, now on the east side of the road through Warren, State Route 627, Warren Ferry Road, and began building a house. This small brick structure has an eye-catching, almost heart-stopping presence, clearly a piece of history caught in time. It's hard to drive past it and not want to stop to admire the place, to be amazed.

There is a fair amount of documentation for the construction of the William Walker house, mostly through insurance records. "It doesn't need to be called circa," the present owner, Emily Marsteller, says. It was begun in early 1803, William Walker took up residence in December, and it was finished by 1805. Unfortunately, William Walker died young, before his house was completed. The construction was overseen by his brother, James, a carpenter and millwright. Oral tradition links the design of the house to Thomas Jefferson.

It seems remarkable, Emily Marsteller notes, that a house of such sophistication was erected "in what was then the hinterlands." The 32'x34' building has been called "a little jewel" by Susan DeAlba (*Country Roads, Albemarle County, Virginia*) and is noted by the Virginia Landmarks Register as "diminutive," with "subtle and sophisticated simplicity." It was meant to be, of course, an outstanding feature in a growing urban environment, broadcasting the status and taste of the builder.

Charlottesville architect Donald A. Swofford made the William Walker house the subject of his Master's thesis at the UVA School of Architecture, studying it as an example for adaptive restoration. He forges as many connections as his research allows to Thomas Jefferson, concluding not that Jefferson actually drew the house plans but that he influenced them and may possibly have suggested them. "There is a formidable link between Jefferson and the William Walker house design." (Don Swofford, "William Walker House, Warren, Virginia: A Study for Adaptive Restoration," Master's thesis in architectural history, UVA, 1976.)

The compact brick structure now faces the river, as originally intended; in the early twentieth century it had been reoriented with porches and a new door to face west towards the road. The family living quarters are on the raised main floor, originally built as two small bed chambers east and west of the center hall, with a parlor and dining room at the rear of the building. Currently the parlor is a single spacious room across the back; ceilings are 12 feet tall. Below, in a high English basement, are the kitchen and a second room for servants.

Emily Marsteller and her family, who had UVA connections and friends in Charlottesville, bought the house while living in

Roanoke, 1983. They used it on weekends and for holidays. It was in good condition, and the family "fell in love with the little place." Emily was particularly pleased with the front hall, with its neat proportions and wooden mouldings.

*The cooking fireplace in the Walker kitchen.*

The Anderson family owned the William Walker house since 1892, and the house had been inherited by a number of the relatives and finally was lived in by 90-year-old Annie Anderson. There was no running water or electricity; her grandfather "didn't like changes." Hugh Weaver bought the house in the 1970s and had it restored and modernized, as well as returned to its original look; he stayed at Lumpkin's, Emily remembers, while the work was underway. Swofford was consulted frequently, and the plans he developed in his thesis were used as the basis of the restoration.

Marianne Ramsden, later the head librarian at Scottsville Library, cleaned house for Weaver, who was an art and antiques dealer from Richmond and used it as a summer house. She did small repairs and got rid of dust and spiders. Many changes were needed to restore the house. Around 1871, roofed porches had been put across the south and east facades, as well as the north (which may have been in the original design, Swofford notes); the interior was changed to suit Victorian tastes, with some doors blocked, and the door between the salon and dining room enlarged. A lean-to was erected on the west side as a shed.

Surprisingly, the original portico, so central to the house's design and look today, survived intact during these changes. Damage being done to the bricks and roof by the newer porches was repaired. The six fireplaces and much of their original Federal-style moulding remain. Emily still has the iron crane used for large cooking pots in the kitchen fireplace. The "prettiest fireplace," she shows, is in the southeast chamber, its detailed eighteenth century surround painted an appealing soft sea green. The new basement floor is Alberene stone set in cement. Bricks for the house, Swofford writes, were "possibly shipped from a commercial brickyard to Warren, arriving via the Kanawha Canal; they are similar in size to those used at two of the Pavilions on the UVA Lawn." They are laid, Swofford observed, in "economical three-course American bond (three rows of bricks lengthwise topped by one row short end out.)" Wood for the house's beams was locally milled, probably at Walker's own mill. A local blacksmith produced necessary hardware. Square nails are used, for the most part, where the structure isn't pegged, Emily says.

How does Swofford tie all this to Thomas Jefferson? He found documentation that Walker's brother, the house-builder James, was an employee of Jefferson's who excused himself from completion of Jefferson's mill because of the press of other work—perhaps this house. "Design details" and the fineness of the work set the house apart, Swofford says, from typical construction of the period in the Piedmont but align it with several Jefferson-inspired or designed houses in Albemarle County, such as Glen Echo, Bentivar, and even the Bruce House in Scottsville, which he outlines in detail. Finally, as this house shows the classical influence of the Italian architect Palladio, it's important to note that

*The pegged rafters. Photo by Ruth Klippstein*

Jefferson owned one of the few available copies of a translation of Palladio and himself drew house designs based on Palladio. Swofford shows the several ways William Walker House is, as others say, a "perfect example of Palladian architecture," while being, in his words, "somewhat more relaxed and functional...[with] regional and restrained modifications."

Jefferson could not have envisioned the demise of Warren, hastened by the opening of the Staunton Turnpike to Scottsville in 1827. Citizens were leaving in droves; in a March 1818 letter that Swofford found, Margaret Nicholas wrote that her daughter and family were returning to Baltimore. She doesn't blame them: "I think they are perfectly right not to remain in so dreary a place as Warren."

*The entry hall and door to the southeast chamber of Walker house.*

Scottsville grew and flourished all through the 1840s and '50s, whereas Warren lost its bid to become an urban center. Fortunately, there are remains. Emily Marsteller credits Don Swofford with "saving the William Walker House," since he carefully documented it, demonstrated its importance to our architectural heritage, and "got people interested in it." A December 22nd, 1974 *Washington Post* article by, according to Swofford's description, "the great art critic... Sarah Booth Conroy," publicized Swofford's ideas before his thesis was finished. "She heard about me at a cocktail party," he says, "the way things were done in the '70s and earlier." Her article, appearing just before the sale of the house to Weaver, catches the sense of

103

excitement about verifying the links to Jefferson and the long, useful life of the house. She notes the "two chimneys with their beautifully detailed chimney caps…slate roof and its neat double-hipped form. It leaks here and there," she says, "but then so do some new houses." Conroy suggests that while Warren is "hardly even a wide place in the road," this Jeffersonian design displays a vision for a small, domestic design—within Jefferson's large view of America—that we can enjoy, emulate, and learn from. It is, Swofford writes, a "visual tie with the past," part of our "architectural heritage which is irreplaceable at any cost today…."

*Originally published October 2014*

# 16.

# A History of Maple Hill

"Daddy, there's a house in the road," Gene Harding's kids yelled at him as he was driving home from the Scottsville pool, coming over a rise on Route 20 near the Catholic Church. It was June 13th, 1984, and there was, in fact, a house taking up the two lanes of highway. The surprise of it gave Gene "the weirdest feeling," and he says now he had no idea what it was and so almost ran into it.

*Daily Progress* photographer Jim Carpenter showed it to us all the next day, but many people remember it. Some took photographs, though so much time has passed that it's been impossible to recover them. Marianne Ramsden recalls seeing it "not too far from where it was going. The moving man did a great job. The house looked huge, and we had to wait. But it was OK—we figured we'd never see that again!"

The Maple Hill Cottage, as it's called in K. Edward Lay's *Architecture of Jefferson Country*, was originally built on the Maple Hill estate, "almost directly across from where the Catholic Church is now," says Sam Spangler, who bought and moved the house. It is such a strong, well-built structure, Sam says, that it could once have been the original main dwelling, becoming, with the addition of the more modern building there now, a tenant's house. It has the classic two rooms on each floor but is made larger with a full English basement. Sam thinks the construction shows it to have been built c. 1790, and Tom Phillips, who has owned it since it was repositioned, agrees. Tom thinks this house and Stuart Munson's Colonial Cottage on Main Street (*Scottsville Monthly*, May 2014) were probably built by the same person.

Tom, a former restoration consultant and implementer, offers details that bolster the date: hand-hewn nails and beams of 12-inch pine, stronger and denser than any you could buy today, and the construction of the two chimneys on the ends of the house: they are attached to the structure halfway up the second floor, and then, when there'd be no need to access them from inside, they are free-standing, the small gap quite evident from the ground. Tom points out the vertical marks of the pit saw that created the beams, as well as the broadaxe that smoothed them. In fact, Tom says, the beams are only smoothed where it is important for them to be even, and

*The 1790 stairway, still in use.*
*Photos by Ruth Klippstein.*

that is under the floorboards or behind the wainscoting, where an even surface is presented. On the living floor beneath, the beams are left in their rustic condition. Due to the chimneys, the first course of beams around each floor, starting on top of the brick foundation, is a summer beam, tied into the center beam and perpendicular joists and carrying the entire structural weight of the house.

Sam Spangler, then employed at Southern States (now Augusta Coop), was delivering fertilizer to Maple Hill when by chance the farm manager, Charlie Owen, told him the property owner, John Kluge, wished to get rid of the house, which he didn't need and which was now in the middle of a cornfield. Owen didn't want to destroy the building, and Spangler agreed; "Give it to me," he said. Charlie Owen opined that he couldn't do that, but they agreed on a trade for three loads of fertilizer. This, Sam thinks, was about $3,000.

He didn't, however, have a place to put it. Describing his hope to preserve a piece of old Scottsville history to Jack Manahan, history professor, genealogist, and owner of nearby Fairview, Manahan was happy to come to the rescue. He sold Sam two acres of pasture about a mile south from the house, on the west side of the road. "It couldn't have been farther than that, or I couldn't have moved the house," Sam says, "though its solidness made it somewhat easier to do."

Sam confesses to "not being 100% sure [he] could do it." He prepared the new site with a brick English basement, built by Sharkie Massie and S. J. Boatwright of oversized brick so that it would be thick and similar to the original, and contacted a house mover his father knew in Fredericksburg; "I have to give credit to this man," E. E. Ayers, he acknowledges. Ayers had moved some large tanks for Southern States and later moved another house for Sam. They made a house-wide cut in the bank leaving the Maple Hill land  you can still see this today.

Spangler had the power company come to raise the power lines so they could get under them, and they cut the house from the basement. Moving the structure with its chimneys intact was unusual and difficult, but—in the end—possible. A cable through the house tied the two chimneys together. They didn't even take off the porch but drove out of the Maple Hill field, tipping like a boat in water,

Sam says, in what he thought a dangerous way. "Stop!" he called; "Go slower." Ayers said he had to keep up speed to proceed at all, and they turned onto Route 20, virtually touching both sides of the road, and drove south about a mile to the new site.

Today it would be on YouTube before morning, but now we have to imagine the stately procession: cars waiting both north and south, as well as the ticklish repositioning of the building on top of its new foundation and entrance. The original glass was still intact, and Sam had Stuart Tapscott dig up the old boxwoods from Maple Hill with "big scoops of dirt. They never left the bucket until we put them in the same sized hole at the new place."

The house on its current site.

There are tall cedars around the property front now, almost hiding the house, but if you know the place, you'll see that it has recently been re-sided in cypress, reroofed, and repainted, all with attention to correct historical detail. Tom is not the first nor second person to modify the house. Around the time of the Civil War, there was a remodeling, resulting in the front porch with its columns; the window surrounds show the windows to be from that era. Then in the early 1900s, the rear addition was added, creating more living space. Tom purchased the house the summer it was moved, and without hookup to his well or septic, he moved in, chasing out all the animals that had found free lodging there: "dogs, rabbits, rodents of all kinds, birds everywhere."

Tom's first big job was cutting out the rotted beam on the original rear wall of the house, ruined when the back addition tilted towards the building and held water against it. His replacements were 12x12s from a South Carolina cotton mill. To add winter warmth, he put studs against the main floor walls, hung sheetrock, and finished with original wood wainscoting. He re-hung doors from two of his last professional jobs, an 1820s house in Philadelphia and a church in Boston, and added trim, getting hand-planed beaded, three-part trim: door stop, beading piece, and final trim. These wood elements are painted a rich, attractive blue-green. Upstairs, he added a second floor addition to give space to one of the rooms and re-configured the stairway to add a hall, giving separate access to each room. The low ceiling was changed by raising the collar ties, Tom explains; the short doorways—he had to stoop to get in them—were raised. Places for closets had to be devised everywhere; wardrobes would have been used at the time the house was constructed.

The original stairs presented problems: each one was a different depth of tread and rise. The inspectors allowed him to keep the stairs intact if he made the handrail the mandated number of inches above each one, and consequently, it zig-zags up to the second floor. Tom points out that the house is so well-proportioned that it looks small and tidy, though in fact it's roomy inside, with big windows and a large door opening.

Tom shows the original Rumford fireplaces, designed in the late 1780s using Count Rumford's new physics of heat: comparatively shallow, high, and wide fireboxes, with the back wall curling outward toward the room to radiate heat and direct smoke. By 1790, this state-of-the-art fireplace was in use around the world. This, as well as the half-lap rafters with no ridge beam in the roof, helps date the structure, which is similar to the small white building north of the former Professional Building on Valley, possibly made by the same builder. Tom says he knew he wanted to own and restore an eighteenth century house; as "challenges presented themselves," he has dealt with them. "It's something you have to do because you love it."

*Undated and uncredited, this flea market find shows the house at its original site on Maple Hill farm. Photo courtesy of Tom Phillips.*

Joe Bishop and Russell Gaines each spoke about living in this structure as children, before it was moved, fulfilling its role as tenant house at Maple Hill. Joe, now living in Buckingham, recalls walking into Scottsville to work at his father's sawmill. He recalls two tenant houses as well as a cook's one-room cottage behind the main house. Russell Gaines was there until the mid-1980s with his seven siblings and parents, Sally and Benny. Benny worked on the farm, Sally at Traveller's Rest hotel in Scottsville. Virginia Lumpkin would drive out to bring Sally to work, Russell says. He went to the Scottsville elementary school house that burned in 1980; a bus would pick them up, though he had to walk if he missed it. "It was a lovely house. We grew up in it, that's for sure!" It seemed big to him, and it was remodeled during his time to include a more modern kitchen.

John Kluge owned the Maple Hill estate when the house was moved. After that, Dave Matthews bought it and, in 2003, created a conservation easement to protect the land. It has been owned more recently by local corporation Two Times Five, LLC. The property, in relation to relatively current Scottsville memory, is thought of as George Omohundro's, who sold it to W.D. Morris. Further back, Sam Spangler says, it's spoken of as Moon property. Tom Phillips relates a tale that the house was built for a circuit-riding preacher who visited churches in the area.

There are many stories left to uncover, thanks to the fact that the house has been saved. Sam Spangler's final word on the project: "That was one of the most fun things I've done in my business."

*Originally published September 2014*

## 17.

# Pine Knot Still Standing

We gathered in the parking lot, water-bottled and L.L. Bean-booted—hardly clones of the old Rough Rider, Teddy Roosevelt, or his cultured wife Edith—but eager to see and identify the new life spring was bringing to Pine Knot.

As in past years, the house and grounds were open April 19th for a morning nature walk led by Tom Dierauf, research director of the Virginia Department of Forestry for 38 years, and Chip Morgan, expert naturalist and tour guide. Paula Beazley, chair and president of the Pine Knot Foundation, was with us as well.

Dogwood and redbud were blooming, with spicebush adding its acid green, and fiddlehead ferns were curled low on the ground. Tom Dierauf described our general geologic location in the Scottsville Triassic Basin, and Chip Morgan brought us more up-to-date by describing the land around us, at 711 Coles Rolling Road, State Route 712, as mostly farmland when Edith Roosevelt purchased the modest house and 15 acres. Roosevelt, who himself enjoyed cutting down trees to improve the view of the distant Blue Ridge Mountains from their porch, styled a piazza. Paula explained that the Edith and Theodore Roosevelt Pine Knot Foundation would "like to revert the property to what it was."

Time has, in many ways, been kind to the little structure, as trees such as oaks, black gum, and tulip poplar have sprouted up where conditions suit them and where they help shield the already out-of-the-way house. In 1976, a biologist from Purdue University, Alton Lindsey, wrote about Pine Knot as "now forgotten although still standing"; another researcher had to use courthouse records and coordinate latitude and longitude to find it. But, of course, nature hasn't stood still, and as well as sheltering trees, there have been inroads by invasive species such as multiflora rose and Japanese honeysuckle. Loblolly pines were planted around the house after timber was harvested, and it was patch-cut in 1994.

Pine Knot was originally part of the 5,000-acre Plain Dealing estate owned by a friend of the Roosevelts, William Wilmer. Edith Roosevelt had seen her husband tire under the pressures of Washington politics and the demands of the presidency, gaining weight through lack of outdoor exercise. While he was absent in Denver, on a trip combining hunting and politics, she visited Wilmer in May 1905, saw the cabin he was building for a farmworker near Miller Creek "on a 180-acre tract called 'Spring Hill,'" according to William H. Harbaugh, Roosevelt biographer, retired UVA history professor, and chair of the advisory board of Pine Knot in *Magazine of Albemarle County History, Vol. 51*, 1993. Edith liked the two-story cottage "with its ochre clapboards, brown trim, and green blinds," totally innocent of insulation, electricity, and plumbing, and bought it for $280, including the changes she wished to make, without alerting her husband. He did not see it until early June.

Pine Knot was always meant to be a family place and never a working retreat such as Camp David. Roosevelt started dictation on the return train to Washington. Reporters did occasionally get to the door and were treated cordially, but the Roosevelts on their eight visits were mostly left alone to ride, hunt quails and rabbit, attend church at Glendower, read, gather wildflowers, and look at birds. When domestic staff accompanied them or were engaged locally, they stayed at the nearby houses. Administrative staff were left in North Garden, and the Secret Service did not show their faces. The closest grocery store was in Keene. Roosevelt apparently never came to Scottsville.

Edith had a wide porch attached to the rear (or north side) of the house, which she made the front entrance. It was then, as it is now, supported with slim columns of trees left in their natural state. Edith moved the central stairway to the rear wall, opening the single room in a lodge-like space, and created a small, third bedroom upstairs. She had two external chimneys put at the ends of the house, the stone likely from Schuyler, and fireplaces where the family originally cooked; restoration of the chimneys was among the first chores for the Pine Knot Foundation.

*Rear view showing one of Edith's Roosevelt's new chimneys. This was the original front of the structure. Photo by Ruth Klippstein.*

The Roosevelts got to Pine Knot by more than a half-day's travel.

First they boarded a private railroad car, one of them named Rover, attached to the steam-powered Southern Railway line, Number 35 for the Red Hill/North Garden depot, and they travelled the last nine or ten miles by horseback, carriage, or larger "stage" pulled by four horses. The Red Hill stop allowed them to see Wilmer's brother Joe either at the depot or his home at nearby Round Top, or for Wilmer to meet them. Many stories and anecdotes are now attached to the Pine Knot saga, but a few news items from the time exist to document what the reporters could see: the president's children in attendance, the horses, the length of the trips; other information comes from Roosevelt's letters and the family diaries.

Our own nature walk led from the open front area through mixed hardwoods and the loblolly pines down the somewhat over-grown paths ("Are we lost?" someone asked; Paula said the Foundation is "trying to find our trails again") to the moist lower ground of Miller Creek and the spring used by the Roosevelts for water. Violets and pink spring beauties were just beginning to bloom; the song of a Louisiana water thrush was identified. It was too cold and early for the lady slippers. Chip and Tom pointed out black haw viburnum, lady fern, a short leaf pine, and talked about natural succession in dry land and wet.

We returned to the house for cookies and lemonade, a chance to read the printed exhibits and handle an actual pine knot, and ask questions. The porch, whose deep roof covered the original second story windows, still looks inviting, suggesting the visitor imagine the Roosevelts sitting there in the evenings in their rocking chairs, listening to whippoorwills, or eating their breakfasts in May.

Often Edith read or relaxed at the cabin while Teddy was out on horseback or tramping through the woods, hunting game birds, watching the warbler migration or the arrival of the cuckoos after a hatch of caterpillars. There were rare guests—Edith's sister; Dr. Presley M. Rixey, surgeon general of the Navy and the family's physician; and three or four others. On what became the Roosevelt family's last visit, May 8th-10th, 1908, the naturalist John Burroughs was their guest.

Burroughs was a preeminent essayist, required reading in

schools across the country, and a strong voice for land stewardship. He and Roosevelt respected each other's scientific approach to field study and each other's breadth of knowledge about the natural world. Burroughs accompanied Roosevelt on a camping trip to Yellowstone after the president created this first national park. He was 71 at the time of the trip to Pine Knot, but not just for that reason did Burroughs have to ask Roosevelt to slow his pace while hiking through the woods; Burroughs was sure his friend's enthusiasm would scare away the wildlife.

*The road leading to Pine Knot.*

Together they compiled a list of 75 species of birds over the three days. It is most likely, one ornithologist has said, they could have identified more birds if they hadn't also been botanizing. Burroughs, around this time, wrote an introduction for The Nature Library's volume *Bird Neighbors*, 1908. "To the real nature-lover a bird in the bush is worth much more than a bird in the hand, because the nature-lover is not after a specimen: he is after a living fact; he is after a new joy in life."

This attitude of joy often characterized Roosevelt, though he did shoot specimens and game in the wild. At 13, he learned taxidermy from an assistant of Audubon's; at 14, he travelled and collected bird skins on the Nile and in Palestine. He majored in biology at Harvard and published his first work on the bird life of the Adirondacks. Roosevelt had "extraordinary powers of observation," Burroughs wrote in *Outlook*, 1907.

One of the reasons Roosevelt invited Burroughs to Pine Knot was the possibility of seeing passenger pigeons. Roosevelt had, almost exactly a year before, reported to the director of the U.S. Biological Survey his sighting near Pine Knot of what he was sure was "a flock of a dozen passenger pigeons. I have not seen any for twenty-five years and never dreamed I should see any again; but I could not have been mistaken (though I did not kill any for I did not have a gun, and in any event nothing could have persuaded me to kill them). I saw them flying to and fro a couple of times and then they all lit in a tall dead pine by an old field. There were mourning doves in the field for me to compare them with, and I do not see how I could have been mistaken."

John Burroughs got a similar letter and wrote back to the president that he hoped he was "sure about those pigeons." The massive flocks that could darken skies of the Midwest were gone before the end of the nineteenth century; accounts of sightings in the early twentieth century were usually judged to be confusion with mourning doves or distant flocks of shore birds. The last known passenger pigeon died in the Cincinnati Zoo on September 1st, 1914.

But Teddy Roosevelt was the president who had published an account of birds and wildlife in *Scribner's Magazine*, October 1907, called "Small Country Neighbors," giving his recommendations for bird books and relaying various observations made at the White House, Sagamore Hill, and his summer estate on Long Island. In this article he detailed his reasons for certainty in identifying the passenger pigeon. "They were unmistakable," he wrote, due to their flight pattern, flocking, and lack of whistling sound mourning doves make with their wings. To be more sure, he wrote, he asked Wilmer to get corroboration from Dick McDaniel (of Esmont), the "colored foreman at Plain Dealing," who was "a frequent companion of mine in rambles around the country, and he is an unusually close and accurate observer of birds, and of wild things generally. Dick had mentioned to me having seen 'wild carrier pigeons,' as he called them; and…I began to wonder whether he too might not have seen passenger pigeons." Wilmer said he, as well, thought McDaniel had "unquestionably" seen the passenger pigeons between Plain Dealing and the woods.

Some controversy has attended this report, occasioned in part by Burroughs later withdrawing his opinion that Roosevelt must have seen them, but descriptions of Roosevelt's birding skills and his procedure in reporting convince us that his sighting was in fact, in Lindsey's words, "the last time a trained, qualified naturalist ever saw wild passenger pigeons."

Though Burroughs never got to see the Pine Knot passenger pigeons, he and Roosevelt listed the Bewick's wren, extirpated now from Virginia, and a loggerhead shrike, a rarity in our area since the late 1990s. Likewise, the evening grosbeak they saw is now only an occasional visitor. Burroughs, who began to feel bullied by Roosevelt, didn't publish an account of the visit and their list, though the president often pressed him to do so, until 1921.

Teddy Roosevelt didn't achieve the third term his wife Edith prepared for by purchasing 75 more acres around Pine Knot. He died in 1919, and no one from the family visited again, though Edith held onto the property until 1941. She allowed Boy Scouts and Girl Scouts to use the place—a number of the Scottsville boys carving their names, still there, in the upper floor rafters; and finally sold it to a neighbor and "hunting buddy" of Roosevelt's, George Omohundro, Sr., who rebuilt the piazza and painted the house red. Fifteen years later, he gave it to his son, George, Jr., who owned Omohundro Hardware on Main Street in Scottsville.

George, Jr. added a metal roof but generally treated his ownership as a stewardship, and he allowed the Scottsville Lions to use Pine Knot for their annual dinner. In the early 1970s, Archie Roosevelt, the president's youngest child and the one who most enjoyed time at the cabin, revisited and reminisced. Then in 1986, Omohundro offered Theodore Roosevelt IV the property, and he bought it. He placed it on the Virginia Landmarks Register and National Register of Historic Places, and in 1992, with financial assistance from John

Kluge, Roosevelt gave Pine Knot, with a conservation easement around it, to the Theodore Roosevelt Association. The trees will continue to grow, the flowers by the flowing spring to bloom, and the house—minus the passenger pigeons—will remain preserved for us all.

*Originally published June 2014*

# 18.

# The Tangled History of 345 East Main Street

The Scottsville location we now designate 345 East Main Street was once forested lowland with a view of the outside curve of the James River. Known to beavers, perhaps, raccoons certainly, and maybe bobcats, it was land hunted and used by the Monacans. When Europeans arrived, looking for places to settle that had water and access to trade, it became real estate, a house, a history. It became 345 East Main.

It might have seemed a tangle to the new wave of settlers, though it must have offered wild fruits, fish to catch, and ample water to use. A main street for the new settlement was laid out, building lots were drawn, the ferry began to run. Nearby houses were built here in the county seat of Albemarle, more than 100 years before the canal, the old tavern across the street.

The small house now called Colonial Cottage, and known also as the Fore House—for an early 1950s resident, house-painter Jim Fore, according to Gene Harding—was documented in the autumn of 1936 by R. E. Hannum of Union Mills, who wrote descriptions of several Scottsville and Southern Albemarle places for the WPA's "Historic Virginia Inventory." These priceless records, often including maps and photographs of now-demolished buildings that were part of our state's everyday life, are readable online through the University of Virginia Library.

Hannum labels the house simply "Dwelling adjoining Pitts' mansion." Up until the 1950s, the cottage was next door to a most imposing two-story brick structure, sensibly built on a basement with 18-inch thick walls, originally with an unroofed porch on the rear, later a roofed porch across the front as well, and entered by "heavy double doors." A date left on a corner gutter gives the house's construction as 1831. Miss Mary Agnes Pitts, the owner in 1936, told Hannum the cottage to the east was "traditionally thought to be as old as the Pitts' home," and Hannum assumed it was "probably a little older." The Pitts mansion is now the site of East Main Garage.

K. Edward Lay, professor emeritus of the UVA School of Architecture, visited 345 East Main Street twice in the early 1990s to make drawings and write a description, and he included the structure in his 2000 book *Architecture of Jefferson Country*. "Perhaps built about 1780," he says, "for Samuel Tompkins in Scottsville, the hall-parlour-plan Colonial House features a double-ramped chimney, beaded weatherboards, nine-over-nine window sash, wooden wainscots, six-panel doors with wooden box locks," and other features that illustrate its period. In his archived papers at UVA Special Collections, Lay notes the house was built on land Tompkins purchased from John Scott. "This modest house is an excellent example of the middle class vernacular architecture…. In both plan, shape and decorative features the home closely resembles Mt. Walla, John Scott's residence." We do not know of an architect; it is more likely Tompkins employed the common process of hiring craftsmen who combined regional ideas for houses with local resources and adapted them to fit the client's site and pocketbook.

Hannum describes the house as "an 'L' shaped, story-and-a-half frame building with a three-roomed basement" from prior to 1731. Ed Lay also says, in his notes, the hall-parlour, or part of the house facing East Main, was built prior to 1831, and the "L" addition was built ten or fifteen years later. This same information is used to describe the house in Scottsville's 1976 application to the U.S. Department of the Interior for inclusion in the National Register of Historic Places. An undergraduate student of Professor Lay's, Marsha Glen, in her 1976 project "Architectural Survey of Scottsville…," available to read in the Scottsville Library Local History Corner, says the two buildings were connected "early in the nineteenth century." There is a third element, to the north of the rear wing, east of the original house, added on with a shed roof.

This leaves us now with several conflicting possibilities for the Colonial Cottage dates. Hannum does not suggest there was anything but one L-shaped house, built before the 1831 Pitts house next door. Professor Lay's UVA. papers say the two parts of the "L" are separate constructions ten or fifteen years apart. Jean Cooper's 2007 *Guide to Historic Charlottesville and Southern Albemarle County* and Susan deAlba's 1993 *Country Roads, Albemarle, Virginia*, both in the Scottsville Library, date the front section, facing East Main Street, as being from 1780, and the rear wing, which would have had a door to the west and be well set back from the street, as being from 1732. Professor Lay's 2000 *Architecture of Jefferson Country* says they were "perhaps built about 1780…." The Scottsville Museum states that the rear section was the original house, the front the newer wing, whereas the National Register description says 1732 for the front and "about 15 years" later for the rear, or circa 1747. Ah, the mysteries of Scottsville.

The house has two standing seam gable roofs and two chimneys; inside are four fireplaces, though the one in the living room is not operational. The windows add an elegance that hardly seems "modest" in terms of today's houses: nine panes over nine, with double-hung sashes and their original glass, give an arresting look and soft light to the living and dining rooms, with their original pine floors, the boards in varying widths and complete with insect holes. The rear addition with 20x20-foot rooms includes a kitchen with hand-hewn beams on the basement floor, a dining room above. Ed Lay notes the "chimney pent or closet" next to the fireplace in the kitchen, an unusual element for this area. The second floor, over the front part of the house, is reached by a staircase

*Stairs to top floor.*

in the front room that is open for the first several steps, then turns to ascend along the perpendicular wall and is enclosed. There are chair rails in the west room, wainscoting in the east.

*The connecting section of the house, from the back yard.*

Besides Samuel Tompkins, this house has been owned by Mrs. Pete Hamner, who sold it to D. H. Pitts in 1870. Pitts willed it to his sisters, of whom Mary Agnes Pitts, Hannum's informant, was one. In the 1970s into the 1990s, Frances Joseph, who also owned the Canal Warehouse, held the deed. Lewis Ramsey, a house collector and restorer who had lived in Slate River, Buckingham County, bought the house in the 1990s from his sister Frances for "much less than it was worth," John Snoddy remembers him saying, because the person living there was sure there was a ghost. There was, in fact, John says, a drunk who regularly crept under the house at night and rummaged through his empties, making, apparently, ghostly noises. Lewis did the bulk of the renovation on the Colonial Cottage, finding the entire basement floor covered in many feet of silt and virtually abandoned. Luke Ramsey, Lewis Ramsey's son currently heading Ramsey Restoration in Wingina, says he and his father lived in the Colonial Cottage after Lewis purchased it. "It was hardly livable when we moved in," Luke recalls; "it didn't really have a basement because that was filled with silt." Lewis laboriously dug it out and restored the kitchen; Luke remembers sleeping there because the rest of the house was so cold. "We'd stuff plastic bags in the windows to keep out the wind." After much effort, inside and on the landscaping, Lewis restored the house to its simple elegance. Current owner Stuart Munson

Peter and Jae Suska had it while they were transitioning from ownership of High Meadows in 2000. Peter says they were "always fascinated by the middle level of the house, many feet off the ground. There, above the elevated brick basement, was our own flood line." There was an exterior staircase leading up to a 9x10-foot open area looking out on a two-person balcony on the west. Suska engaged David Ramazani, a master craftsman of Charlottesville, to build fine bookshelves in the area connecting the two parts of the house. Ready to move to a quieter location, the Suskas' last improvement was to have a Nellysford nursery remove the bamboo, installed as a screen to the west, and plant the evergreens growing there now. John Snoddy moved into the Colonial Cottage in 2004. When he married, his wife Lindsay Check—"lured by the house," he laughs—joined him. "We loved that little house," she says. One child fit in well, but the prospect of two children seemed a stretch for the small space, and in July of 2012 they moved, necessitating John's leaving Town Council and his position as vice-mayor.

So in 2012, this structure was once again real estate, billed as an "Amazing Historic Home Right in the Heart of Downtown Scottsville." In Seattle, Washington, Stuart Munson was looking for a place to live nearer his family in Charlottesville. He'd seen everything for sale along 29 North and had one reaction to it: "Ugh!" When he saw a picture of the Colonial Cottage, he "totally fell in love" with the house but "had no idea where Scottsville was—I had to Google it!" Ahead of his appointment to tour the house with the agent, he came to town, walked around, and got into conversation with folks. He enjoyed their friendly openness and sense of humor, and he felt at home. He loved the house, the river where he could kayak, and the next day made an offer.

Stuart, who works in Richmond and is a docent at the Scottsville Museum, is clear that the odd spaces of his home show it was two separate houses, but he has not yet uncovered much more information. He's hunted deeds but wishes for "the good part," the stories about the house and the people who lived there. He hopes to help develop such house histories with Dan Gritsko and the tourism committee to promote Scottsville as the summer season begins.

Stuart has done little to change the house, though he adds his own touch—and old ship models. He worked closely with the Scottsville Architectural Review Board to create a needed garage, between the house and the levee, that mirrors the house's architecture. He's also had to have the front door taken apart, due to water leakage, and rebuilt with new elements; he's added a storm door and fixed the gutter to keep the problems from recurring.

John Snoddy dealt with the water problem, too. He had various gutters re-piped to take water away from the foundation, sending it under the yard to the storm drain. "The kitchen floor was damp brick when I moved in," John writes in an email, "and we removed that surface and about two feet of substandard soil underneath it. Drainpipes were installed to pipe a spring [which had given] access to indoor, fresh water (as evidenced by drain pipes found under the stairs during the 2005 excavation) through the southwestern kitchen wall, under the yard, and out to the storm drain." Water is still a problem, and it's only due to the A. Raymon Thacker Levee that the last real estate ad, 2012, could confidently declare the place was "a stone's throw from the James River."

FEMA has recently recertified the levee against another 100-year flood, so the Colonial Cottage is covered by insurance—though Stuart has a plan for evacuation he can use if he has warning. Marshall Lee Johnson, who remembers living in the house in the late 1940s, when he was a child, says it "got quite exciting in the spring when the floods came." Marshall remembers walking from his Main Street home to the primary school at the site of the current library.

This fine place, once a wooded river bank, then developed as Scottsville grew, now recognized and preserved, lives on into the 21st century. As it's changed, Stuart Munson says, "many of the original aspects—the banister railings, floorboards, and narrow stairs—have been saved," though he has ample room for his computer and microwave. The National Register of Historic Places includes structures for their "age, integrity, and significance" and helps owners consider strategies for renovation and repair. We all benefit. The WPA project's final line Hannum had to fill in, number 28, asks, "Does occupant seem to appreciate old architectural features?" "Yes," was the answer.

*Originally published May 2014*

# 19.

# Scottsville's Bygone Days

*Looking south down Valley Street in Scottsville, c. 1925. Photographer: William Burgess; Payton Thacker Collection, Scottsville Museaum, Stcottsville, VA*

The Scottsville Museum, the structure built in 1846 as Disciples of Christ Church, reopened for its 1993 season March 28th, 1993. James Barclay's church had been transformed with a major community effort, led by Bob Walls, almost 25 years earlier. To commemorate the effort and celebrate the opening of a new season, the board and board member Bob Spencer convened a panel of Scottsville natives to reminisce about "Growing Up in Scottsville."

Bob quoted Dwight Eisenhower: "One of the best things that can happen to a person is to grow up in a small town.... It is a great and priceless privilege." Bob set the tone of the afternoon by saying, "Scottsville has had lots of stories written about it, and those of us who've lived our entire lives here know that the attitude 'time has stood still in Scottsville; the long-lost traditions and values we search for are still present here' is characteristic of the town."

There have been many changes, Spencer noted, something those born here know well, but Scottsville still "holds an ambience of bygone days." He invited panel members, who spanned almost seven decades of the town's life, to recall "the wonderful things of childhood." Bob opened by listing the things he missed: Dorrier's general store on the corner (the James River Tavern now), Bruce's ice cream and soda fountain (across West Main Street, now Balance yoga studio but when he spoke, a drug store without a soda fountain); the Traveler's Rest hotel (five stories, not a right angle in the structure, on the northern corner of Main along Valley Street) with Edith Taggert (the central telephone operator) sitting on the porch; the old Victory theatre; the two-room school (on Bird Street at Page, burned down in 1980 and now the site of the Scottsville branch library).

The first panel member Bob introduced was Jacqueline Beal Grove, 1918-2001, Mayor Barry Grove's mother, who was then on town council, her signature hat this time a brimmed red felt. Jacqy emphatically stated, "There couldn't possibly be any better place to grow up." She, like many on the panel, went to "the little school," the first and second grade building across Bird Street from the high school. In fact, she went an extra year, as she used to listen to the lessons while sitting on the front steps until one teacher, Ms. Hancock, told her she could come inside "if I didn't say a word." After two legitimate grades, she went to the high school building where "we had the best time in the world." She thrived on the large number of young people in town, the river, as well as the movies and stores; she remembered with warmth Charlie Lenaham sounding the noon whistle daily.

Raymon Thacker, mayor at this time, recalled his 83 years, 81 of them spent in Scottsville. He spoke of his father coming to Scottsville to be a grain miller; of the cooper at the mill, who charmed the young Thacker by "making music with his hammers" on the barrel hoops; of Mr. Sutherland, the policeman, who lit the streets' gaslights nightly "with a little stick" and then "cut them off around midnight." Thacker recalled the town's dray services, the installation of the first plumbing, the first car—Dr. Stinson's red Maxwell "sputtering along the road like a lawn mower."

Thacker hinted at less positive stories—"I've seen the good and the bad occur"—but feels he's lived through many highlights. He and Bob Spencer talked about Victory Hall, with three different movies a week, sometimes all 360 seats filled and the pot-bellied stoves, the only heat, glowing bright red in the dark. Thacker touched on his political and fundraising efforts to get the levee and dam built, to which Jacqy commented, "Aren't you glad I came back to help you!" The Mayor responded, "You also give me a lot of trouble!"

*Haden Anderson and MC Bob Spencer.*  *Jacqy Grove and Mayor A. Raymon Thacker.*

Roy Hamner, 1909-1997, and his son Jack were next introduced. Roy said his family was characterized by its closeness; they hunted, fished, and played together. He told of his father's many pet animals, including parrots and monkeys. His father was one of the first car dealers in town—Plymouth-Chrysler—and Roy told of the three days it took to drive a new model from Richmond to Scottsville on the difficult roads. "Cars coming to Scottsville was a big deal." Jack Hamner went to school in Scottsville and became a teacher in Albemarle and, always interested in local history, an important member of the new Scottsville Museum.

Haden Anderson, 1920-2012, Bob said in introduction, was associated with W.F. Paulett & Son; Haden's father, he remembered, was in the Scottsville Orchestra. Haden thought that being one of six children left him blissfully unsupervised as a boy. He swam in the

James, built dams across the creeks, fished, and ran around as he pleased. There never was much money, but he did own a pair of clamp-on roller skates, which he held up to show the audience, and spoke of "skating on every street in Scottsville."

*The Payne family: Amanda, Mildred, and James Bolling.*

Haden recalled the names of "four colored businesses in Scottsville," saying he used the NAACP term by choice: there were two grocery stores, run by Leonard Lewis and Luther Lewis; a clean-and-press shop owned by Tom Pierce; and Charlie Terrell, the blacksmith. Audience members recalled a black butcher, too.

Haden appreciated going to a local school with local teachers, as well as the sense of everyone knowing and helping each other. He told with a grin of Bob Pitts' grocery store on Main Street, where whole fish were displayed out front for sale. One day, a man came in off the street and said to Mr. Pitts, "There's a cat sitting out there with one of your fish in its mouth." This didn't bother Pitts, who replied, "Yeah, he got one a while ago, too."

Bob Spencer next introduced three members of the Payne family: Amanda Payne Hall, Mildred, and their brother James Bolling Payne. Amanda said that, like her cousin Jacqy, she went to the little school and has a "memory I'll never forget." Her second grade teacher Ms. Hancock was pleased with Amanda's progress in reading, and arranged for her to read to the high school students at a daily assembly from her Baby Ray book. (These Elson Readers were popular in the teens and 1920s; the same author wrote the later Dick and Jane books.) "I went down, shaking in my boots," but the high schoolers listened respectfully ("Can you imagine today?") and clapped for her. Afterwards, Ms. Hancock invited her home for tea, and while Amanda dreamed of elegant cakes and a fancy party, all she got was "milk and a bowl of rice. I was never so disappointed in my life!" Amanda also told a story from one of the many house parties in Scottsville—"this was a large part of our entertainment at the time."

Mildred told of the passenger trains stopping in town, and "everybody went to the depot." The mail was taken off and everyone trooped to the post office and visited while it was sorted. "That way we got to see everyone in town every night." She also told of her siblings often getting a dime each to attend the Scottsville movies. "One night we were missing a dime," so no one could go. But the kids remembered a dime that had dropped in the piano, so their "father took the keys off the piano so that we could all go to the movies!"

Roy and Jack Hammer.
*Photo courtesy of the Scottsville Library.*

James Bolling Payne, 1930-2007, said he got the job of making ice cream at the drug store. "The first time I made it, I forgot to stir it to mix in the air, so it froze but had no volume. The people who ate it said that was the best ice cream they ever had in Scottsville." He also would deliver groceries in his wagon from James River Market. One day, when a live chicken was loaded in from the coop kept out front, he lost the bird on the way. "Someone else got a fried chicken dinner that day!"

Mildred remembered always going home from school for lunch. Bob Spencer recalled the many after-school groups offered by "people who seemed to care for us" and the benefits that gave them. Millie then spoke of Bob starting his magic shows at the school, and she told of the Saturday morning theatre Bob, Donald Coombs, Wilson Harrison, and Robert Taylor arranged in Bob's basement, entertaining any child who came from ten to noon.

Pat and his wife Baxter Allison Pitts were introduced by Bob as first-grade sweethearts. Pat said he felt as children they "literally knew the town high and low. There were few roofs we didn't climb or buildings we didn't play underneath." He told of an elaborate practical joke involving a wallet on a fishing line and boys hiding in the storm drain on Main Street, and another of boys with Roman candles on top of Victory Hall. That one ended poorly, at Dr. Moody's office up Valley Street. Pat commented, "Scottsville was pretty self-sufficient. If you couldn't get it in town, you didn't need it. I miss that."

Baxter reminisced about her swingset, snow-sledding down the hill from Belle Haven, roller-skating down the sidewalks to visit friends, getting ice cream cones to take home from Mr. Jones' drug store. "It was an easy way to grow up. Life in Scottsville is a few decades behind, I guess."

Scott Ward, 1936-2014, recently returned to his namesake town, recalled his birth in the apartment above Agnes Beal's grocery store with Dr. Percy Harris and his father, "having a sip of good water," mixing up his middle name and the place of birth on the certificate. He says he didn't know his middle name was Scottsville until he joined the Air Force. Scott recalled playing football behind Bruce's Drug Store, kids at the Saturday movie matinee, and another rooftop escapade with Arthur Thacker and cherry bombs.

Tom Allison, 1915-2000, spoke last, "The 'Fesser," Bob called him, teacher and principal, who "had a lot to do with childhood in Scottsville." There was banter about the big tree stump on legs in the principal's office, where "naughty boys" were paddled," and Allison said he knew stories no one wanted to hear again.

Allison, a physical education and agriculture teacher, was assigned to teach aeronautics. "I was given the book—I didn't know one end of a plane from another. But we all learned." Bob recalled him teaching biology and chemistry in a classroom with one table, one microscope, one set of cabinets for supplies—including the frog they dissected and on which Allison demonstrated some basic principle by applying an electrode, alarming the students.

The afternoon ended with thanks to museum president Don Hunt, hostess Mary Williams, and the many board members, docents, and volunteers who brought the museum into being and keep it running. Today those names are different, but the attitude of volunteering is not, nor is the pleasure of living small town life in Scottsville. Be sure to attend the museum opening this season, Sunday, April 6th, at 3 p.m.

*Looking north on Valley Street in Scottsville, showing the Victory Theater with billboards of the current movie being shown. c. 1925. Photographer: William Burgess; Payton Thacker Collection, Scottsville Museaum, Stcottsville, VA*

*Originally published March 2014*

# 20.

# Papers Tell Scottsville's History

A trove of damp, mildewed papers, retrieved last year from under the stairs behind the freight elevator in the James River Brewery, has shed light on commerce in Scottsville around 1946. There is still much work to do to uncover the complete history of the three-story building itself.

Most recently purchased by Scott Minor, the structure is undergoing development as the brewery grows. Some people in town remember it as the Western Auto store, run by John Williamson up into the 1980s. Lucinda Wheeler recalls part of the

*Ruby and Harold Parr, in front of Parr's Furniture Store; 1944; posted on Ancestry Library.*

ground floor was used prior to that by Dr. W. E. Moody as his office "for years and years." Lucinda also remembers when people bagged sand there to keep the James back during floods. The Scottsville Council for the Arts, around 1990, she says, considered buying the historic building from owner George Dansey, "but it was too expensive and we couldn't handle it." By 2010, it was the 1804 House, with furniture, and then the Flying Pig, an art gallery and artists' studios.

The exact date of construction of the building is not known. Jean Cooper, in *Guide to Historic Charlottesville and Albemarle County*, gives it as c. 1850; the James River Brewery is using c. 1840; and Scottsville's application for the National Register of Historic Places gives the date as 1835. When the Scottsville High School seniors compiled a booklet of "Historical Sketches of the Town of Scottsville" in 1927, they used the designation "tobacco factory" from the period when Harris and Merrick manufactured plug and chewing tobacco under the brand names "Tuberose" and "Mason's Select." In business until about 1880, they also transshipped hogsheads of tobacco. Mayor Raymon Thacker, on the museum website, says he recalls, as a young boy playing on the third floor, seeing bales of tobacco left there.

*View of third floor window renovation. Photo by Ruth Klippstein.*

The building was used by the Virginia Braid Company until 1940 to manufacture uniform and upholstery braid. I talked to employee Margaret Duncan in 2006 for the *Monthly*. She dropped out of high school during the Depression to work there, along with about 15 others; her original ten-hour days brought her $2.50 a week, most of which she paid to her parents for room and board. Eventually, though there was no break built into the day or sick leave—she once was fired for staying home sick after lunch—she made $8 a week. The earliest days of the structure are not clear. Jean Cooper says it was originally a mill, set as it is beside a bend in Mink Creek, and "was part of the Scottsville General Hospital during the Civil War."

The building was a function of a strong, varied Scottsville economy in the late 1940s. As war loosened its grip on the home front, and prosperity looked possible again, new homes were built in Scottsville's Paulett Town, and returning soldiers took up their lives and work. Harold Parr—his given name was Hallstead Hedges, and he often went by the initials H. H.—began his career buying damaged furniture in Richmond, according to Mayor Thacker; his business was then on Main Street. Harold's nephew, Tommy Parr, believes Harold began his working life hanging wallpaper. "Then he and Ruby ran the creamery at the ice plant," (near the river, at the foot of the current bridge).

Harold is shown with his class at the school on the hill, above Jackson Street, in William Burgess' 1909 photograph archived on the museum website. He attended the Scottsville Methodist Church and its adult Sunday school. During the 1940s, he was fire chief and a saxophone player in the Scottsville Orchestra that played for dances at the canal warehouse. It's likely, people remember, that he belonged to a civic club; he was well-known and liked in town. Chub Walsh recalls an incident when Harold was playing with the orchestra at Victory Theatre. Mrs. Gibson, sitting with Mrs. Ruby Parr, commented on what a "crazy character he was," and then repeated the story to Mrs. Pauline Mayo, not realizing she was his sister.

Chub says Harold was a good businessman. He had the only furniture store in town, at a time people didn't often travel far to shop, and he certainly made money. He was able to invest in real estate in town, and eventually to buy Chester, now the bed and breakfast on James River Road. Monty Duncan says, "I knew Harold and Ruby—they were nice people. He was a little grouchy, she was very sweet, as nice as could be." At Chester, he recalls, they had a community Easter egg hunt.

Monty also says that Harold was "very liberal with his credit. If you weren't so affluent and your refrigerator went out or something, the word was 'Go see Mr. Parr.'" He repaired furniture, too. Eddie Adcock sends us these memories.

"I was still pretty young—I don't know how young—but had probably started to school. What I remember is my older brother Bill paddling around downtown Scottsville in a boat during a really high flood [there were five of note in the '40s], back and forth, rescuing people and property. He had a very kind heart and was always helping people. And I believe this happened around the time Bill went to work at Harold Parr's Furniture."

"Eddie was the baby of the Adcock family," his wife Martha adds, "with two sisters—Nancy and Willie—and four brothers—Harvey, Bill, Clarence, and Frank. All the children were musically inclined, but it was older brother Bill who was responsible for bringing home, one at a time, a variety of instruments collected at Parr's Furniture, and introducing an avidly interested young Eddie to their delights."

Eddie continues: "Mandolin, guitar, fiddle, and four-string banjo.... If it hadn't been for Bill Adcock bringing those instruments home from Parr's, I don't know if I'd have had the chance to become the kind of musician I did. It was a good thing Bill knew how to tune them!"

Martha says it is not known exactly how the instruments came to be at Parr's, whether they were taken on trade or not. Eddie says, "I don't recall that Parr's sold musical instruments. Just furniture, pretty good furniture, and some appliances, and maybe wood heaters. The first floor was furniture, I think, with repairs made on the top floor. My brother Bill loved working at Parr's. That's where he learned his repair and upholstering craft. He could do invisible repairs" and eventually moved to Alexandria to work in some "mighty fine, wealthy houses there."

(There must have been a good enough connection between the Adcocks and Parrs for Harvey Adcock to have given Harold as a reference when applying for credit for a purchase of $41 at Sears Roebuck in Charlottesville. Why Harold did not fill in the request and return it to Sears is as unknown as how it got bundled up with other papers under the stairs in the back section of the store, probably during the period when the business was still changing from the braid factory to the furniture store; a new cinderblock wall was added then as well.)

Lucinda Wheeler recalls that Ruby "had a sharp mind for business. She was quiet and reserved, ladylike." It was she who kept the books. Harold's nephew, Tommy Parr, says she was "tight, held onto every dime." So why were invoices and other papers from late 1945 and randomly through 1946 under the stairs? We can guess—or, as Virginia Woolf writes, "Let me imagine, since facts are so hard to come by," that it was some kind of filing system, or safeguard, or just a desperate last-minute attempt to clean off a desk. The papers do show us Scottsville at work.

Parr's Furniture and Mrs. Parr's Garment Shop further south on Valley did business with other Scottsville businesses. They got their newspaper, the Scottsville News and Albemarle Courier, and had printing done at George and Dorothy's. They bought tape, as well as medicine, at Bruce's ("Drugs and Stationery, Whitman's Candies, School Supplies, Garden Seed, 'On the Corner.'") W.G. Mason did a plumbing job for them, though the ink on the bill is too faded to read. Both Paulett's and Omohundro Hardware company provided such necessities as lumber, ball twine, needles, nails, brushes, and stove polish. Heat came from coal—one ton purchased from Omohundro Coal Co. in Scottsville cost $16.16, delivered, May 1st, 1946. Valmont Dairy provided most of the Parrs' milk, the bills enclosed in envelopes addressed H. H. Parr, Scottsville, Va.; the stamps are green one-cent George Washingtons from 1945.

The Parrs kept the local service stations busy: Branham's on the corner could afford to send an envelope and bill in 1946 for five gallons of Amoco gas, total $1.24; Harold also had tires fixed there ($.85) and the car washed ($.75). At Pitts Chevrolet Sales, on Valley Street, Harold had his right front door fixed in July, and links installed, for a total bill of $1.85. A larger job in November, including rings, spark plug, grinding valves and tuning the engine, itemized a spring for that pesky front door lock, totaling $42. In 1946, Parr owned a Ford truck; the insurance card is included with the papers.

There were individual bills from C. R. Dorrier and Co., General Merchandise for salt in January 1946, and from Scottsville Flour Mills ("Manufacturers of Blue Bird Flour"). There are multiple telephone bills, electric bills, and tax bills—to the town, for water, and the federal government for excise tax. Also included is an assortment of doctor bills and charges from Miller and Rhoads and florists in Charlottesville. Parr banked with the Scottsville branch of National Bank and Trust, Charlottesville.

*The cache of invoices and miscellaneous papers that were found. Photo by Ruth Klippstein.*

During this period, whether for Harold selling stoves or Ruby selling a mink stole, the Office of Price Administration sent notices of their regulations on maximum prices. Sometimes wholesalers included notes that the OPA finally had allowed a price hike.

What were the people of Scottsville—or Buckingham, Schuyler, and nearby Fluvanna—buying in Scottsville? They could fit out a new house, from linoleum and rugs to curtains; from chests, tables, and chairs to cribs, beds and bedding; pictures for the walls and a radio or record player and records. Parr sold lamps, metal and wooden stools, saucepans, wastebaskets, and sink-stoppers. Ruby offered work shirts, socks, and overalls; sweaters, skirts, coats, and suits; hats and bags, shoelaces and handkerchiefs, and in December of 1946, she had one dozen "bloomers" she bought for $8.50. Her dresses included, in September, a single black check, black and pink, a plaid wool and a tan gabardine, a dress in gold and one in aqua. These cost her from $5.75 to $8.75. She also offered girdles, blouses, and bathing suits.

Harold's father, William H. Parr, is listed in the 1910 U. S. Census as a farmer; his mother, Mary Miller, was postmistress by the 1920 census in Payne's. Harold and Ruby are listed in 1940 as living on Jefferson Mill Road; they had one daughter, Betty, who died recently in Florida. H. H.'s brother, Goulay—Tommy's father—lived on Route 6 in Fluvanna; Tom's birth was attended by Dr. Stinson.

Tommy recalls big family parties at holidays, both his mother Francis and his aunt Pauline Mayo being excellent cooks who "could put on a nice table." Tommy remembers Harold having to move all his stock to the top floors during floods and that, when Tom established his own home in York County, Harold took him to Highpoint, NC, to pick out furniture and charged him only the wholesale price. Harold wasn't really grouchy, Tom says; "that was just his presentation."

The James River Brewery rebuilt the old stairs to make them less steep; other changes to the building have been, as Chris Kyle says, "authorized by the Virginia Department of Historic Resources," and include the restoration of third-floor windows, some structural work to shore up the building, and the Beer Garden along Mink Creek. With the hope that the Scottsville economy will develop into a durable, vibrant network, the brewery is "preparing the building for its next 100 years."

*Originally published February 2014*

# 21

# "I'm the Most Famous Poor Person You'll Ever Meet"

Smiling and sincere, Eddie Adcock played more than half his recent show accompanied by Martha Adcock and Tom Gray at Victory Hall, with driving banjo and flights of fancy on the guitar, conjuring the glory days of the Country Gentlemen, before telling a favorite Scottsville memory to his enthusiastic fans. He and Rex Meyers, Eddie said, would jump from the hill behind Victory Theatre onto the roof, with straws they purchased at the dime store, and shoot peas at passersby in the street. They never knew what hit them, Eddie is still pleased to report; they never looked up.

Eddie Adcock's life has stayed entertwined with Scottsville, where he lived until he was 16. He and Martha have been committed to the refurbishing of Victory Theatre and come yearly from their Tennessee home for this concert, which also gives them time to see family and friends. They were happy, after the show, to invite everyone to join them at the Tavern on the James. Scottsville looks good to them.

Eddie was born here in 1938, one of seven siblings whose birth dates span more than twenty years. He lived his first seven years on Howardsville Road about three miles west of town. Then his father hand-built a house near Jefferson Mill Road, a place that became the source of the family's sustenance. "We lived off the farm," Eddie remembers, and as a youngster he did daily chores, helping with the cows, chickens, pigs, and gardens.

"Everyone in my family was musical to a certain extent," Eddie now says—except, perhaps—well—his mother, who "sounded like a squeaky hinge." But they sang; brother Harvey played the harmonica, Frank played guitar, Bill took up fiddle, and sister Nancy had a beautiful voice. His other sister, Willie, sang all the time around the house, anywhere. The children were often in church or school choirs, as well.

Eddie doesn't think of his family as a major influence in his life of music, though Bill gets special credit. Bill worked repairing, upholstering, and delivering furniture for Parr's, located in the three-story brick building now housing the James River Brewery. Harold Parr, who owned Chester—an estate on James River Road built in 1847 and now Chester Bed and Breakfast—would sometimes get instruments in trade, or Bill would be given an unused instrument when he brought furniture to people's houses.

Eddie started bringing a guitar to school in the sixth grade. His first grade teacher, Parr's sister, Mrs. Pauline Mayo, took a special interest in him and taught Eddie to read and write music. "She had a black acetate record with all the sounds of the orchestral instruments—the winds, the brass—and she would play them back to test me. I learned all the different sounds," he says. Expanding his musical world beyond the "hillbilly sounds of local groups, and even the Scottsville Orchestra, Mrs. Mayo got me wrapped up tight in all forms of music—opera, jazz, country," Eddie remembers. "I've given her credit for that in every interview."

Gene Harding, a classmate of Eddie's, says he's heard Eddie tell that story at concerts. But what he recalls is Mrs. Mayo saying, "'Eddie, put that guitar down and do your schoolwork.' I don't know which version is true!" Gene says Mrs. Mayo recognized Eddie's talent and wanted to encourage him; she was always patient.

Most of his musical training, Eddie says, came from listening. He learned guitar first, then mandolin, then tenor banjo. He was "relieved," he says, when his Scottsville friend Joe Smith showed him the proper way to hold the G chord, which was much easier than what he'd devised. Joe and his brother Wes were in a different band in town and "advanced, musically." Joe says his father played the fiddle and got him interested in music by teaching him guitar. He and his brother and a neighbor would play for dances and sometimes played with Eddie and Frank. Joe remembers that they occasionally played on the street in Scottsville, especially near present-day Baine's Books and Coffee. One night someone opened a window above them and yelled, "'We're trying to sleep in here'—and [they] walked off playing and singing 'So Long, It's Been Good to Know You.'" One night, Joe says, he and Eddie walked home to Joe's, up Albevanna Spring Road, playing and singing all the way.

Despite having help from Joe ("the one person he's taken advice from," says Martha), Eddie, throughout his career, has forged his own way and made his own sound. "It costs you to do music the way you want," he says, "and I'm the most famous poor person you'll ever meet." But eventually people caught onto his style and technique, and he says he's hearing popular musicians now playing as he did twenty years ago.

Eddie went to first and second grade in the old primary school on Bird and Page, then to Scottsville High School into seventh grade. His asthma kept him back in first grade, and in third grade his teacher, Mrs. Phillips, thought he should repeat, though he had passed all his work. He didn't question this until later, but being two grades behind his peers was a difficult challenge, he says. Mrs. Mayo, his favorite teacher except for Miss Caldwell, was hard on him but, seeing his worth, helped him get as much out of school as he could.

*Eddie playing a banjo from a "Scottsville Sun," 1956 photo.*
*Photo provided by Eddie and Martha Adcock.*

There was a small pavilion, a type of bandshell, behind Scottsville High School, on the playground. It was roughly where the recycling dumpsters are now. Eddie and "anyone else musically inclined," according to Gene Harding, would play there informally during recess. Baxter and Pat Pitts remember this as a highlight. Gene says Frank, though not as serious about music as Eddie, was a "terrific player." Eddie formed a group called the James River Playboys.

Eddie feels he couldn't always concentrate on school, due to his chores. His older siblings "got out as soon as they could." Wartime was a strain; the family worked hard to provide themselves fruit and vegetables, meat, milk, and flour—which they had ground at the Scottsville Mill on Main Street. They bought only sugar, salt, and coffee, Eddie says. His father often made only $5 a week. His mother had a series of nervous breakdowns; his father, cancer. Eddie lived with an aunt for a while. He had a paper route for *Grit* and for *The Daily Progress*; he mowed lawns, including the Scottsville Cemetery, all with a push-mower. He didn't have a job at Victory Theatre but "helped out" there.

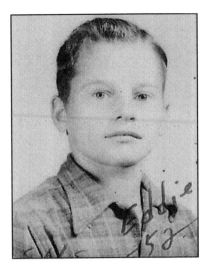

*Eddie Adcock as a young school boy.*

Eddie, at 14 or 15, was raising a calf and feeling that he would like to be a farmer. He says he read about it, "got excited about farming. But music was burning in my soul." Occasionally, he'd earn pocket change—$4 or $5—busking at Duke Johnson's Republic service station at the Main Street end of Valley. That was an odd-shaped lot on the east side of the road, he says, where two cars would fit, and four would make it "plumb full." He stood in front of the drink machine, where folks would be sure to find him.

His first professional music job was on WCHV, Charlottesville, where he played on a gospel show with Frank. He'd met the preacher at a tent meeting on the high school grounds. Then, in 1954, he heard Smokey Graves on the radio say he needed a five-string banjo player, "and farming went out the window."

His mother sensibly noted that he played tenor banjo, not five-string, but Eddie knew he could learn. Without a phone, he wrote to Graves, who responded by inviting him to try out for the job. "I'll be there in two weeks," Eddie wrote; "there's some stuff I have to clear up around the farm." Eddie sold his calf and bought a new Gibson banjo at Stacy's Music in Charlottesville. "I stayed glued to the banjo and the clock. My finger bled. I got to where I thought I was good enough to fake the rest. Smokey understood I was a musician and thought I'd continue learning," so Eddie was hired. He left home in 1954 to join the Blue Star Boys in Crewe, Virginia. His mother helped with the banjo payments, and when he started making $35 a week, he sent money back to her.

"I lived in the YMCA in Crewe," Eddie says, "and later with a family." Besides giving him professional experience, this time also exposed Eddie to a deep degree of racial animosity he never knew in Scottsville. The band did regular radio shows and played for dances or concerts. Whenever shows didn't prevent him, he hitchhiked home to his mother's, usually two or three times a week.

"When they came back to the Victory Theater," Martha Adcock says, "he was a hero!" This is the period in Scottsville Eddie remembers as the best. Three hundred and fifty people would fill Victory Theater for two shows a night, seeing the best acts in the country—Kate Smith, Flatt and Scruggs, Roy Acuff, Gene Autry. There was a guaranteed crowd for the music in Scottsville; acts never went to Charlottesville. "Victory Theater was poppin'!"

"Scottsville," Eddie says, "when I was a kid, was so crowded you couldn't walk down the sidewalk on weekends. You had to step off into the street. There were horses and wagons filled with produce, as well as cars. Everyone was out." It was an expansive time, "peacefully optimistic," Eddie recalls, through 1956; three or four years later, "it looked like a desert." But Eddie was off to broader horizons: a job with Mac Wiseman in 1955 and Bill Monroe in 1957. His most renowned group, the Country Gentlemen, was invited to play at Carnegie Hall in 1961; Eddie stayed with them until 1970. This group, through Eddie's determination to play music his own way, pushed the boundaries of bluegrass, and broadened the appeal of its sound during the folk music explosion of the '60s. "I released all my insides, all my creativity, into the band," he says now. "I was ready to say something on my own—and that's where I made my mark."

Throughout a wide-ranging career and many awards, including the governor's proclamation of June 14th, 1987 as the first "Eddie Adcock Day," Eddie treasures most not his fame but Martha Hearon. They met through music in 1973 and married in 1976. "That was my life completed," he says simply. Today, after three dramatic, difficult deep brain stimulation surgeries to correct a tremor in his right hand, Eddie continues to play special concerts with Martha, be involved in various musical and other charities and educational efforts, and to run a recording studio.

At the October 5th concert at Victory Hall, Eddie and Martha, joined by former Country Gentleman Tom Gray on bass, played on the 60th anniversary of Bob Spencer opening the curtain for Eddie's first solo performance at the theatre. Their pride and pleasure at being in Scottsville was evident, and the music was fine. It was a hometown night, full of smiles, laughter, jokes, and love, all blended with soaring song.

*Originally published November 2013*

# 22.

# The Night the Books Burned

"The night of the fire, as I was putting hoses back in the firetruck, my daughter cried," Duane Karr told a meeting of Scottsville citizens in late 1980. "I asked her what was wrong. She said, 'Somebody burned my library down.'"

One slightly soothing revelation of that awful night, Saturday, September 6th to Sunday, September 7th, 1980, is that it wasn't a person who started the fire that demolished the Scottsville branch library, formerly the town's primary school, at the corner of Bird and Page Street. Lightning struck during a severe storm around 8 p.m. *The Daily Progress* reported the sound was "like bombs," and a tree was set on fire elsewhere in town.

Neighbors George and Lucinda Wheeler, Cenie Moon, and Hamner Goodwin all heard the loud crack. Lucinda says her family was at dinner when the storm hit, and they jumped up to close windows on the porch. "We thought that lightning had struck our house," she says; both she and son George felt the electricity in the air. George, Sr. checked out the house, determining all was well, and dinner resumed. That was the strike that hit the library, however, and when Lucinda rose at 12:30 to see if her daughter Sue had returned from a date, she thought perhaps someone had broken into the library—she could see light behind the windows. George came to look and declared, "'No, that is a fire in there!'"

George, who was in the Scottsville Volunteer Fire Department, went running outside to be sure, and he found the library door glowing "orange-reddish." He returned to his house and dressed, then took his truck downtown to activate the fire siren at what is now

Coleman's Outdoors store. Lucinda remembers that young men, out late on a Saturday night, guessed that George was reporting a fire either at his house or further down Bird Street, at the rubber plant. The boys drove right by the actual fire: "They missed it!" Lucinda says, in their eagerness to get to the plant. Turning back to Page Street, they found that the fire department had arrived at the library. That corner got so busy that Sue could not find a place to park when she finally got home from her date.

The fire, which "hid up in the ceiling" for hours, as firefighter Gene Johnson reports, engulfed the building. "A brave effort" was made to save the structure, reported Jefferson-Madison Regional Library director Christopher Devan. "It was a bad night," firefighter Duane Karr remembers. Joe Jordan says that while extensive records are kept now on the Scottsville Fire Department's responses, to send to county and state, at that time this wasn't required. Joe, Duane, and Gene remember little in detail from that night, except that by the time they were called, as Karr says, "it was pretty well involved, and we poured a lot of water on it until it cooled." The roof fell in, on top of 13,000 books.

Peggy Boatwright, one of the two members of the library staff, had been at work that Saturday. "I was the last one out of that building," she says, and she remembers that, before she locked up, she looked back inside; it was "nice and clean, the books all put up on the shelves. I thought how pretty it was. I loved the library."

The building had a long, significant history. The land it sat on was donated to the town by Captain John Lee Pitts, who had purchased Belle Haven, further up Page Street, around 1900. Born in Scottsville in 1863, John Pitts became captain of one of his father's three canal boats at 14, hauling hogsheads of tobacco on the two-day trip, as the Scottsville Museum website says, from Warren to Richmond. He later went into railroad construction and "prospered." John Lee Pitts was "an influential Scottsville citizen."

His daughter explains for the website that school principal William Day Smith "had much to do with the acquisition of the site." She describes the building as two rooms housing the first three grades: "Grade One and Two were held for only half a day. The new building also had running water and flush toilets," unlike the school on the hill.

Raymon Thacker was in the first class to attend the school, and his picture appears on the museum website—with him donning knickers and a belted Norfolk jacket, flanked by the rest of the students in 1917, standing on the school's steps beside the columns gracing the façade. Bobby Pollard thinks he was probably in the last grade to use the building, in the mid-1960s, when the two classrooms were devoted to two first grades. "Miss Tindall's was on the left side of the door, and Miss Caldwell's on the right." He had Miss Caldwell. Bobby also remembers that the school's "old swing set was there for years after they turned it into a library." The elementary grades moved to the Scottsville High School when, in 1967, grades 10 and up were sent to Albemarle High School.

The library had been an independent, mostly volunteer service in various locations in downtown Scottsville before this time. Marianne Ramsden wrote about the library's history in the January 2007 *Scottsville Monthly*. In 1959, Scottsville joined the JMRL system to bring broader services to the area; the new branch was "a great success." Approximately 5,000 books were moved into the 14,000-square foot school building, and various clubs and the Scottsville Chamber of Commerce helped with renovations. For 15 years the structure was improved and the collection enhanced. Mrs. Louise Holt became branch head in 1975, and during her tenure there, she added activities for everyone and was always encouraging people to take out more books. "A human dynamo," Joe Turner described her as at that 1980 meeting, and the old school quickly became small and crowded as a library.

Louise would have been notified of the fire and went to see what could be done for her beloved library. "'I just wish I could get in there and see if any circulation records were saved,' said Mrs. Holt as firefighters doused the remains of the blaze," early Sunday morning (Overton McGhee, *The Daily Progress*, 9/8/80). "Firefighters raked through coals from the remains of the ceiling and attic. 'There's the children's room,' Mrs. Holt said. 'It was built with volunteer labor, and the book club raised the money for it. You wouldn't believe all the love that went into it.' Mrs. Holt rejected as unimportant several offerings the firefighters brought her from inside." Finally, "a firefighter appeared with a tray containing two rows of slightly scorched cards and pieces of a wooden box that had contained them. 'That's it,' said Mrs. Holt. 'That's it, and I thank you very much.'"

The next day, says Peggy Boatwright, there were "just four-foot tall jagged peaks left." But all the volumes Louise had pressed patrons to check out, estimated at 2,000-3,000, were saved. About 3,000 water- and smoke-damaged volumes from the shelves were dried and cleaned by the library system; many of the rest were sold as a fundraiser. Virginia Moore gave the first gift to start a new library, a collection of her poems, and an unnamed little boy gave a book from his own shelves. Someone from Richmond sent 1,100 good quality paperbacks, and the library service McNaughton gave 200 books as a gift.

With books in hand, a building was now needed. Within ten days the unused cannery on the school grounds was refurbished and the Scottsville library was re-established. Cenie Moon called everyone she thought could help to volunteer time and keep the library active. Louise constantly lobbied for a new, larger building on the original site and brought the town together at a November 1980 meeting at the Scottsville Methodist Church. All interested parties, the library director Devan said, from the insurance company to the county Board of Supervisors and the library Board of Trustees, "want[ed] to hear from the people of Scottsville" about their hopes. One proposal was to put a library in the old high school. Chris Wade pointed out that the community was "not interested in rescuing books from the flood."

Helen Wieneke, later a member of the JMRL Board of Trustees for Scottsville, summed up this meeting by saying, "On a note of hope, like the phoenix who rose from the ashes more beautiful and stronger than ever, I am confident that a new library more beautiful and functional will be in the future." The people of Scottsville stood firm in their support, and the new building on the old site, with a community room for meetings, was let out for bids in January 1982. The library opened in May 1983, with salvaged columns from the front of the old school—the same ones seen in the picture with Raymon Thacker—installed in the children's area of the new building.

*Originally published October 2013*

# 23.

# Memories of Golf, the Rubber Plant, and Days Gone By

*Where the golf course used to be. Photo by Ruth Klippstein.*

"It was wonderful to have these opportunities in a little town. We could play golf or tennis with no questions asked," recalls Pat Pitts, one of the young men who learned to love golf by watching older men play at the Uniroyal plant in the 1950s and early '60s. "I never had a lesson in my life. We'd watch the employees play and scout the creeks to find golf balls. It was great fun."

The coming of the rubber plant to Scottsville is a success story often told. Mayor Raymon Thacker, who was instrumental in identifying the property for the U.S. Defense Corporation and encouraging owner Dr. R. L. Stinson to sell it, has recorded his memories of the plant on the Scottsville Museum website. Virginia Moore, in *Scottsville on the James*, calls it "a major event." The cornerstone was laid in May 1944 with a town barbeque, and the $2,240,000 building "went up fast." In November 1945, U.S. Rubber, which had been running the operation, bought the plant—its forty-third—from the government for $1,837,500.

Donald Carroll was the first manager. Through the 1950s and '60s, Don and the company were proud of the employees' "outstanding production record during the War...their craftsmanship and teamwork" and the "most modern textile plant in the U.S., bringing greater progress and more people to Scottsville" (advertisement in *Sun-Press*, Scottsville, 1964).

Writing in 1951, George T. Starnes, "The Labor Force of Two Rural Industrial Plants," noted that after the strong development of manufacturing during the war, "of outstanding significance in Virginia's transition to peace have been the generally good industrial relations that have prevailed in the State during the period of reconversion. The condition of harmony has been in marked contrast to the labor turmoil and strife in many other parts of the country."

Besides the modern production room inside the plant, development on the 51-acre site eventually included a fishing pond, a tennis court, croquet lawn, and a four-hole golf course. As amateur photography was new and seemed expensive, no pictures have surfaced of the golf course, and we rely on the memories of those who played there.

Bill Mason recalls it fondly. He left Scottsville for a period in 1956, so he knows he played on the plant grounds before that. "Anyone could play," he says, and many did. He states that players started in front of the plant, went east, parallel to the river and the spur railroad serving the plant on the south side of the driveway, and then crossed the road for one more hole. "There wasn't enough room for more than that. You looped around to play and overlapped and criss-crossed" for nine holes. He believes the course, which extended to the rear of the cannery, the block building now used as storage by the apartments, was about 25 acres. "The greens weren't real fancy," Bill notes. They were sand, Pat Pitts says, possibly oiled to keep dust down. Jack Hamner, another young player, says, "The 'greens' were simply round areas of sand with a hole and a flagstick. They were designed and built by Russell Brill, I believe [a local landscaper known, Pat Pitts says, for having the equipment to move boxwood and small trees]. These 'greens' were very susceptible to the elements—every time there was a hard shower, gullies appeared in the sand and had to be raked smooth. Also, before putting, the 'greens' had to be smoothed of footprints, debris, etc. with a burlap 'sweep' attached to a long pole." Dave Catlett remembers dragging the greens for the next players, and Pat Pitts recalls a long 2 ½-inch pipe with a smaller T welded on the end used to smooth the sand.

Pat provides us a map of his memory of the four holes. He shows the first tee box on what he calls the plateau, where employees parked. He recalls that a creek ran alongside the holes on the south side, now marked by a thick band of trees and greenery, and players had to twice cross a small creek perpendicular to that. This was part of the spring, now blocked, remembered to have been near the single hole on the north side. Several players remember getting drinks of water there, even after the plant declared it as "unfit."

These holes were maintained with regular mowing no different from the rest of the grounds. Jack Hamner remembers that George Wheeler, a "delightful jack-of-all-trades," was employed by the plant for maintenance but is not positive he is the one who kept the golf course mowed. Bill Mason recalls that Steve Wharam's grandfather Walter, "a legend, a real character," worked on the grounds and groomed the greens. Steve contributed the name of Johnny Wales, a "super nice man" who used to work on the grounds. Steve and his sister Virginia Higgins recall their grandfather, as well as their mother, working at the plant. "We talk all the time about the way it was."

It seems likely the U.S. Rubber Company, which produced the "Sensational New Spun-Latex" golf ball in 1935, developed the golf course for employees; some people have suggested it must have been put in for upper management. Golf was still new to the American public just after the war. Though the first public golf course in the

United States, in northern New York City, was established in 1896, the development of golf equipment—as well as of leisure time and the surge of post-war discretionary income, creating the new concept of "lifestyle"—helped popularize the game. Clubs were standardized in the 1920s and '30s, losing colorful names like "mashie" and "niblick" to numbers; the golf ball, originally of wood and then gutta percha, became a core of rubber wrapped in rubber. The *Encyclopedia Britannica* says this "was easier to hit and gave its strikers a greater sense of power. Older men found it easier to play, and hosts of women and children were drawn into the game." In the 1950s, Ben Hogan, Sam Snead, Byron Nelson, Jimmy Demaret, and Babe Didrikson Zaharias were champions on the new, longer golf courses. Professional golfers dominated amateurs in tournaments, and the game finally came to television, finding in Arnold Palmer the "perfect star for the new age…."

Amanda Hall thought it possible her husband Conrad, plant manager in the 1970s, developed the golf course for his own pleasure. But it is more likely that since the course was in operation during the '50s, it had become unused and Conrad refurbished it after 1972, when he became manager. "I've got to get those four holes back," Amanda remembers him saying; he played often after work or after dinner.

Robert Lloyd, a later plant manager, first came to Uniroyal in 1968 and "vaguely remembers" the golf course. He does recall that Conrad Hall "was a golf nut" and probably "the driving force" behind the course after the damages of Hurricane Camille in 1969 and Agnes in 1972.

Bill Mason lists "some of the really great golfers of the time" as Dave and Danny Philpot, brothers who worked at the plant; in 1952, Dave was Scottsville High School P.T.A. president as well. There was also G.C. Golladay, an Appalachian Power Company maintenance worker; Willie Marshall; Ed Turner; and Herb Craft. Bill Mason says Mayor Thacker's son Arthur played, as well as young Maynard Spencer. Pat Pitts adds the name of Kent Carter, stepson of Scottsville's druggist Tom Bruce, and Red Rittenhouse. Marie Lane tells of her brother, Donald Combs, loving golf and later learning tennis at the plant. He always emphasized how much fun he had there with his friends. Don Combs and Dave Catlett were both on the 1952 Scottsville High School baseball team; the school did not utilize the golf course.

The teens would stand back to watch if older men were on the course; sometimes they would caddy for 50 cents. "We'd take a sickle down along the ditches. You could always find balls, and we were young—we had all day." Bill Mason also says Dave Catlett was the best of the young players, although Dave denies it. He does remember that the course boasted ball washing stations. He lived in the house west of the current library and so could quickly walk to the course—"it was my front yard!" He says he'd play three times a week. "Barney Philpot was the best, I'd say." Dave adds that the nineteenth hole, the last stop of most games for the older players, was Lee's Restaurant on Valley Street, where upstairs they'd get beer.

*Where the golf course used to be. Photo by Ruth Klippstein.*

Bill and Jack were both left-handed. "There were very few left-handed clubs back in those days," Bill says, and he learned right-handed. His original set of clubs was J.C. Higgins he thinks he bought for $24.95: "a bag, three balls, a putter, a wood, and three irons." Jack says he never felt comfortable playing right-handed and switched when he could afford new clubs. His rubber plant foursome often included Pat and Billy Pitts, Walter Townsend, or Kenneth Quick, "and anyone else who happened to show up!"

Walter Townsend recalls that "it was nice. We used to love going around to practice playing. It was like a park...and a very cute layout for a course." Most people learned to interrupt play when the 4 p.m. shift let out and cars streamed down the drive. But Walter's first car, a Pontiac, had its grill broken by a duffer hitting low across the road.

Bill Mason remembers, besides golf at the plant, roller-skating on the sidewalks under the floodlight. Mr. Luckado, night watchman, would let kids inside for a drink of water. "Everyone learned to ride a bicycle there," Pat Pitts says, as well as how to fish in the pond. George Goodwin, with his friend Alan Philpot, would wait for Alan's father to play—he was always smoking a pipe on the course—while learning to throw a Frisbee. Their dogs, Happy and Lemon, accompanied them, and George learned to play tennis at the court there. "The plant was always a good corporate citizen that took care of the community," he notes now.

The plant, Walter Townsend says, "was a respected place to work and a big loss when it closed." Employing up to 340 people at its peak in the late 1960s, it closed at Christmastime in 2009, putting 106 people out of jobs. Although the Scottsville ordinances allow for the development of a golf course "in the floodway district" if all environmental and other regulations (including four parking places per hole, plus one per golf course employee) are observed, there are no current plans for such development. George Goodwin, town administrator, reports that a town dog park has been proposed to Dr. Hurt, the current owner of the plant. Meanwhile, Scottsville's golf-teaching professional Richard Singleton will give group or private lessons, arrange special clinics, make a digital movie of your swing, or play a round with you. He had a practice range at his West River Road home and is a golf pro at Farmville Municipal Course. Fore!

*Originally published August 2013*

# 24.

# Scottsville Bricks: The Puzzle Remains

*George Godwin, grandson of Brick Co. founder, with blotter advertising the bricks.*
*All Photos by Ruth Klippstein.*

Every day in Scottsville we can pass by structures made of Scottsville Brick Company bricks. Often called sand bricks, with a yellowish-grey color, they are made of concrete. This we know; much of the rest of the story is gone.

There are Scottsville bricks in Victory Hall, Lucinda and George Wheeler's house on Bird Street and garage on Page, and most likely the train depot. Local information always says the bricks came from a foundry across the James, on the flood plain at the Snowden estate, run by John Staples Martin (1853/8-1933). I started with this information, as well as an ad from the June 29th, 1921 *Scottsville Enterprise* that says, "Scottsville Concrete Bricks Make Beautiful Buildings. They last longer—cheaper in the end. With our enlarged plant of modern machinery we are now prepared to make prompt delivery. Write for prices." While the ad undoubtedly ran elsewhere, I have only been able to see it in the *Scottsville News* for August of 1922.

George Goodwin and Mayor Raymon Thacker told me that George's grandfather, Tyler Goodwin, was also a principal in the company and owned the large Snowden property, now called Belle Mead. George has an advertising blotter from the company, found by Jack Hamner, framed in his office in the Municipal Building, built of those bricks. He said that Jack Hamner has located some miscellaneous metal on the property, unusually called "the low grounds of Snowden," including a doorknob, as well as a red brick foundation, but nothing conclusive.

In Thomas Jefferson's notes, he says that the property was his father Peter's home (1708-1757), deeded to his younger brother Randolph. It was speculated among the Jeffersons that "Snowden, Wales, was the supposed birthplace of the family."

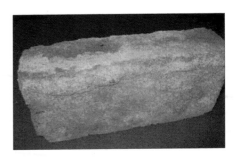

*Portrait of the brick.*
*This is a Scottsville. Co. brick.*

The original home was on the high bluff overlooking Scottsville and was burned by 1857; a new house was built in a different spot on the bluff. According to the WPA's 1940 *The Old Dominion*, Snowden was originally 1,900 acres owned by a now-unknown Mr. Snowden, with Captain John S. Harris acquiring it in 1857.

John Schuyler Moon got it in 1870—he was married to James Barclay's sister and bought the place at auction; his younger brother Jacob Luther was married to John Staples Martin's sister. There were then no structures on the land. In 1937, the Scottsville High School students wrote and mimeographed a booklet of local information, identifying the property as Buckingham Cliff and attributing the ownership to "Mrs. D. W. Hancock, Mr. F. L. Holt, Mr. Howard Ragland, and Mr. Tyler Goodwin." George Goodwin says that the land was divided several times, often among relatives. He thinks the best way to describe the possible site of the brickworks is about three-quarters of a mile along Valley Street and across the river, past the apex of the James River's Horseshoe Bend.

Raymon Thacker remembers that Tyler Goodwin was instrumental in establishing the Disciples of Christ Church with James Barclay, as was Thomas Staples, in 1846. John Samuel Martin, John's father, married Martha Ann Staples. In a scrap of history from 1859, recorded in the *Scottsville Register*, May 7th, we read that Staples and Martin are "in receipt of their Spring Goods" and are selling clothing and groceries. The elder Martin also farmed. Thacker says that later, Tyler Goodwin and John Martin, the son, had a real estate business, with an office on the north side of Main Street. "I used to go and sit and talk to Mr. Martin. He was the nicest man." Census records show that he owned a home, situated in Scottsville, and was never married.

The Scottsville Brick Company enters what I can find of official records with a line in the "Annual Report of the Secretary of the Commonwealth...for the year ending 9/30/21." This records the charter of the Scottsville Brick Company, Inc., December 27th, 1920—formerly the Scottsville Sand and Silica Company, Inc., itself entered into the record February 21st, 1920.

It is possible these companies were related to one listed in the 1909-10 "Bulletin Issues 6-9, Virginia Division of Mineral Resources," the Pure Silex Company, with "office and bed or pit" in Scottsville. A different publication, the "Biennial Report on the Mineral Production of Virginia during the Calendar Year 1909-1910," by Thomas Leonard Watson of the Virginia Geological Survey, also lists the Pure Silex Company, and says it was a producer of sand.

The Biennial Report describes the term "sand-lime brick" as "all brick made by mixing sand or gravel with a relatively small percentage of slaked lime, pressing the mixture into forms in a brick mold, drying or hardening the product either by sun heat or artificial methods. The manufacture of sand-lime brick in Virginia commenced only a few years ago..." with only two producers in 1909, neither of them in Scottsville. This seems, however, a possible model for the men of Scottsville Brick; the Pure Silex Company is another question left without an answer.

A journal named *Concrete Products*, published in Chicago, says in Volume 18, June 1920, "Scottsville, Va. is the home of Scottsville Sand and Silica Co., which has received concrete brick-making machinery for installation in their new plant which is nearing completion. The company is composed of local capitalists and owns a vast deposit of silica sand which is located just across the river from Scottsville, in Buckingham County, Va. The company has been operating for several months a small plant to demonstrate the possibilities of the material, and their experimental work was so satisfactory that the new plant was started which will have a capacity of 30,000 bricks per day. It is also proposed that the company will manufacture concrete roofing tile."

*Bird St. front of the John Martin house, c. 1914*

*The Scottsville depot.*

The Romans developed concrete in the first century BCE from burned limestone as a binder mixed with crushed rock or possibly some volcanic ash or cinders. Portland cement came into use in the U.S. after 1872, as the Preservation in Action website writes, "and was a significant milestone in the history of our built environment." Sears sold a concrete block-making kit in the late 19th century so that the "average man" could make his own block. Today, concrete brick manufacturers note their product's low maintenance, fire protection, and sound-deadening qualities, as well as their variety of colors and finishes; it is considered by some more ecological to produce than clay bricks. Clay brick producers disagree on the value of concrete bricks, noting that they will often shrink and are less durable than clay.

Scottsville Brick Company and its forerunner, Scottsville Sand

and Silica, duly registered their charters with the State Corporation Commission; these are housed now in the State Library archives, in fragile leatherbound volumes numbered 106 and 110. The first company, Scottsville Sand and Silica, listing its office in Scottsville, states its "purposes are to lease, buy, hold and operate sand deposits and sand lands and silica deposits and silica lands and mines and other mining and mineral lands...and the manufacturing, buying, selling and disposing of concrete brick, concrete roofing tiles, concrete drainage tile and other concrete materials and other kinds of brick and tile and material of that character and the handling [etc.] of sand, cement, lime, timber, slate, and all kinds of building and roofing material...and also the...dealing in...goods, wares, groceries, and all kinds of merchandise, and also the mining and manufacturing of other kinds of mines and minerals; and to construct...roads, tram roads, railroads, pipelines, water pipelines and conduits and all buildings and structures necessary for those purposes...."

*Two handmade clay bricks from an old farm near Point of Fork.*

The officers listed include John S. Martin, President; John L. Pitts (1894-1984), Vice President; F. C. Moon, Second Vice-President; G. T. Goodwin (1871-1944), General Manager and Secretary; with John S. Martin acting as Assistant Manager and Treasurer. The four men were also listed as directors. "The amount of real estate to which the holdings of the corporation at any time is to be limited is Fifty Thousand acres. 14 February, 1920." The document was notarized by S. R. Gault. Frank C. Moon (1860-1925) was one of John Schuyler Moon's 14 children, a lawyer who practiced in Scottsville and Lynchburg, and a state senator for one term from Buckingham County.

Then, in December of the same year, the board of directors met in the Sand and Silica office, with Martin acting as president of the meeting and Goodwin as secretary. The men resolved "that it is desirable and advisable that the corporation name...be changed to Scottsville Brick Company, Incorporated, and that the charter...be amended...."

It was an ambitious set of purposes the band of capitalists proposed, and at this point we know little about their operation. But the bricks were manufactured by one or both companies, and buildings (at least in Scottsville) were built. Victory Hall was

*The garage on the Page St. side of John Martin house.*

constructed probably between 1918 and 1920. Architect D. Wiley Anderson possibly specified these bricks for his design, and Anderson's biographer, Susan Hume Frazer, notes in a private letter that "Anderson may have consciously used brick companies located near a commission. It made good economic sense. Moreover, using local materials showed aesthetic sensitivity.... When Anderson was associated with the Sprenkle Company [in Richmond], he used South Side Brickworks" from that city. "There is no question," she concludes, "that brick companies and other suppliers wanted to work with Anderson, whose knowledge of and interest in building materials was superior...and contributed to his success as an architect...."

Near Victory Hall, north along Valley Street, the White-Dorrier Ford dealership, now the General Dollar store, opened by 1922 in a Scottsville Brick Company brick building. The Pitts' Belle Haven garage, now owned by Jan Glennie-Smith, is of Scottsville brick, as is the chimney of the Main Street house formerly owned by Janie Caldwell. The Historic American Buildings Survey description of the C&O railway station, now owned by CSX and located between the river and the levee, says that "according to local tradition, the white sand bricks (made of cement and sand) used in the [1915] building may have been produced on a site across the James River by…James [i.e. John] Martin, brother of Senator Thomas Martin. This type of brick was produced for only a brief period…before its manufacture was discontinued." Across the river, left on Snowden Drive, Montie Duncan's Craftsman-style house is said to be of Martin's bricks, and was built in the 1930s, perhaps as late as 1939. "My understanding," Duncan says, "is there's a bunch of buildings in Richmond and a bunch in Norfolk. The bricks were shipped on railroads." Mayor Thacker told him the business flooded three times before they quit. Thacker said to me that the concrete brick never took paint well and couldn't compete with our area's interest in red clay brick. "They did fair for a while, but they weren't very successful. It was a small business, and they never sold a whole lot of brick."

Cliffview, a D. Wiley Anderson house made for John Staples Martin himself, is dated c. 1914 on the Scottsville Museum website. Anderson was, besides an architect, an inventor. In 1901, he filed for a patent on "Brick for Making Structures Fireproof"; in 1903, "strong and durable" brick tile; in 1904, "combined brick and tile"; and in 1926, a flashing brick. His Multifix brick was patented in 1927 and produced in Chicago. A 4x8 inch block with hollow channels, it could be made from clay or cement. A number of current concrete blocks look quite a bit like the Multifix, which was used in structures in Lynchburg and Richmond.

If D. Wiley Anderson specified Scottsville Brick Company brick in his Scottsville buildings from 1914 to 1918, and Montie Duncan's house was built of the same bricks in the 1930s, why can't we find records of the company except for 1920? At the State Library, the charters are stamped "Dissolved," but without a date. No other possible records exist with the State Corporation Commission; perhaps the company simply stopped paying its annual assessment and was dissolved by law.

Despite the paucity of details in this account, it has been long-researched and was a difficult column to assemble. Many local history friends have helped: Jack Hamner found the digital books from Google while he was on vacation; Montie Duncan interrupted his corn-planting to talk to me. Mayor Thacker, at 103, readily offered what he could; Bob Spencer lent me the Scottsville newspapers and lamented the ongoing lack of facts. George Goodwin gave time to show me artifacts he had, hoping this would elicit more. Cenie Re Moon Sturm identified F. C. Moon. Librarians from the Library of Congress, University of Virginia, Albemarle County Courthouse, Jefferson-Madison Regional Library and Albemarle-Charlottesville Historical Society, and the State Corporation Commission all answered requests for assistance. Thanks to Dr. Susan Hume Frazer of Richmond for responding to questions from a stranger, and to Mac Derry and Jeffrey Plank. Thanks to my driver Tom for trips to Charlottesville and Richmond, and to the folks at home for listening to

*1930s photo of Bruce White Motor Co., now the Dollar Store, with the bricks painted.*
*Photo courtesy Frances Moore.*

my tales of research woe. They know more about brick now than they want to.

But none of us knows enough about the Scottsville Brick Company. Dr. Frazer suggested possible information in the D. Wiley Anderson papers at the Richmond Historical Society, but otherwise I've run out of time and leads. How can we lose history less than 100 years old? We save pictures of weddings and wars, diaries of daily domestic life, and even dance cards that old. It all matters; it's all part of the past and future of Scottsville. At least we have the bricks, and we can carefully keep the buildings they made.

Originally published June 2013

# 25.

# Favorite Things in Life: Honolulu and Women

*Ivery was in the Navy during WWII, stationed at Pearl Harbor and saw action all around the Pacific.*

Ivery Davis is "a piece of Scottsville history," says his only child, Denise, as she surveys her kitchen table filled with mementoes of his life, from the U.S. flag flown at his funeral in 2001 and his World War II diary and snapshots of buddies to local newspaper articles about him and all his state chauffeur licenses. Denise finds memories welling up, through laughter and tears, about one of our town's "characters."

Clarence Ivery Davis—Ivery to most, Slick to his friends—was born in Buckingham in 1922; his father, Alan King Davis, who worked for the C&O Railroad, "liked moving around." He attended elementary school at Woodside, on Route 6 in nearby Fluvanna.

He dropped out of high school "like so many of that time to go to work" and, in 1942, joined the service. This was the most important activity of his life, Denise thinks. "Dad went to war and never really left the war," she says; "it never left him."

*Ivery Davis with his wife Gracie Powell Davis.*

Ivery was a Seabee, using his skills doing construction for the Navy. "Dad could do just about anything, especially mechanics," Denise says. He was stationed in Pearl Harbor and saw action all around the Pacific. He was at Iwo Jima, driving a bulldozer to clear the beach of bodies (so that American soldiers could land) and saw horrific sights that stayed with him. "What a hell of a time I had. Some good, some bad. Amen," ends his war diary in February of 1946.

He came home to this area and married Gracie Powell of Appleberry Mountain, near Covesville, on Christmas Eve, 1946, at the Presbyterian Church in Charlottesville; he recalled throughout his later life that it snowed that night. It was a volatile time for Ivery, as transition to civilian life was not easy. Mark Stevens recalls that Ivery told him he was at a bar near Bremo shortly after his return and got into a fight, feeling invincible—but "that guy took my temperature!" Ivery tried to learn to cool down. He worked, among other jobs, as a mechanic at the Texaco Service Station on Main Street, where GoCo is now, keeping and wearing the uniforms much later. He also worked at Valmont Dairy. "Doc" Stinson fired him from that job for smoking, an activity he wouldn't tolerate, even on the person's free time.

Two more significant events occurred: Ivery began driving James Ripley's cab, along with Herman Napier and Ed Aldridge, for his widow Myrtle in 1954. In 1957, he purchased his own cab and started Davis Taxi. Mrs. Ripley sold Ivery's mother, Pinia Davis, the Silver Grill, now Scottsville's police station at the main corner of town. Ivery ran the taxi from the restaurant, taking calls there—the cab said "Dial 2341" on the door—waiting for customers on the bench facing Main Street.

Davis was "one of the last of the country cab drivers," *Daily Progress* reporter Chip Jones wrote. He'd take men to job sites up and down the C&O line, take people to the doctor. He said, "I go five miles out to get someone and bring them in to get some groceries. Shoot, I could make ten trips a day and have it made." He charged $1.10 per mile then, at a time when, the *Progress* noted, gas cost three times that much. Mark Stevens still has Ivery's standing sign: "No Parking Taxi Cab Zone."

Among Ivery Davis' fares were young women, often from "well-to-do families" in Charlottesville, who went to Richmond for abortions. Dr. R. L. Stinson organized these appointments and the trips Ivery took, knowing that he could "keep his mouth shut and drive," according to Denise, and the arrangement worked until 1963, when "'someone squealed on me,'" as he said to the *Daily Progress*. He continued, "'the Law met me at the doctor's. Davis said he served a year in the state prison farm for that particular cab fare," though "'nobody ever held it against me. I've got as many friends as I ever had.'" Denise was young then, eight or nine, and would see her father on

*Ivery as a child, with his brother Carlton. All photos courtesy Denise Davis.*

weekends when he was allowed home from Goochland; she says his sentence was much longer, perhaps 15 years, though he had to serve only one. Someone else drove the cab that year, and her mother took in laundry to help with family expenses.

*The Daily Progress* also recorded that one of Davis' longest cab rides was "through the fields from Scottsville to West Virginia when an avid fisherman paid over $100" to get to his favorite fishing hole. There were "few competitors in the country taxicab business," they add.

Still struggling with war memories, Ivery Davis and his wife Gracie ("they were opposites," Denise says, "they loved each other but couldn't live together") divorced after 19 years. She moved to Charlottesville and remarried. Ivery became friends with her new husband, and Denise stayed in Scottsville, living with him. "Ivery was a ladies' man and didn't try to hide it," and he listed his favorite things in life as "Honolulu and women." Denise says she saw him as a combination of George Jefferson, Archie Bunker, and Ralph Kramden, with some chauvinistic opinions and a strong streak of stubbornness.

But Denise feels he "enjoyed life to the fullest. Well, maybe even a little too much." All the same, he loved his family and was "even-keeled until he got very aggravated." He kept guns and once escorted a man who seemed bent on robbery from his friend Lewis Rhodes' gas station, keeping his pistol to the man's head. "There were regrets" about some parts of his life, Ivery later said, including "the situation with his wife."

Denise feels she learned "many life lessons" from him. She used to ride in the cab with him at times, and they shared a lot. He had firm rules for her: no dating preachers' sons—they are either too wild and crazy or they're sneaking around—and no going on a date in a van. When she completed first grade, he had promised her a car at graduation and bought her a "beautiful black and white LTD with red leather interior" when she was a junior. All he demanded was that she take auto mechanics at Albemarle High School, making her one of the first girls in the course, so she'd know "the difference between a hubcap and a distributor cap." On principle, he paid for everything while she lived with him, though he said she'd "send him to the nuthouse or the poorhouse." He was "very straightforward and treated everyone the same." "Help people out" was one of his philosophies and "the way he was," says Denise; he reminded her that the time might come when she'd need help. Another of his famous lines was, "If you don't want to listen to what I am saying, then you will just have to learn the hard way, but I can guarantee you one thing for certain: you will learn." She also remembers her father's good sense of humor. Ivery, in later years, went every day to the Silver Grill,

which had passed by then to Denise's aunt, Bea Thacker. It was, in fact, a major social event in town, and Ivery would meet and talk with his friends there, including Norman Skeen, Reverend James Jetton, Jerry Ballowe, and Gene Bryant. At the end of the day, he'd clean and sweep up. He also made the coffee, though it was notoriously bad—"the worst," recalls Mark Stevens, of the nextdoor Coleman's. "People bought it every day and complained about it!" Denise says Jerry, who recently died, used to exclaim, "Good god, Slick, how many dirty socks did you put in it today!" She discovered the secret: he used the leftovers from one day along with the next day's batch. Denise took to setting up the coffeemaker each night. "He was a great ol' guy—fantastic," says Mark now. Gene Harding recalls, "I liked him a lot; he might have been controversial, but I liked him."

The day Ivery said he didn't feel like going to the Silver Grill she saw as the beginning of the end. He developed Parkinson's, and Denise was glad to have returned to Scottsville in 1998 and to be able to help him, to "pay him back," and for her children to get to know him better. "I'd never put up with a man like that as a husband," she is sure, but she treasures and honors her dad. "He was quite a character."

*Originally published May 2013*

# 26.

# D. Wiley Anderson: Inventor, Purveyor, Designer

*Victory Hall, c. 1925. Photographer: William E. Burgess. Courtesy of Scottsville Museum.*

*D. Wiley Anderson as a young man. Photo Courtesy of Keith Van Allen.*

D. Wiley Anderson, inventor, bottler, and purveyor of Albevanna Springs water, designer of the Jackson Street house, The Terrace, and of Victory Hall, as well as residential and civic buildings from Brooklyn to Georgia, had strong ties to the Scottsville area, where he grew up and raised his family. His daughter Mollie, born in 1915 and now living in Richmond with her son Keith Van Allen, recently buried her older sister Patsy (Phyllis Anderson

Davis) in the Scottsville Cemetery. "I get so homesick sometimes," she said.

D. Wiley (David, named for his Civil War uncle, later a member of the House of Delegates in Fluvanna) grew up in the thick of Cap'n John Bledsoe Anderson's clan. Cap'n John, 1819-1911, married Mary Elizabeth Morris in 1843 after his first wife died. He inherited about 1,000 acres of land on the Albemarle-Fluvanna border along the Hardware River;

*The Victory Hall Theatre.*

here he raised D. Wiley and his 10 other children. Much of what we know about this strong-willed patriarch, who always stood by his word—a builder and expert carpenter—comes from a grandson-in-law, Thomas Cleveland Sadler, whose "Memories of Bygone Days" has often been referenced here. The Cap'n was, Sadler says, "very rough-spoken and might scare you to death if you did not know him," though he was in fact a kind and tenderhearted man for whom religion, music, and family were important. "Many old houses in and around Fork Union are still standing that he built."

His son D. Wiley joined him in this work during the summers, and this was D. Wiley's initial training for his later architectural career. Dr. Susan Frazer, VCU, the first writer to consider D. Wiley Anderson's designs in an academic framework, resurrects him from "obscurity" with her thesis that Anderson, "after being trained as an artisan-builder in rural Virginia and then completing a six-year architectural apprenticeship in Richmond…became an accomplished building technologist, an excellent draftsman, and a competitive regional architect." Frazer, who presented this material at the Scottsville Museum in 1997, says that Anderson's "stylistic evolution" allowed him a long, important career.

From his father, we presume, D. Wiley learned drafting and business practices, as well as building skills. D. Wiley was a quick student at Scottsville's Stony Point School, always reading; he liked math and drawing. His father's imprint on his work ethic was strong; he taught all his children the various skills still being employed by the slaves who had stayed on at the family's farm. In 1889, he went to Richmond and got a job with architect George Parson. He opened his own business in 1895.

This was only a generation after the Civil War, when Richmond had been ruined and people in the South had very little money. D. Wiley had been exposed to the architecture of Jefferson, and it is possible that he heard Ralph Waldo Emerson speak at the University of Virginia. He later took part of a quotation from Emerson as his business motto, "Not a mousetrap man,

*Wiley Anderson's home, Albevanna Springs, near Scottsville.*

but the world beats a path to his door." ("Build a better mousetrap," Emerson had said, "and the world will beat a path to your door.") Anderson was outgoing and handsome, with entre into Richmond society through Parson and his well-off client Lewis Ginter, whose mansion he built, and through the Civil War veterans who revered his uncle.

When he started his own firm, D. Wiley Anderson was designing in the high Victorian style. Several of his three-story, wrap-around porch, gabled, turreted, and crenellated houses are in the Fan and Hermitage Road District, redolent of the elegance of the upper class as the Richmond population boomed. As land northwest of the city was developed, D. Wiley began to add the newer architectural trend, Colonial Revival—with its symmetry and elaborated front doors, often with fan lights and porticoes with columns—to his Victorian designs, including Queen Anne (the painted ladies) and

Richardsonian Romanesque (with round-topped arches and square-cut stone work).

*Keith Van Allen, holding a photo of his grandfather D. Wiley Anderson; and Mollie Anderson Van Allen, D. Wiley's daughter and Keith's mother, at home in Richmond. Photo by Ruth Klippstein.*

This eclectic approach, while it has been described as an expression of Anderson's lack of formal training, was very popular at the time, and he was offered many commissions from various prominent families in Richmond for large, expensive houses. These include Montrose, Bleniquhain, and Rosedale.

As the twentieth century progressed, D. Wiley Anderson began to design public buildings, churches, movie halls, and train depots. He offered a design in the competition for a new State Capitol in Richmond. While it didn't win, it was considered impressive and important, and Anderson used its inspiration later when he designed the Louisa County Courthouse. D. Wiley also designed the wooden, 10,000-seat Exposition Hall for the United Confederate Veterans reunion, a "huge event," says Frazer, and a big boost to his popularity, as well as a Jewish temple, movie theatres, and warehouses. Keith Van Allen's favorites include his grandfather's Italianate Confederate soldiers' homes in Richmond.

Anderson's son John worked with his father during this time, and was being groomed to take over the business. Keith Van Allen thinks that John designed the small Bird Street Scottsville Elementary School that burned down in 1921. John was killed in the dreadful carnage in France during World War I, and his loss and its effect are still remembered by his half-sister Mollie.

Susan Frazer notes D. Wiley's ability to blend stylistic architectural elements and to utilize the newly available manufactured pieces that could be added to a building according to the client's taste and budget. Perhaps this is how he arrived at his late Victorian commercial design for Victory Hall. As Bob Spencer says, D. Wiley was "of course involved with the idea of having a performance area in Scottsville so the local drama coach, Marion McKay—championed by Mayor Jackson Beal—could stage her shows." When silent movies were available, Willie Burgess put in piano and screened movies, 20 cents a ticket. Later, Chautauqua and travelling vaudeville acts performed there, with many famous entertainers coming to Scottsville. The Victory Hall Company Corporation was founded, with banker Jacinto V. Pereira as treasurer and D. Wiley one of the stockholders, and "everyone in town was asked to contribute," Bob says.

Bricks for the building were made in the John Martin foundry across the James River, in the low ground of Snowden south of the current bridge. The project, commemorating the Armistice, began in 1918; the building was dedicated in 1920. "As Mr. Anderson designed it, Victory Hall was like an old opera house. It had a balcony and a lovely proscenium. There were 386 seats that folded down ("usually filled on Saturdays," Bob says) and a floor sloping toward the stage. The box office opened to the street, and there was a neon sign. While the high school had its senior class plays here, Bob says, "Victory Hall played many roles in the history of Scottsville."

Fred Schneider of the Scottsville Architectural Review Board notes, "Victory Hall is clearly the most impressive of the buildings found along Valley Street at this time, the larger braid factory building [at the north end of the street] notwithstanding. Its prominence is due primarily to the building's deeply recessed arched entry, its most distinctive feature. With this grand gesture to the public, Victory Hall invites us into both the new civic meeting place called the cinema and the twentieth century itself."

D. Wiley Anderson designed the brick house Cliffview, owned by George and Lucinda Wheeler and originally built for Senator Martin, on Bird at Page Street. Keith Van Allen says the interior is a mirror image of the house Anderson built for his own family at Albevanna Springs, three miles northeast of Scottsville. T. E. Bruce, Sr., Scottsville pharmacist, asked Anderson to redesign the 1832 Carlton Hotel at the corner of West Main and Valley as his drugstore and soda fountain. Anderson prepared drawings for restoration and additions at Fair View Farm, on Route 20; it burned in the 1930s. D. Wiley also designed homes for J. L. Pitts and W. E. Moon, as well as The Terrace for the D. P. Powers family, today restored to its former glory and most recently the home of Haden Anderson.

Nearby, Anderson did "a beautiful little church" at Bremo Bluff; renovations of the Boxley House in Louisa; and Ednam—his Albemarle masterwork—in Charlottesville, 1902. Keith Van Allen says that the Boxley project, transforming an antebellum house into "a charmingly exuberant expression of Colonial Revival, flipping the staircase around, making a wild flying balcony underneath the grand portico," was one of "D. Wiley's most fun jobs." The architect and the owner were "cracking jokes the whole time they worked on it." D. Wiley also designed the mansion in Southern Albemarle called Nydrie.

D. Wiley's wife died, and he remarried. He lived various places in Richmond from 1900-1913, then moved to Albevanna Springs. Here Mollie's memories center, as she recalls her ebullient, happy-tempered father and, eventually, 12 siblings and half-siblings, roaming free ("Our mother knew we were safe") on the hills and in the woods. They drove a Model T around the countryside and to Scottsville High School, and they also took shortcuts through the woods to walk to Scottsville.

They still stopped regularly to talk to "Aunt" Fanny Mundy, who had been a slave on the Cap'n John property and whom "everybody loved." Mollie had lots of cousins, who enjoyed the freedom and jollity of Albevanna Springs and often came to borrow Frank, one of the horses. They'd ride him to town, then "pat him on the back and send him home. He'd go into the barn by himself."

Mollie remembers the garden in front of the house on the 133 acres D. Wiley eventually acquired. Money from one of his inventions, an automatic thermostat window opener, paid for this, Keith says. Mollie also remembers Scottsville High School, where she revered W. D. Smith. It was there she met her future husband, Russell Van Allen. "Stop looking at me," she told the brash young man. "It's OK—I'm going to marry you," he replied. Mollie went to the D. Wylie-designed Smithdeal-Massey Business School in Richmond and later worked at Buckingham Slate, where, in her interview, the owner learned of her connection to D. Wiley Anderson and said, "Oh, you can have the job; he's specified enough of our slate to reach around the world." Her father would sometimes talk business with her, calling her "my little secretary."

But it's D. Wiley's love of life, his storytelling, singing, piano-playing, and jokes and stories that Mollie remembers best. All her cousins would "flock over" to Albevanna Springs to see D. Wiley drink Worcestershire sauce "right out of the bottle." The last house D. Wiley designed was in Fork Union, next to one his father built. He died of bronchitis. ("If you have your health, you're a millionaire," she recalls him always saying.)

D. Wiley Anderson concentrated on his inventions during the later years of his life. He received 16 U. S. patents, one Canadian, and was able to attract enough investors to produce his Multifix brick, a flashing brick. He invented a Murphy-type bathtub for crowded apartments and other building-related products. Keith says he predicted fast food.

Anderson bottled and sold Albevanna Springs Ponce de Leon water from 1911; he was still sending it as far as North Carolina, New York, and Ohio in 1935. Mollie remembers gazing into the pooled water of the nine springs on the property. "Theodore Roosevelt bought that water," Keith says, "when he was at Pine Knot." D. Wiley hoped to develop the property as a "hotel-sanitarium or a large hydroelectric power plant," according to Susan Frazer, but the Depression had other ideas. Despite his pleasant, joking ways, D. Wiley Anderson fell into debt. He went to work as a staff architect for a Richmond production builder, living at his daughter Marie's residence while in Richmond and taking the train home to Scottsville on weekends. Sometimes he had to borrow the fare from her.

Albevanna Springs was sold out of the family in the 1970s. Lingering memories include D. Wiley and his pet duck under the garden arbor, the dances they'd have in the big front parlor, or parties on the lawn with Japanese lanterns lighting the evening. D. Wiley would hunt for frogs in the pond he designed by the spring house, and the cook fixed them for his supper. Anderson would love it when his daughter Virginia, or any of the family, rubbed and soothed his head when he was home from Richmond on weekends.

Keith Van Allen, who has done a great deal to preserve and document the life, work, and legacy of D. Wiley Anderson, recalls, "It was impossible when I was growing up to get a bunch of Andersons together without a barrage of jokes spewing forth, each person trying to top the other. But at the same time, talk of building or scientific study or philosophy could be spouted out equally. All this before eating. Family reunions at Albevanna were wonderful, with several styles of chicken to choose from, then various country meanderings afterward. I miss all that."

*Originally published February 2013*

# 27.

# Dear Old Scottsville High

"Dear old Scottsville! Blessed the day
When we knew thy helpful sway,
Learned to follow wisdom's footsteps for our guide.
Filled with study, play and song,
Hours which now we would prolong.
Scottsville, Scottsville, Scottsville! Happy days with thee."

*The high school in an undated post card view. Scottsville Library Collection.*

This is one of the verses of the Scottsville School song, written by William Day Smith, who served as principal from 1907 to 1937, and remembered still. It conjures the strength of feeling, the devotion and memories, of students who attended the school.

Scottsville has had several schools and a long history of education. In fact, the first high school in Virginia to be accredited by the state was Scottsville's in 1913. School was held in the brick Brady building, on the southeast corner of Valley and Main Street, from 1876 to 1906. It was superseded by the large frame school on the hill above Jackson Street, originally without running water but with the particularly memorable teacher Miss Willie Hickok, Wild Bill's cousin.

In 1924, the Masons laid the cornerstone for Scottsville's last high school, at the end of West Main Street. At the time, Scottsville's population was growing, and the town had two large flour mills, an ice plant, braid factory, theater, two hotels, two drugstores, a

*Scottsville High SChool's Class of 1934. Photographer Unknown.*
*Photo courtesy of Scottsville Museum.*

boarding house, and several restaurants.

The new school was progressive, with the first school library in the state and a large auditorium with classrooms ranged around it, Bill Mason recalls. Physical education and domestic science were on the curriculum, and there was an honor system. It must be remembered that the school was exclusively for white students and teachers.

The youngest students, grades one and two, attended classes in the now-vanished building where the Scottsville Library stands. In third grade they would go to the high school building—"a move up, I guess," says Larry Stallings, though their class was held in the basement, across from the furnace room. "It was nice and warm."

For years, high school was composed of grades eight through eleven; twelfth grade was added later. But when school opened in the autumn of 1968, Albemarle County moved the high school students into Albemarle High School, leaving Scottsville School as a junior high and elementary school. An undated 1967 *Daily Progress* photograph shows valedictorian Mary Curtis and salutatorian Keith Rittenhouse looking "sadly at the building that holds many pleasant memories." Reunions have helped keep the memories alive and recement the bonds. At the 1988 reunion, there was a representative from the class of 1919, Ruby Omohundro.

The yearbooks and literary magazines survive. "Ripples," started in 1932, offered sports news, theatrical schedules, a meditation by principal Mr. Smith, and gossip. From the May 6th issue: "The other day, the school was hit by a miniature cyclone. This was no other than Jacqueline Beal who had lost precious notes. Not only that, but someone had found them. Jacqueline wouldn't reveal what was in the notes, but we imagined, asked her and received no answer— Well, silence gives consent." And further on, "The Junior Class was rather bad on Wednesday 13. The assignments Mr. Noble Smith had made were not done, and consequently, the lid blew off, the class was confronted with more lectures than they ever had in their gay, young lives, and now the Juniors have reformed."

The "Scotty," the high school yearbook, has pictures in 1956 of students in a variety of clubs: international relations, commercial, public speaking, safety patrol, and library. There was a band and a flute choir, basketball for both boys and girls, a student council, and Future Farmers of America. Classes for vocational agriculture students, taught by Tom Allison, later the school's principal, were in the small block building near Bird Street and the current library. School life was full and rich, an important element of the town.

Chub Walsh recalls the dirt basketball court and how the older boys would sit outside, "smoking our cigarettes and watching the girls go by." Students could leave school grounds for their noon meal; "town would be loaded with kids at lunchtime," getting a hot dog and soda at the restaurants or service stations. Some students, he says, would do the family grocery shopping, if their parents didn't have a car, and take bags home on the school bus.

*1955 Scotty snapshot. Courtesy Scottsville Museum.*

Chub says there was chapel in the auditorium every Wednesday, with preachers rotating from various churches in town. First graders sat in the first row, second in the second row, and so on sequentially through the eleventh graders. Older students also had study hall in the auditorium, though he doesn't remember a lot of studying going on. In Chub's day, Leslie Walton was principal. "Shorty," people called him, "but not to his face. He used to paddle you if you didn't behave yourself." Larry Stallings, who admits to never having been paddled, can describe the oak stump on legs, with the annual rings dated—it was more than 100 years old—over which Walton "would fold you and paddle you." The stump is in the museum, and other physical discipline, like

187

slapping—which Larry did endure—is also gone.

"The really nice thing about it was it was small, and you knew everyone," Baxter Pitts says. "Teachers knew the families, your siblings. You weren't anonymous and couldn't get away with anything—it kept us out of trouble. It was a good place to go to school," she recalls and notes that she was well-prepared when she entered college, having had Hamner Goodwin for the last three years of English. "We all learned." Language electives were French and Latin, and there was math up through Algebra II. Also offered were general science, physics, chemistry, biology, shorthand and typing, home economics and shop, and the vocational agriculture class, which Baxter's father taught.

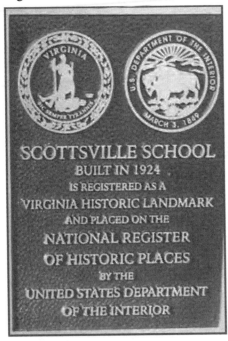

*New plaque at the high school building.*
*Photo by Ruth Klippstein.*

For physical education, all the grades, eighth or ninth through twelfth, were together. Seniors chose squads, which then stayed together as the games rotated through softball, volleyball, and basketball, a week at a time. P. E. was offered just before lunch.

Other extracurricular activities are remembered, too. Bill Mason says he usually wore a six-inch hunting knife in a scabbard to school, or brought an icepick stuck into a cork, for mumbletypeg, and "no one said anything about it. One boy was known as a knife trader; he could hardly keep his pants up, he had so many pocket knives." Mumbletypeg competition got more and more complex and difficult as the game progressed.

Larry Stallings recalls touch football and four or five of his friends going down to the little creek at the south end of the grounds to play. They'd beat down the six-foot tall weeds with sticks—again, no one said anything about the sticks—to make a clubhouse or tunnels. "That was nice."

*Jeffrey Plank addresses group gathered to celebrate re-dedication of the apartments. Photo by Ruth Klippstein.*

Games and sports were always important at Scottsville High School. Principal Smith originated Rally Day for all county schools. It "attracted statewide attention," according to the Bicentennial History of Public Education in Albemarle County. Scottsville won the first year and often afterwards. Bill Mason recalls the various relay races, with flags or blocks that had to be stacked, and especially his favorite game, dodgeball. Rally Day was at Lambeth Field, part of the University of Virginia along Emmet Street.

Everyone recalls good teachers at Scottsville School. Two special stories from Larry Stallings feature Katherine Phillips, the "loveliest woman and one of the best teachers I've ever had. She was a wonderfully nice woman, a humanitarian, not a disciplinarian," who introduced him in sixth grade to Steinbeck's *Of Mice and Men*. He also tells of Leslie Walton, "quite severe," he recalls,

189

"coming regularly into his fourth grade, taught by Miss Boggs, from West Virginia, to read Uncle Remus stories." He read very well, but what the students didn't know was that this was the beginning of his courtship of Miss Boggs, whom he eventually married. Larry left high school to support his family when his father became ill. He worked at the rubber plant, went into the Navy during the war, and returned to Scottsville to finish high school—in the same class as his third youngest sister in 1949. Many possibilities and promises left Scottsville with the closing of the school, but the venerable building, now on the National Register of Historic Places, has had a rebirth. In 1991, the Jordan Development Corporation bought it and converted the classrooms into 34 apartments for the elderly and disabled. In 2011, Piedmont Housing Alliance took over the project and began planning substantial, expensive, renovation. Work on both exterior and interior began this past January, and the apartments were rededicated with an open house in November.

Remarks by representatives of the many groups and banks responsible for developing and funding the project indicate the broad support for it and the sense of celebrating a job well done. "What a great occasion," said Forrest Kerns, president of Jordan. Stuart Armstrong spoke for the Piedmont Housing Alliance and recognized Martin Horn, Inc., who did the construction. Renovations brought the building back to its original external look and added state-of-the-art heating and air conditioning to the rooms. Harold Trent of the Virginia Community Development Corporation congratulated everyone concerned; "I am quite impressed," he said. "It is impeccable work and looks great." The careful renovation earned historic tax credits from both state and federal governments; the building will have to maintain compliance for 15 years to retain the credits.

Rick Funk, vice president of dBF Associates, the architects behind the renovations, found the experience of bringing high-quality rental units to seniors, so they can stay in Scottsville, "a most rewarding aspect of the project." Jeffrey Plank, chair of Scottsville's Architectural Review Board, said in his address, "What a splendid job, what attention to detail, what care, and what restraint." He noted the importance of the structure in the downtown Historic District and pointed out that "its restoration ensures that an iconic public building and the function of its first life, that of an every-grade public school, will remain part of the town's landscape."

"In this building," he concluded, "we see the continuity of our built environment—a 1925 building picking up on the features of our 1825 buildings and this 2012 renovation giving it new life in the 21st century, a building full of life and memories for all ages, and now for all of our people."

Clarence Michens and Bea Proffitt, residents since the opening of the apartments, cut the ribbon between the columns. Inside, at the ample buffet tables, Bea and her sister, also a resident, spoke about attending Scottsville High School. "It was a close-knit school," said Frankie Turner. "I remember the apron I made in home ec and embroidered with my name, Frances." "We're from a large family," said Bea, "and we're a large family here. I'm living in the apartment that was the classroom where Mrs. Sutherland tried to teach me math."

*Originally published January 2013*

# 28.

# Scottsville Celebrated Its History in Style

*Planning committee: from L: Jean Dansey, Jackie Grove, Amanda Hall, Fred Schneider, Frankie Ward, Sandy Small, Linda Jones, and in front, Bob Spencer and Mayor Raymon Thacker.*

"All roads seemed to lead to Scott's Landing," reads the Scottsville Museum website, after the September 4th, 1744 Act of the Virginia Assembly divided extensive Goochland County, one of the eight original 1643 shires of the colony, to form Albemarle. The plantation of Edward Scott was ordered for the original convocation of magistrates, a mile west of today's town.

This meeting, held on February 28th, 1745, has a long history of conjecture, as does the subsequent building of the first county courthouse. While archaeological work attempts to document the exact location of this building, the choice of Scott's Landing, as the community was called, is more obvious. In the geographic center of the new county, Scott's Landing was the first major riverport above Richmond, "crucially important to the settlers," as historian Virginius Dabney writes. Mary Rawlings, in *The Albemarle of Other Days*, says that, until the advent of the railroad, Scottsville was the "most important settlement in the county. Even at this early date, its natural advantages [offered] a promising location."

The story is often written of how "time has covered up most traces," as Virginia Moore says of Scottsville's great promise and how poorly history and the weather have often served us. A burgeoning population in the old county caused the legislators to split off Amherst and Buckingham counties from Albemarle, leaving Scottsville at the edge of its administrative area, and in 1762, newly formed Charlottesville was named county seat. As Eryn Brennan says in *Images of America: Charlottesville*, "A settlement did not exist at the site, and a simple grid was used to lay out a town." The legacy of Jefferson did the rest.

In the early 1990s, as Scottsville expanded in area and population after a boundary adjustment with the county and secured protection of the flood levee, citizens began thinking about their special relationship to Albemarle and chose to celebrate the county's 250th anniversary in 1994, as well as their own. As Matthew Lee wrote in *The Daily Progress*, January 2nd, 1994, "the County of Albemarle will likely be upstaged in [anniversary] festivities by the Town of Scottsville, which also celebrates its 250th this year." In fact, the reporter found, some of the supervisors didn't even know it was the county's sestercentennial.

But Scottsville was busy. A Celebration Planning Committee formed almost two years in advance, with Robert K. "Bobby" Spencer, a town councilor, as General Chairman. Mayor A. Raymon Thacker took an active interest, and the other committee members were Jean Dansey, Jacqueline and Jesse Grove, Amanda Hall, Linda and Latham Jones, Steven Meeks (who chaired Albemarle County's

250th anniversary committee), Marianne Ramsden, Sandra and Tim Small, Roberta "Frankie" and Scott Ward, and Frederick Schneider. Sandy was recording secretary, and Frankie was treasurer. "We really did work hard," Frankie remembers.

*Rob Coles, Jefferson descendant in "Meet Thomas Jefferson" at the Museum.*

Looking back on all that was accomplished in the four-day Labor Day weekend celebration, one can be pardoned for not believing the scope of the work. Tim Small says, "Bobby Spencer emblemized leadership, getting things done. Without him, it probably wouldn't have happened. I couldn't praise him enough." Bobby, retired from teaching, had just then been diagnosed with cancer and says he was "so proud of how the committee continued functioning and following through with plans and preparations." It was, he thinks, "one of the best Scottsville events in my lifetime." "It was lots of work," echos Scott Ward, Marianne, and Tim.

Friday, September 2nd, started with the Opening Ceremony outside the Scottsville Museum and continued with a tour of five historic homes and four churches. In the afternoon, the museum's special show, "Work in Progress: Scottsville's Working People," by Evelyn Edson and Ruth Klippstein, was open, and the UDC hosted visits to the Confederate cemetery on Hardware Street. In the evening, everyone gathered near the Uniroyal/Goodrich plant, at the

194

west end of Bird Street, for "Of Town and the River, Folk History of Scottsville," written by John Randolph Phillips and revised by Bob Spencer as a U. S. Bicentennial celebration, with direction by Mo Cahill. Kathy Coleman and Ken Smith narrated vignettes showing the development of the town since the Monacans came to the banks of the James. Bursting firecrackers in an oil drum heralded Sheridan's Civil War raiders, dramatically riding in on horses supplied by George Dansey.

Saturday was Jamesfest Day, with free carriage rides, citizens dressed in Colonial costumes (of which Norma Schneider crafted a great number), walking tours, and a Market on the James set up on the site of Bruce Park. Under this big tent, Marianne Ramsden gathered "some fantastic crafts and demonstrators—quilting, sewing, a blacksmith, herbs, calligraphy," she remembers now. "The town was full of people and really spruced up, with flowers in front of each business." Harry Koenig sheared his sheep for a sheep-to-shawl demonstration, and strolling entertainers enlivened the proceedings. The Buckingham Lining Bar Gang demonstrated old-time railroad work on East Main, under another big tent, and performers on the

*Mayor Thacker and Jefferson (Rob Coles) meet an unidentified Civil War soldier.*

Chautauqua stage included Kirkwood the Colonial Magician. Eddie and Martha Adcock played at Victory Hall in the evening.

On Sunday, an interdenominational church service was conducted under the Main Street tent, and the new town flagpole, at the corner of Valley and Main, was dedicated in memory of George T. Omohundro, Jr., by the Lions Club. A community picnic and Charlottesville Municipal Band's concert, with a bluegrass group at the Market Square, rounded off the day.

Labor Day began with Scottsville's first 5K run, circling town, and the official anniversary ceremony, addressed by Governor George Allen, with music by the Fort Lee Military Band and a gala birthday party afterward. A reprise of the pageant wrapped up the day and the festivities.

A time capsule was buried on the museum lawn, to be opened in 2044. "I hope to be around," says Steven Meeks. Many souvenirs

*Chautauqua singers. Photo courtesy Marianne Ramsden.*

were created for sale, from bumper stickers to the brass cipher created by Beverly Sims. Fred Schneider's 250th anniversary logo was featured on T-shirts and a commemorative plate. "In my years of working with other events and festivals, this is undoubtedly one of the best event logos ever designed," says Steven Meeks. "It was an idea I had floating around," Fred says, "and this was a good occasion to bring it to light. It was a labor of love."

*Bob Spencer and Mayor Thacker at the opening ceremonies.*
*All photos courtesy of Bobby Spencer.*

Another monumental effort made was Gaye Bowen's and Jeanine Reagan's painting of the batteau mural on the side of Main Street's Maxwell Furniture store; Heather McQuale, now Rolfe, painted the county seal and name in beautiful script. "It was a wonderful experience," she says. "I had fears and doubts and trouble sleeping over it, but I persevered and pulled it off. I remember my two small children cheering me on as I executed the first letter with a huge brush. I felt such support and gained confidence."

The committee produced a Monopoly-style game, with many businesses and individuals who contributed named on it. Remember the *Pig 'n Steak*, *Family Haircuts*, the ice cream parlor and *Flower Cart*?

Charlottesville has done much this year to celebrate their story and Albemarle's heritage. Steven Meeks has again been instrumental in that, documenting "what has been lost and the lasting values that we benefit from today." But as Fred Schneider says, "We feel proud of our event. I like to think that Scottsville set the bar on how to celebrate a 250th anniversary. This will live in history."

*Originally published September 2012*

## 29.

# The Lost House of Scottsville

Parts of Scottsville's history are lost quite easily. Old roads become faint traces through the woods, and the houses once conveniently built beside them fall down or are otherwise forgotten. Yet sometimes—when we're lucky—those bits of history can re-emerge with just as little effort or foresight.

This is the story of finding one of those forgotten houses. It's on land to the east of Antioch Road, State Route 637, about two miles from Driver's Hill in town. This parcel of roughly 80 acres, rolling hills in grass bordered by mixed woodland, was, in the early twentieth century, transected by a road that ran across Antioch Road, veered toward the Hardware River, where it forded a tributary creek, and about two miles later came out in the vicinity of Fox Memorial Church on Route 6, near the property called Spring Hill. (Various dead-ending sections of unimproved roads

*Margery standing at east chimney.*

199

are shown in this green space on the 1967 USGS topographical map.) That part of the road just off Antioch is now called Old Spring Hill Road, its former name.

Much of the land around that section of the road was sold in 1897 by William J. Isham and Mary J. Cleveland to someone named Tillman. In 1899, M. Ida Hughes and Lucy M. Morris, a daughter of William Cleveland, sold it to Bartholomew T. Kidd. Kidd, who married Lucy Harris Field, died in 1952, and his son Don Pedro (and Don Pedro's wife Lucy Bell Kidd) inherited the property. In 1959, six acres of it were sold to John Rittenhouse, and after his divorce in 1976, Don Pedro Kidd conveyed the property to his son Edward B. Kidd. In 1977, Edward Kidd, who had not lived at the property as an adult, sold it to Margery Edson-Gould, who was moving to Scottsville from Northern Virginia, planning to start a horse farm. It was she who worked to develop this chain of title from the county deed books.

*Dovetail notch detail. Photo courtesy of Ruth Klippstein.*

*Date on chimney detailed.*

Margery was not interested in keeping the old farmhouse next to what seemed to be a driveway when her contractor reported that restoration would be very difficult due to deterioration. She organized help to take the house down while she continued living in Alexandria. As the framework and walls started to disappear, a log cabin stood revealed.

Margery hired Herb Stahl, now of Charlottesville, to consult on saving the cabin, and Herb brought in his friend and work partner Tom Joseph, who had experience moving and re-establishing old log cabins. "We found log walls chain-sawed through to make room for interior door openings in the former 'new house,'" Herb recalls, "right over the cabin. The entire roof structure and attic were missing, but the chimneys at each end of the cabin were intact. And the roof line pitch was firmly engraved in the stone chimneys. I was amazed at how steep the pitch was. In fact, when we shingled the newly constructed roof, we simply leaned the ladders from the ground all the way up to the peak. We also came up with a neat design for panels and windows to fill in the missing, chain-sawed, sections of now exterior walls. We designed a kitchen area for the first floor and put in a new bathroom."

Evelyn Edson, president of the Scottsville Museum and Margery's daughter, remembers that the Kidd family was notified to retrieve items from the farmhouse, among them a sidesaddle. Heavy horsehair furniture was salvaged, and Evelyn was left a crumbling leather-bound ledger book. It is inscribed with at least 14 different names on the covers and was used from the back end as an account book with entries starting in 1839, mostly about cotton and wool spun and woven into cloth. The front section contains recipes often found in nineteenth century household books: damson pickle, Sally Lunn cake, green wool dye, and a salve to "cure Cancer." It is not clear how this book relates to the log cabin, and it was possibly just a random possession.

Tom Phillips, who has been a restoration consultant and implementer, now retired, observed the exterior of the cabin recently. Tom owns a 1922 and an 1860s log cabin. He pointed out ways such structures can be dated. Marks of a broadaxe are seen here in the wide logs. While people could use this technology even after the advent of sawmills (as well as pit saws and lumber made with a two-man saw), it might not have been accessible. "If anything," Tom considered, referring to a date scratched into a stone in the east chimney, "the 1880s is too late for this building. It's possible, but I would have guessed earlier." The steep roof pitch "adds credulity to the age of the house." There is another mark on the north side of the stone chimney: the very precise initials, with serifs, "JCC."

Tom noted, as well, the size of the logs, appearing large enough "to be from native growth trees—here and mature when white folks showed up 300 years ago." (My own counting on a first course log at the west side of the cabin reached 111 annual rings.) The dressed logs average 12 inches, with some considerably larger.

While the "wood of choice" for a permanent cabin was chestnut, Tom says, with its distinctive color and durability, he thinks the wood of this cabin is oak. The notches of the squared building are dovetailed, a special notch that creates "a lock, as the logs on top want to go downward." These notches were made on the spot to "mate," Tom says, two specific logs into the house. The chinking is two to four inches in width.

The logs are about four feet long on the west side of the cabin and three feet on the east, with a new framed section in the middle, surrounding the front door. There are two rooms inside and a loft above; chimneys are at the gable ends of the cabin, the one on the west made of brick and, on the east, the original fieldstone with brick at the roof. Tom described how chimneys were often made of stone up to the roof, finished with small round logs canting away from the house and braced with a pole. This section could be easily pulled down in case of a chimney fire, saving the roof from being set aflame. The bricks, Tom says, look handmade.

The house is set on rock piers at each corner, without a full foundation. The interior fireplaces are stone, plastered over and with some of the original red paint still adhering. The old ceiling beams show the nail holes from lath work, points out Allan Ebell, Margery's nephew, who currently lives in the cabin. The property is for sale.

Allan points out the footprint of the demolished farmhouse,

concrete pads extending out from the front door and along the front of the house and out the rear of the cabin, now covered as a screened porch, with a deck projecting towards the Hardware. To the east are stone foundation walls, about two feet high, used now to enclose a kitchen garden and flowers. There are several outbuildings, including a shed that possibly served as a chicken coop. A cistern was found under the area now used as a deck.

This information corresponds with the little bit we can learn about the vanished house built over the cabin. Joyce McGuire, who lives at the corner of Antioch and Old Spring Hill roads, was born at Hardware and came here around 1956 with her husband, Jimmy McGuire, who worked at the rubber plant. "Pulling down the old house was the first we knew of the cabin," she says. "It was a big house," and she only visited inside a few times, once after a kitchen fire. "Don Pedro must have been cooking there, at the back of the house. There was a well in the kitchen," she says.

Don Pedro, Joyce recalls, had a rough manner but was friendly; she had a garden on part of his land. She remembers taking the old road across to Route 6 and thinks there was another, now vanished, cabin along it, possibly belonging to Joe Harris.

Forrest McGuire, Joyce's son, recalls that Don Pedro drove a mule team and wagon, according to Allan. Ben McGuire, who also lives off Old Spring Hill Road, has good stories about Mr. Kidd. He told the cousins they could ride their motorbikes off into his fields and woods. "I never saw him doing

*Margery's cabin in snow.*

any work," Ben says, but Don would sit with his friends on the front porch, talking convivially and enjoying the day. "A party house, you could call it. Women in the neighborhood didn't like it."

Once, after the boys rode through and the men waved and called out in a friendly fashion, they heard "beating and banging on pots and pans," with the men singing a song they were making up about the boys riding their bikes. It had a rude refrain expressing very dire hopes for the boys' future, "laying us out. We were actually scared." But when they had nerve enough to ride by Don Pedro's again, everyone was "as nice as could be." Joyce likewise found that Don Pedro's "cussin'" was bluster, and he was pleasant once she talked with him.

Lee McGuire says that Don Pedro never owned a car, though they were common then; Lee's father would stop by to see if Kidd wanted a ride to town, otherwise he would go by horse and wagon. The two-story house, Lee recalls, was L-shaped, with a big front

*Margery's cabin this spring. Photo by Ruth Klippstein.*

porch where he would play while his father talked with Kidd. Lee thinks Kidd, living alone, used just the rear portion of the house, the old cabin.

In the woods east of the fields around the cabin, marked by a tall magnolia and iron fencing, is a small family cemetery. The Fluvanna County Historical Society and Point of Fork chapter of the DAR gathered the names on stones there in *Family Cemeteries of Fluvanna County, Virginia*, in 1996. They describe the place as "abandoned and overgrown," though it has been known to family members, who visited when Margery was living. The stones are for W. L. Bragg, 1896-97; Sarah Cleveland, 1797-1879; William Cleveland, 1795-1874; and one erected by William H. Ancell, 1885, in memory of his wife, Virginia A. Cleveland Ancell, 1829-1884, and their children.

The road that used to pass near it "in the old days," Ben McGuire says, "was fairly busy." We have still these markers, the path the road took, the cemetery stones, and the log cabin, once covered by a farmhouse, to remind us of the families and the ways that are gone.

*Originally published July 2012*

# 30.

# The Booming Scottsville of the 1840s

The past—and not so terribly long ago—is not just a different time; it's a different world. Scottsville—without cars, paved roads, electricity, or running water and certainly no wifi, TV, or Chinese carryout—was still busy, the town's residents engaged in everyday routines: going to school, to the shops and to work, listening for the "trahnahn-ahn" of the ten-foot long tin packet boat's horn as another craft came into town, calling for the canal's lock-keeper. This was the world of Scottsville in the 1840s and 50s.

Despite improvements to river traffic along the rival Rivanna, as John Hammond Moore notes in *Albemarle, Jefferson's County, 1727-1976*, "Scottsville continued to prosper." The James River and Kanawha canal opened in 1840 from Richmond to Lynchburg, and the Plank Road—planked at least a part of the way from the Rockfish Gap to Scottsville—brought more and more of the Valley's produce to town for shipment to the capital and markets to the west. Moore writes that "a traveler reported in May 1845 that he saw at least 50 heavy wagons on [the road]," and in 1850, after continued improvements to the turnpike, "70 mountain wagons" were counted one day in Scottsville.

The produce of the fertile Shenandoah Valley—wheat, tobacco, meat, beeswax, and more—was loaded on boats from warehouses around the canal turning basin, now the grassy heart of Canal Basin Square. Flour was inspected, an important activity for the town's economic life, and the prosperity all this trade generated gave Scottsville "twenty-one stores, twenty-four mechanics shops of various kinds, three taverns, a tobacco factory, and four churches." According to Moore, "Canal transportation eastward was conducted by nine freight boats and two packets," and "produce and freight valued at over one million dollars was being shipped annually."

Partaking of this prosperity, and adding to it, was the Tutwiler family. Martin and his wife Mildred owned property on both sides of Main Street, and in 1832, they sold a lot to the Methodist Church for its building. Martin ran Tutwiler's Tanyard and was a partner in a "100-foot long tobacco storage" building, according to Tim Small, co-project manager of Canal Basin Square. Some of Martin's property was in the path of the proposed canal, and he received money for it in compensation. He was also contracted to build several locks west of town and other canal-related structures, according to Tim.

Martin's son Wesley Clark Tutwiler, born in 1823, bought two partial lots on Main Street in 1860, numbers 115 and 90 on the plat, to open a boatyard serving the canal. (Tim researched this through deeds recorded in Fluvanna County, where the lots were then officially located.) This land is immediately south of the street at the termination of the levee. When Wesley owned it, the property went from the edge of the canal to the street. Currently, while the street is still in place, the canal has been replaced by the railroad, and the CSX owns most of the area that was the boatyard.

Wesley married Amanda Maria Moon, and in the federal census of 1860 are listed Thomas P. Tutwiler, their eldest child, and five others, including Lily, who married Luther Pitts. An unrelated man, age

22, was living in the household as well. Two more children were born later. Wesley was astute enough to make "special precautions to ensure his wife…would retain control and profit from his investments, most notably the boatyard," Tim writes. "After her husband died in 1871 at the age of 48 years, she, only months younger, continued to operate the yard until the closing of the canal a decade later."

Tim has found other documents detailing the work of the boatyard, and much of his research appears on the informative plaques at Canal Basin Square. "The new Cora Lee sold for $975; the R. B. Snead, a full-sized deck boat was defaulted…. Another new boat sold for $950…built by Tutwiler in the early 1870s." Toward the end of the canal period, the business would have focused mostly on repair and sale of used boats. The Exchange sold in 1874 for $900, and the full-decked R. E. Lee sold in 1873 for $350. Tim says that "John H. Briggs was superintendent of the yard and acted as agent in the sale of Tutwiler boats." Thomas, Wesley's son, later acted as agent. Other names associated with boatbuilding in Scottsville, most likely at Tutwiler's, are William H. Anderson and Benjamin F. Childress, as well as Daniel Moon, William Bugg, and Luther Pitts. According to a *Scottsville Courier* newspaper ad, Tutwiler employed B. F. Daggett for lettering the boat's name and said his "skill in this beautiful art cannot be excelled. He is entirely original in the conception of whatever work he undertakes."

Much else must be left to conjecture. Even the oil painting shown here, on display in the Scottsville Museum and signed by J. W. Tutwiler, does not give us much information about the working of the business, though it shows the Cora Lee of Scottsville, Worsham and Pitts Packet Lines, passing two brick buildings (one with a sign over the door reading "Office") as it is pulled toward Richmond.

The large freight and packet boats would likely have been built outdoors, and the forms and tools needed might have been kept in that brick building or the frame one that still exists. A photograph from Milton, PA, shows such boats under construction—so big that ten men have ample room to use their adzes along the massive hull—in a dirt-bermed enclosure that could be broken open to float the finished boat into the canal.

In one of his *Courier* ads, Tutwiler mentions having "good pine and oak" for boatbuilding. Atlantic white cedar, formerly widely growing in wetlands along the East Coast, had been preferred in boatbuilding for its durability and light weight; it was clear-cut and became scarce in the early nineteenth century. Local white oak was used for boat hulls, with different woods supplying interior ribs, decking, and other needs.

Barry Long, who recently built two Melonseeds, a nineteenth century Chesapeake Bay gunning boat, talked about what sort of tools Tutwiler's men would have used. The drawknife and adze were necessary to shape the long planks of the hull and carve the stem, where the planks join at the front. Finishing would be done with handplanes. An internet source on boat building in the nineteenth century (www.gaudet. info/LEARNING) says, "the average number of planes owned by the 'old time craftsman' is about fifty. Commonly used planes were the modeling, smoothing, rabbet, jack, long or trying, jointer or floor, and cooper's long jointer."

Barry says that it is important to begin with well-seasoned, dry wood, which, when put in water, will swell to fill the seams. The seams are also caulked with cotton batting and a

*Boathouse view along Main Street, looking east.*

chisel-like tool called a caulking hammer. It is common, he notes, to work from a pattern for the ribs, so they are all alike; otherwise, a form around which the wood is bent could be employed, allowing the wood to take the shape it will. "In the end," Barry notes, "the wood will win and take its own shape."

In general, boat construction techniques in the nineteenth century were the same as other carpentry techniques, and most information and skills were passed on orally and by experience to apprentices. Construction practices probably varied from boatyard to boatyard. Barry suggests it might have been possible to erect a derrick to help in the heavy lifting but says that most work was done by hand. The boats needed large crews, and Scottsville was able to provide all kinds of workers for this phase of the canal economy.

Tim Small points out that other support industries would have been found in Scottsville at the time: horse and mule stables, a brick

*Painting by J. W. Tutwiler of the Tutwiler Boat Yard, 1860-1880, Scottsville Museum*

kiln, an iron forge, and other workers needed, including a toll-taker at the gauging station and tobacco inspectors.

Tim is constructing the packet boat to fill the northernmost boat slip at Canal Basin Square, using photographs of original boats. His objective is to make the craft look like an original, not necessarily to follow nineteenth century building techniques. He plans to call it *The Lizzie* after a boat Tutwiler advertised as having "a name as sweet and dear as the boat is beautiful and good."

The white frame structure on Main Street, once part of the Tutwiler boatyard, is now owned by David Becker, Jr., who bought it from Jane Caldwell's estate. It is across the street from his house, and he uses it for storage. He says he's learned that the railroad used it as their baggage claim area. There is a walled-off office in the southwest corner. Newer shelves on the east walls attest to its use as a grocery store within memory of some Scottsville citizens, and Dave has found a sign on the rough plank floor suggesting it was a place that served breakfast at some point.

The original part of the building has two floors built on a field-stone foundation. There is a flue for a stove but no chimney. There are two additions toward the river, one in block and one metal, and a second roof covers the original structure and the first addition. "The oldest part of the building is in better shape than the add-ons," Dave says, indicating the rotted floor joists. He has a number of deeds that came to him with the property, showing that it was sold by Helen and Charles Harris in 1907 to G. W. Lewis of Fluvanna for $200, that Dr. L. R. Stinson owned and sold it in 1917, and that Leonard Lewis sold it to J. Walter Moon for $500 in 1932.

Dave, who grew up locally, "always playing on the river, the Rivanna or the James," says he now "gets on the river every chance I can, especially in my kayak." Using the James for recreation rather than work has been typical of the twentieth century, but Pat Pitts remembers when, boating as a boy, he would see few others except fishermen out on the river. He had a wooden rowboat made by local mail carrier Pen Thomas, who lived nearby on Drivers Hill. His construction method, Pat recalls, was to pull out a piece of wood, look at it, and then cut it. "A damned good guess is better than a poor measurement any day," he told Pat, who has found that to be true. The boat Thomas made, "for the joy of it," was heavy, with oak gunnels and a marine plywood bottom. Pat's father had found the wood and had Thomas build him a boat, too.

The river continues to flow past Scottsville, bringing us riches, even if it is no longer the basis of our economic prosperity. Our world has changed, but remember what the Water Rat tells Mole in Kenneth Grahame's *Wind in the Willows*: "Believe me, my young friend, there's nothing—absolutely nothing—half so much worth doing as simply messing about in boats."

*Originally published June 2012*

# 31.

# Of Rivers, Wells, and Springs

By Ruth Klippstein
Correspondent

Photo courtesy
of Scottsville Museum

*c. 1912-1915, photographer uncredited; in Robert Goldstone's 1953 thesis "Historical
Geography of Scottsville, Virginia," Masters thesis UVa.*

Water is always important in the siting and success of either
cities and towns or a house standing alone in the woods or
fields. Scottsville needed the James River for commerce and growth,
but while it has been used for drinking water, Scottsville has needed
other sources as well.

"When I was a little child we didn't have electricity," Raymon
Thacker has stated. "Don't think we were poor though. We had run-
ning water: three times a day I ran to the town well." Immediately to
the west behind the Methodist Church (then further east on Main
Street), the town well could be found directly in front of the 1835
Tompkins House on Jackson Street.

The well, Thacker says, had an "arrangement of little cups on a
belt you cranked to bring up water." There was also a rock-surrounded

spring with "the nicest water"—still there, he says—in the woods below Mt. Walla, near Ferry and Jackson Street. Gene Harding describes this spring as "straight up the hill. As kids, we played on the hill, running up and down." It was also "where the winos met." Once, while careening headlong, he stepped on a napping "wino, who let out a 'Woof!'" Gene ran away all the faster, not considering that, if the man couldn't stand, he couldn't chase him.

Gene says that "there used to be lots of springs in town. On Poplar Spring Road, up on Driver's Hill from the laundromat, there was "the big one in town. It was dug out and covered; water ran out in a four- or five-inch pipe." There the boys learned how to close the pipe with an ice cream cup so water would spray out a small hole. Halfway up the other side of the hill on Route 6, in Fluvanna, another spring was used regularly into the 1950s, until the county put a sign on all the springs stating that they were contaminated. "I don't know why," Gene says.

Gene also remembers a prank played by local youngsters on a man who brought his water jugs to fill in a kids' red wagon. One day they slipped a frog into a jug as the man went elsewhere in town, leaving the wagon at the Pitts' grocery store. This caused great consternation and dismay on his return.

Mayor Thacker didn't always have an easy time running to and fro with his family's water. "I would make at least two trips a day," he told a gathering at the library in 1985, "one in the morning and one in the evening.... One evening, I was returning from the spring with two small buckets of water when I stubbed my toe and fell, with water splashing all over me. A distinguished-looking gentleman visiting the Pitts [across Main Street from Thacker's home] seated on the porch began to laugh at my predicament. Oh my, he made me mad! Mad at myself because I was clumsy, mad because I had lost my water, and mad at that old man. My mother consoled me and said that she would go back for more water, but I eventually went back for another bucket, still smarting...." The next day he was told the man was Captain Lamb, a Confederate veteran and friend of Robert E. Lee, who, as curator of the Confederate museum in Richmond, gave the boy a lifetime pass he has continued to use.

Ruth Brooks, growing up in the large Gardner family in Esmont, recalls going to the local spring as a daily chore she and her seven siblings performed. Going with neighboring children meant there could be playing and socializing along the way, but even the littlest one carried a pail, perhaps a small one that had been purchased with molasses in it—maybe holding a half-gallon. "When I was older, I used a gallon size. We had to come through the woods, up the hill and down the hill." And imagine how much cooking and laundry there was to do at home! The family collected rainwater in barrels, too. Washing was heated on the cookstove, so it was always very hot in the kitchen, summer and winter. Schoolwork was done by lamplight, the glasses of which the children cleaned. "Sometimes now, when things are so convenient, I wonder how did we make it," Ruth says. The spring, as far as she knows, is still bubbling out of the ground.

Thomas Cleveland Sadler, who lived near Antioch Church, northeast of town, described early twentieth century home water systems in his "Memories of Bygone Days," available in the Local History Corner of the library. "There were some wells, but everybody had a spring right close to the house. They would build a large box, or sometimes a small house, right below the spring so that the cool water from the spring would flow through it. They would keep their milk and butter and anything else in it that they wanted to keep cool."

Springs, says Virginia Moore in *Virginia is a State of Mind*, have always been honored here. Pocahontas' "real name," she recounts, was Matoaka, "meaning a spring between two hills. By the 19th century, they were in high repute medicinally and romantically. Thomas Jefferson frequented the Warm Spring in Augusta County...." Closer to home—three miles west of Scottsville, on former State Route 622 and just over the Fluvanna line—is Albevanna Springs. "Bottled at the Springs" as their brochure advertised, and sold through a Richmond dealer, the water was touted by satisfied customers as "beneficial for stomach diseases, gout and affections of the kidneys." "The phosphoric acid it contains is good as a nerve tonic and restorative." "Worth its weight in gold." "The Albevanna

Springs are beautifully located," wrote a Dr. Dillard, "in one of the best sections of Albemarle, and I can see no reason why they should not become very popular as a health resort."

In fact, architect D. Wiley Anderson, owner of the house and springs, had just that in mind. As described on the Scottsville Museum website, he "drew up plans for a resort on the property in 1923, to be called Albevanna Springs, Hotel, Sanatarium [sic], Health and Pleasure Resort." The Great Depression intervened, and the plans were never developed. But people continued to come to the springs for water. The nearby Wingfield family even made it a Saturday ritual. A 1910 picture postcard shows the spring with a small house over it. One Albevanna Springs label in Jack Hamner's collection gives the name "Ponce de Leon Water," and he also has some of the five-gallon bottles used by the springs.

In the 1860s, Fannie Patteson recalled a "spring under the chestnut trees"—of course, they are gone, too—"at the foot of the hill straight down in front of the Baptist Church," where a children's school was held in the 1860s and '70s. "Around that spring was once a lovely place to linger."

In 1934, Susan Hill Dunn remembered back to the late nineteenth century, to both the well "by the lane leading up to the Powers' House," behind

*Jack Hamner uncovers the late nineteenth century horse watering trough on north Valley St. Photo by Ruth Klippstein.*

the Methodist Church, where the children would "frolic around a bonfire at Christmas," and Foland's Spring, in the 1880s, "uphill from the school," where children also gathered. Peter Foland, for whom the spring was named, was a merchant and mayor of Scottsville in 1909.

Bill Mason recalls an enclosed spring under the "huge maple trees" on the rubber plant grounds in the late 1940s. Dr. Paul Mc-Farlane, interviewed by Charlie Fry in 1987, recalls going to school on the hill behind Victory Hall around 1910. "And the nearest water supply was down on Main Street, opposite Blair [the dentist's office beside Mink Creek] and the power building [behind the current police station]. And we carried water up in a bucket. And that was the senior boys' job, every day to carry the bucket, and it was rotated among the four or five of us." But the appointed boy invariably would not come to school that day, except for him. "I came every day, so I was the sucker. I bet I carried more water up that hill.... It was our drinking water."

During this time, most likely, a trough dug into a spring off the other side of this same hill was available for horses that came down Valley Street—or Plank Road, as it once was. Jack Hamner was told of this: "It's just word of mouth. I assume it's true. My daddy told me about it when I was a kid. There was still water running in it then." Jack recently dug out about a third of the trough, braving thick roots, heavy soil, and cars passing close by on Route 20, south from C & S Motors and on the east side. He found miscellaneous bricks, a circa 1920s McCormick's vanilla bottle from Baltimore, and the concrete pad in front of the trough, where a horse could stand while drinking. There's an iron pipe on the uphill side, and water was beginning to fill the trough.

Virginia Moore called this time "New Century, New Hope," in *Scottsville on the James*, though "plumbing remained in a rather primitive state. There were few marble tubs; most were movable tin ones filled and emptied by bucket. Water came from dug wells using windlass and chain."

The Scottsville Water, Light, and Ice plant began to offer services in 1916. A bill from 1919 states that water cost "$2.25 per Quarter in advance, for which 6,000 gallons may be used for one toilet and one faucet." If the house had a bathtub as well, the bill would be $4.50 per quarter. The plant was a fixture in town, and the town bell in the tower was rung at noon by Charlie Lenaham, who also wrote out the bills and kept the generator working.

Pat Pitts says, "When I was a kid, there was a water tower behind where the jail was, beside where you go onto the bridge." In corrugated metal, painted silver, it had a concrete base. It pumped water from the river and filtered it in the tower—"but the river wasn't very clean, it was used for dumping." Jack Hamner recalls that his parents would not let him swim in the James, as the sewers emptied directly into it. Ice was made and sold at the plant. Miss Met Powers, on Jackson Street, bought ice on 25 separate days of July 1931, paying $6.81 for it all.

Last month, we looked at the failure of downtown hydrants during the disastrous fires of the mid-1970s. These had been installed in 1966, and previously, firefighters ran Scottsville's two-hose reel carts to a fire or manned a bucket brigade. Virginia Moore calls it the "problem of Scottsville's wretched water system," with many people still "toting drinking water from the old Albevanna Spring." In 1968, Totier Creek was dammed and the reservoir created, and thus Albemarle County Service Authority took on responsibility for Scottsville's water. It is processed chemically and physically at the Scottsville Water Treatment plant, where calcium hypochlorite and fluoride are added. The Service Authority reports yearly on water quality, with detailed information available on their website. Testing for 2010 revealed an "excellent" quality. Citizen concerns helped stop a 2005 plan to pipe water from the James to help Charlottesville's shortage.

Lucinda Wheeler remembers the well that served residents of Paulett Village off Route 20 to the north of town. The water was always "cloudy and dingy" for the 20 years her family lived there, and all houses had to take care of their own wastewater. "I was sick and tired of it, so I was thrilled to move to Scottsville 37 years ago. The pressure is always good, the water so clear, and we have a wonderful system." She remembers Johnny Lan, who "used to keep it in operation and did so much for the town." Lloyd Barns now runs the treatment plant in Scottsville.

We've come a long way from Matoaka, Virginia's spring between two hills, but we will always need—and savor—clear, pure water.

*Originally published April 2012*

# 32.

# Parlor Games and Tricks

The small-town web of Scottsville—connecting the elite and middle class families, buildings, and social events to form a cohesive community—is exemplified by this photograph. Taken by William Burgess around 1912 and archived by the Scottsville Museum, it shows the Powers, Blairs, and Bells on the front steps of The Terrace on Jackson Street.

"They were certainly leading families of Scottsville," says Bob Spencer. "It's a great story, the story of The Terrace." This two-story Victorian house was built in 1897 for Dr. David Pinckney Powers and his wife, Sarah Staples Powers. The Powers' house, from 1840, is next door to the east, and is noted by Susan DeAlba's *Country Roads, Albemarle County*, for its "original beaded weatherboarding."

David Powers first ran "one of Scottsville's smaller, lesser-known hotels," according to Spencer; Virginia Moore describes the Powers House as "the current [1969] site of the supermarket on Main Street," now housing Dr. Joyce and Bruce's Drug Store. D. P. Powers was the first Albemarle County school superintendent, from 1870 until his death 30 years later, and is remembered as "a quiet, firm man of great character," says Virginia Moore. Sarah Staples was part of a long-established Scottsville family that donated the land for the 1831 Episcopal Church at Glendower. She married Powers in 1853 and produced two sons and five daughters, the extended family all living in The Terrace, a "palace," Spencer says.

The boys were William and Philip. The girls were involved in many activities in town and are mentioned by Susan Hill Dunn in *With Love from Mother*, 1934, available in the Local History Corner of the Scottsville Library: "The [Powers] daughters you all know: Miss Annie Bell, Miss Susie Blair, Miss Mett Powers and Miss Lucy Powers. They've been our friends always."

This "first family," as Spencer calls them, was the topic of an early 1890s article in the *Scottsville Courier*, cut out by her mother, one supposes, and saved by Susie Blair in an undated scrapbook now in the Barclay House of the Scottsville Museum. Pasted in with a 1923 article on commencement exercises at the University of Richmond and one on a poetic parody of rationing is "Miss Powers' Potato Walk," the text of which Virginia Moore uses to describe the "easier" conditions in town as Reconstruction ended. "A very novel game introduced in Scottsville, Va," is the second headline.

"September 4: For some weeks Scottsville has been unusually gay. A number of enjoyable entertainments have been given. But the 'event' of the season was a party given at the Powers House by

*The Powers, Blairs, and Bells on the front steps of The Terrace on Jackson Street. "Family Gathering at The Terrace" c. 1912; Photographer: W.E. Burgess. Photo Courtesy of Scottsville Museum.*

Miss Lucy Powers last evening. The tables were beautifully decorated with flowers, fruits and melons, and the rooms and hallways with evergreens and Japanese lanterns.

"The feature of the evening was a 'potato walk,' which was most novel and amusing. To take a large, knotty potato from the floor in a small teaspoon in a given length of time and carry it the entire length of the room may seem easy, but it is not."

There follows a list of the prize winner and losers, as well as a description of the dresses worn by the women: "Miss Lucy Powers, very pretty in a pale blue gown, baby waist, white lace and ribbon; Miss Marietta Powers, a debutante, blue gown and ribbons; Miss Rose Farrar, in blue veiling, white lace; Miss Theodora Blair, cream dress and flowers; Miss Auralia Blair, lovely in blue; Miss Serena Hamner, in white dress, blue trimmings, very graceful; Miss Mary Bull, white mull [similar to muslin] and ribbons, no ornaments, very pretty; Miss Nora Dillard, black lace, graceful and pretty; Miss Jennie Patteson, black lace; Miss Nannie Davis, black net and amber, handsome...; Miss Grimsley, handsome red China silk, bouquet of poppies...; Miss Susie Powers, white muslin, old lace, diamond ornaments, extremely pretty...."

The men attending are mentioned by last name but not otherwise described. Their names are a roll call of Scottsville's up-and-coming, or already arrived: Harris, Blair, Bell, Carter, Moore, Tompkins, Farrar, and Hill. Might they have worn stiff, high collars and three-piece suits, then gaining popularity? Or, in keeping with the women's diamonds and lace, were they more formally attired, with dark tailcoats and white bowties? Did they leave walking sticks and top hats at the door? I like the idea of tailcoats for the Potato Walk. This parlor game, apparently never played before in town, was one of many offered in books such as *Games for Everybody*, which in the early 1900s demonstrated that children's games could be adapted to adults; included were Tableau Vivant and Forfeits. This type of fun was evolving from the harsh days of the Civil War and its aftermath, and from earlier social stereotypes that allowed children to play games indoors, but not adults. These parlor games, offered in a special formal room set aside for entertaining, clearly indicate a society with more leisure time on its hands. The workers were working, of course—the farmers, railroad hands, lumber and coal men, the many domestic servants and laundresses—but the wealthy, when not reading, sketching, or playing music, were playing games.

Blind Man's Bluff; Charades; Pass the Slipper; and Squeak, Piggy, Squeak—these were somewhat boisterous, sometimes creative activities that we still might play today, like Musical Chairs. They do have an aspect, in a more circumspect society, of "decorous titillation," as the website Victoria's Past points out. Squeak, Piggy, Squeak, for example, involved a blindfolded player, whom the "Farmer" turned around until the player became disoriented in the center of a circle of seated players. The Farmer would drop a pillow in the lap of a seated player, sit on it, command, "Squeak, piggy, squeak," and the disoriented player would try to guess by the sound in whose lap the Farmer was sitting. Not quite Spin the Bottle, but close enough! As the *Foxfire Book of Appalachian Toys and Games*, 1993, notes, "Nothing levels people as effectively as a good laugh at themselves and others in the same funny situation." The *Courier* article did not

*Charlie Albert Lenaham "Citizen Charlie" standing among roses at "The Terrace" --Queen Anne Victorian Home, Scottsville. Photo by Samuel A. Spencer. Photo from the Robert K. Spencer collection.*

say if Mr. Frank Hill, awarded the booby prize in the Potato Walk, was laughing.

Following Scottsville history down through the years, we find a number of Lucy Powers' partygoers pairing up and marrying. Miss Lucy herself did not. "The famous Miss Lucy," as Spencer calls her, ran a nursery school (*Scottsville Monthly*, September 2007) with a teaching friend who lived with the family at The Terrace, Miss Kate Stith. Miss Mett—Marietta—her aunt, remained single and worked "at the tiny little library next door to the Methodist Church," Spencer says, and as secretary to Scottsville banker Jacinto Pereira. Annie Powers married A. Gilbert Bell, uniting those families, and Susie Powers—she of the white muslin, old lace, and diamonds— married Scottsville's dentist, Dr. Joseph Blair, whose office was on the second floor of a now-vanished frame building on the south side of Main Street, next to Mink Creek. Blair's ad ran in a 1911 *Scottsville Enterprise*: "Will visit Alberene, Schuyler, and Esmont." He was chairman of the Albemarle County School Board for 37 years and member of the Scottsville Town Council.

Joseph Blair is remembered in John C. Hill's memoir, *Recollection of Scottsville, 1870-1886*, as "the embodiment of everything that a young man should be.... [He] was a clerk in the Harris [grocery] store, and his salary was $30.00 a month [but] he had his heart set on becoming a dentist." To make enough money for medical school tuition, Hill remembers, Blair asked his friend Thomas Staples Martin, "a power in politics long before he became a United States Senator," to help him get a job as a railway clerk, which gave him "a run from Charlottesville to Hinton, West Virginia.... Joe saved money fast on that job...." After graduating from University of Maryland's dental school, Blair took his friend Hill as his "first patient—he filled a tooth for me." Some of Blair's dental tools came to Bob Spencer from Hayden Anderson, who found them in the attic of The Terrace when he bought the house.

Susie Powers Blair's daughter was always known in Scottsville, with great respect, as "Miss Susie." Susie Nicholas Blair, 1896-1980, was remembered by Virginia Moore in a Scottsville Baptist Church history supplied by Spencer, as "growing up in a large family—parents, aunts, uncles, cousins—this 'only child,' unspoiled, must have been, as prophecy of the future, an earnest young person with a quick sense of humor." She taught English, drama, Shakespeare at Hollins College, and was well-loved in Scottsville as a member of the Scottsville Baptist Church, where she directed the Christmas pageant. She was also an original board member of the Scottsville Museum and helped stage the ambitious cast-of-100 Bicentennial Pageant with Spencer and Randolph Phillips.

"Wise," as Virginia Moore describes her, "with the wisdom which comes not from books…but from life itself." She also remembered for Moore many of the games that were played in her childhood, including Drop the Handkerchief, outdoors at Cliffside. Miss Susie, last of the family to live in The Terrace, stipulated that it was to remain the home of Charlie Lenaham. He and his mother had been servants there and "took wonderful care" of the family, Spencer says.

The Scottsville Museum website describes The Terrace as a "storehouse of artifacts and memories" of the town and these intertwined families. As author Michael Ondaatje writes, "The past is always carried into the present by small things"—dental equipment, a corsage of poppies, and a Potato Walk.

*Originally published March 2012*

# 33

# The History of Main Street's Empty Place

*Paulett's Hardware Store in the 1960s. Photo courtesy of Ace Hardware.*

There was lots of activity on Main Street in December as the Pleasant View Developers from Staunton started work to help prevent damage to the Scottsville Methodist Church building and parking lot. The steep bank behind the building had been severely eroded by a heavy downpour about three years ago, says church trustee Larry Dorrier. When considering how to fix the problem, members saw that the northeast corner of the church was their biggest concern, where an existing wall was leaning toward the building in a threatening manner.

The church decided, Dorrier says, to take down the 10-year-old, not well-used picnic shelter at the top of the bank, close to Jackson Street; re-grade the hill, making a gentler slope; and build a new retaining wall. A landscape architect drew up plans, the town approved, and the earthmovers started work.

John Izzellow, owner, ran the excavator, and Tim Bishop laid the block. "We found some blackened dirt," Tim said, possibly from wood or soil charred by fire, and Jack Hamner found three horse-shoes in the pushed-up fill. How had this large empty place come to be on our Main Street?

The 143-year-old Scottsville Methodist Church building and the entire block on the north side of East Main Street, from the muse-um to Valley, never had a chance for the historic preservation guidelines Scottsville has used since 1996 to develop its historic district. In two spectacular night-time fires, February 26th and 28th, 1976—thought to be arson but never prosecuted—first the 1909 Traveler's Rest Hotel and Turner's Exxon Station were destroyed, and then the church and Paulett and Son, building materials, as well as five structures filling most of the rest of the block all burned

*Tim Bishop laid the block for a wall to help keep the Scottsville Methodist Church and the parking lot from further damage.*
*Photo by Ruth Klippstein.*

to the ground. As one Scottsville firefighter was reported saying in the February 28th *Daily Progress*, "This is just as bad as when the Yankees went through here."

The fire's destruction was enhanced by the poor functioning of the water system. Although 17 trucks converged on Scottsville to help with the blaze that started in the shuttered hotel, only three of Scottsville's 22 hydrants were operating, according to Chief Grover Mowbry in the *Progress*. "The Mayor [A. Raymon Thacker] angrily blamed the water supply problem on the Albemarle County Board of Supervisors and the Albemarle County Service Authority, which owns the system.... 'They promised me they were going to fix it. I'm mad—really mad!'"

The *Progress* reported that there had been plans to raze the hotel on the corner for a "downtown mall." Paulette's was the town's largest business. It was estimated that millions of dollars' worth of damage was done, and as February turned to March, people were reported to be anxious about another outbreak of arson, some of them, according to a *Washington Star* article, "spending nights in back rooms armed with shotguns."

*Pleasant View Developers of Staunton dump trucks line the Main Street area. Photo by Ruth Klippstein.*

Main Street had seen 18th and 19th century development, based on the canal warehouse and turning basin, and later the railroad depot, with hotels, taverns, boarding houses and businesses. Long before the Traveler's Rest, the corner was occupied by livery stables. Mayor Thacker remembers next the home of a "colored man who dug graves all around the area. Next to that was a blacksmith shop; Billy Londeree ran it. Next house down was a shoe shop, and then Mr. Philip Palm's funeral shop—he made coffins and wagons." According to the Scottsville Museum website, Palm was a Swedish immigrant, who served as the town's undertaker around 1910. Raymon Thacker and his brother Homer had their own funeral home office contiguous to Paulett's, though they moved to Valley Street long before the fire.

*Pleaant View Developers of Staunton at work.*
*Photo by Ruth Klippstein.*

Even earlier, the high ground next to the church had a memorable use: John C. Hill, in his manuscript memoir, available in Scottsville Library's Local History Corner, says he was born the night, in September 1870, when water flooded his family's house across Main Street. Dr. Reuben Lindsay took his mother out an upper floor window and carried her in a rowboat over "about 10 or 12 feet of water to dry land" across Main Street. He tied up "to the old well to the left and at the rear of the Methodist Church" and delivered baby John.

The land east of the church, where Paulett's had been, was donated to it by Mr. and Mrs. George Omohundro, Jr. "for use as a parking area," as their printed history says. Dorrier notes that several area contractors at a pre-bid meeting last October did not bid on the job, possibly due to the precariousness of the old wall left by the fire.

The last small piece of retaining wall, the rear of the former Paulette's building, was removed from the edge of the parking lot recently, and a new fence was added to the hill. In season, grass and wildflowers will be seeded. Scottsville persists—and grows—as it has in the past.

*Originally published February 2012*

## 34.

# Memories of the Scottsville Mill

Photo by Ruth Klippstein

The Scottsville Flour Mill, burned to the ground in a spectacular 1977 fire, is passing out of our common memory as an important business where wheat flour and cornmeal were ground. Responses to a request for information now tend to elicit one of three responses (other than "I can't remember"): "It was a huge building," "It sold a nice range of feed and seed products," and "It was a great hang-out for men."

But first, of course, it was a mill. A. Raymon Thacker, whose father was the miller from 1911 to 1917, describes it as "somewhat sophisticated," a new steam-driven mill run with a coal-fired engine. "It was a beautiful, big, nice mill."

Located on East Main at Ferry Street, the lot occupies the area between Route 6 and the railroad. From the front, the frame structure rose two stories over the porch-covered main floor, plus the windowed horizontal dormer running the length of the gabled roof's ridge. From the rear, the building clearly had, in an undated photo in the museum's collection, a basement in the stone foundation, plus three stories topped by the windowed dormer. The mill therefore had a total of five levels, though these were not necessarily visible from the street. The aerial photograph taken when the James River bridge was still located nearby shows the mill as the major feature on Scottsville's waterfront, more massive than the canal warehouse.

Tom Woodson, who worked at the mill when it was producing animal feed, describes the interior as very impressive, with 12" by 12" wooden beams running the length of the ceilings and "a huge open space throughout." He says that augers powered the grain from a trough on the porch facing Main Street up to storage bins. "When that machine was going, you could feel it through the whole building."

The original flour mill was built in 1908 by a consortium of Scottsville merchants, including Luther Pitts, Captain John Pitts, a Mr. Bugg, and one or two others, according to Raymon Thacker. He describes the "huge steam engine and belts going up and down all over the building, taking wheat from where it was ground to where it was bagged."

The owners had no one knowledgeable to operate the mill and tracked down Arthur Thacker "running one just like it in Stuart's Draft. Mr. Pitts went and asked him," Raymon Thacker says, "and offered a considerably bigger salary. He thought about it and eventually said he'd come to Scottsville if he could bring Mr. Powell, his assistant." So the families moved together to Scottsville in the spring of 1911.

"It is still interesting to me how my father could pick the right stones to grind corn and wheat correctly," Thacker says. "It was intricate work; he had to dress the stones frequently with a small hammer." Most fascinating to the young Thacker was the nearby cooperage, to the south of the mill, where barrels for the flour, as well as other goods, were constructed. George Logan was the cooper—"Uncle George" to the boy—and would set him up where he could watch as the staves were bound with iron bands. Logan used small hammers in this work and could "make music" with them to entertain the child.

Luther Moore lived next door to the Mill and was the fireman who ran the steam engine. Coal was stored in a tower further east on the river, at the railroad track. People brought "wagonload after wagonload of wheat for years," Thacker says. During the bitter winter of 1917, with snow up to his waist and the James frozen hard, Arthur Thacker wrapped sacks around his legs to walk to work. That year, the ever-present dust compromised his health, and he left to work at C. R. Dorrier's hardware store.

Richard "Lud" Nicholas describes the mill as "a big operation." He remembers "riding there with my father with wheat to be ground, around 1940. The loading, travelling from the farm in Buckingham County, and unloading at the mill would take most of the day."

The mill, according to Bob Spencer, was a stock-holding company and in its heyday was managed by David Pitts and J. S. Dorrier. "The Pittses and Dorriers ran the show in Scottsville for many years," says Bob—a Pitts on his mother's side. In June 1911, they had an ad in the *Scottsville Enterprise*: "We will give one Barrel of Straight Family Flour and sixty pounds of Offal for 5 1-2 Bushels of Dry Wheat." Their operation is further elaborated, in a 1914 letter preserved by Jack Hamner, to a patron in Glenmore: "We are shipping [you] 1 barrel flour which is to be taken out of your wheat when you bring it in.... We think on account of our improved machinery we can put out a better grade of flour than any other mill in this section."

The mill continued to give credit. A 1932 letter to a Howardsville customer reminds him of an overdue bill for one barrel of flour, "loaned almost twelve months ago." The Scottsville Flour Mill kept accounts with many people in town, including, according to Jack Hamner's collection, W. E. Burgess, Mrs. Sclater, L. H. Walton, and the Farmers' Exchange. The business' typed inventory from May 1st, 1917 includes $2,800 in accounts received, $6,617 cash in hand and in bank, $1,073 stock in hand, and $1,700 tied up in "Ware room and Fixtures." The brands of flour they were then producing, listed on the letterhead, were Pine Knot (fancy), Standard (patent), and Golden Road (family). In 1932, E. L. Johnson wrote to another Howardsville customer in regard to his outstanding bill for $3.85 and one barrel of flour: "We have had nothing but promises…[and] will have to take legal action."

Luther Pitts and John H. Worsham ran the Scottsville Flour Mill in the early 1880s, and by 1937 it was owned by Pitts and E. L. Johnson, according to Bob Spencer. They added a general store sometime after this, as the need for milling decreased. Farmers were diversifying crops, and national brands of flour were accessible in stores.

In the 1950s, L. L. Armistead operated the mill, advertising in the Scottsville High School yearbook as a wholesale grocer offering Scottsville Flour Mill's products. "A nice old gentleman," according to Bob Spencer. Later, T. Tyler Robertson owned the mill, continuing both functions, and was assisted for years by Cecil Harmon, whom Tom Woodson calls "a big man at the mill, a character everybody loved."

Tom Woodson worked at the mill as a young teen after school and on Saturdays starting in 1972. No flour was being ground, but Cecil taught him how to make scratch feed by pouring out wheat and corn on the floor, mixing it with a grain scoop, and bagging it in 10- and 25-pound bags tied with a miller's knot, akin to a clove hitch. He eventually became accurate enough to estimate his weights exactly, filling the 10-pound bag to 11 pounds, accounting for the weight of the bag, and the 25 to 26 pounds. Tom also peppered hams, which were sold "sometimes three or four at a time, to people who came from New York." "They were famous for the hams there," says Lucinda Wheeler. One of Tom's additional duties was to shoot rats in the mill.

Tom would work Saturdays from 8am to 6pm, receiving a $10 paycheck to cover all his school clothes and expenses. "The mill was one of my true loves," he says. He was living two doors away the night of February 28th, 1977, when, at 1:30, a fire started in the mill. The corn bins had just been filled, and Tom says "you could see the corn melting." The staff also swept the floors with oil to keep down dust, a possible contributing factor, Tom says.

This was one year after arson fires destroyed other major structures on Main Street. One fireman, of the 12 units responding to the call, told Tom that "if they'd had water right at the beginning, to wet the floor, they might have had a chance." But the hydrants were dry, though the Albemarle County Service Authority had promised upgrades after the 1976 fires, and trucks driven to the river to pump water got mired in mud. The fire was so hot that plastic trash bags on Tom's back porch started to melt. "There was a cat in the building with three or four kittens, and there's no way they could have gotten out," he still remembers.

Ted Childress was there as a fireman that night and says, "It was a very bad, a very hot fire. Once she started, there wasn't any thinking about putting it out." He remembers the mill's good products, delivered within a wide area to mom and pop groceries, and its function as a farmers' hang-out with poker games. "Real nice games, just local people; it was kind of a fun place to go." "The men, not the women," states Lucinda Wheeler.

The mill was owned by Keith Denby in the 1970s. Andy Wilson, new to the area and trying to grow a big garden, remembers that "it seemed very natural for men to be sitting around there. It was a slice of Southern life I'd never seen before and hasn't been in town quite the same way since. But [to a newcomer and novice farmer] those men were intimidating, whether they meant to be or not."

The fire, "the tragedy," as Tom Woodson terms it, was thought to be arson, and a state investigator worked on the issue. Nothing further came of it. James River Reeling and Rafting is on the site now.

*Originally published December 2011*

# 35.

# Scottsville's Old Magic

*Magician Bobby Spencer poses before a Saturday morning show in the "Little theater" in the basement of his Scottsville home, c. 1949. Photo courtesy Bob Spencer.*

Let's dream up some small-town Saturday mornings in the late 1940s and early '50s. The war is over, restrictions and rationing eased, and though nothing will be the same again, children run and play on tree-lined streets with a new prosperity and optimism in the air. Picture Scottsville—visualize Harrison Street.

Those children have been dropped off by their parents: "A regular parade of cars came across Harrison Street," Bob Spencer now recounts. "The parents were delighted" to be leaving their charges at his door from ten to noon, paying a small fee, "a few cents or a nickel or dime," remembers Donald Combs, for home movies, music, and magic. "It was quite a big thing, I thought," says Bob.

"I can remember going to the shows," recounts Baxter Pitts. "We lived in the downstairs apartment, where the Sesame Seed store was, so I just walked up the hill behind it to attend. I was only six or seven, but I remember him doing tricks." "I used to be a faithful attendee," says Bill Mason. "Bobby had a stage, about a dozen chairs; it was a big deal and always pretty authentic."

## Boy Wizard

"Bobby Spencer, Boy Wizard and Company" created a little theater in his basement, and Spencer's life in magic began. "Bobby always seemed to have a flair for entertainment," says Combs, one of his assistants. On October 22nd, Bob will celebrate his 65th year in magic with a special presentation at Victory Hall Theater.

It started with an assembly show at Scottsville High School when Spencer was in third grade in 1944. There he saw The Shrimplins, a husband and wife team of magicians, and was galvanized. This only child of Kirk and Louise Pitts Spencer, who wanted to be a teacher and preacher—who practiced preaching to captive friends and adults—determined he, too, would make magic.

Bob had also identified the deep strain of theatrical interest in his make-up by this time. "Whenever a play presented by a high school drama group required 'a little brat' in the cast, I was the chosen one," he has written. He had, as well, begun to haunt Victory Theatre in Scottsville, home of Chautauqua acts, popular singers, and regular movie showings. Eventually, he became a ticket-taker and usher, cementing a lifelong commitment to the building. Combs, too, was a ticket-taker—and the wages, he notes, were free admission to all the movies.

A "Blackstone, Master Magician" comic Bob bought, as well as a Gilbert Mysto Magic Set from Christmas 1945, sent Bob on his way. He practiced—he'll tell all young aspirants that endless practice is the only way to magic—and would sometimes, A. Raymon Thacker says, stop people on the sidewalks of town, "get them to stand real still," to unfold a new trick he'd learned for the faculty at Fork Union Military Academy, where he taught English and organized social and entertainment events on campus. He stayed at FUMA for 34 years, performing many jobs. "My true life's work, combining the ministry, teaching, journalism, and entertainment," he writes.

After retiring in 1992, he was appointed to a vacant seat on Scottsville's Town Council and later became mayor. But what a different town it was from that of his young years. Not only had popular culture and technology changed vastly all across the country, but Scottsville, no longer an important shopping center for area residents, was diminishing. "Anything you wanted you could get" in the

*He practiced—he'll tell all young aspirants that endless practice is the only way to magic—and would sometimes, A. Raymon Thacker says, stop people on the sidewalks of town, "get them to stand real still," to unfold a new trick he'd learned.*

*Teenaged Bobby Spencer giving magic show at Scottsville High School. Undated.*
*Courtesy Bob Spencer.*

238

1940s, Baxter Pitts notes. "There was activity everywhere," says Don Combs: "Western Auto, Bruce-Dorrier Motor Company, Scottsville Hotel, Omohundro Hardware, Moon Service Station, the C. R. Dorrier store, The Hub, James River Market, Beal Furniture, Lee's and Ballowe's restaurants, the funeral home, and pool hall." Combs tells of being a soda jerk at Jones Drug Store: "It was not an authentic drug store because Mr. Jones was not a registered pharmacist. He sold over-the-counter drugs, sundries, and operated a soda fountain. We sold ice cream, cold drinks, floats, sundaes, milkshakes, and sandwiches. He allowed me to make all of the items except one; if anyone ordered a country ham sandwich, Jones would make it. He wanted to make sure the ham was sliced at just the correct thickness. After all, it was a delicacy and expensive."

James "Nip" Chisholm, who reminds us he was "very young in the '40s," recalls the 30-cent lunch in town: two hot dogs and a Pepsi. Lucky Strike cigarettes were 17 cents a pack and many of the older boys smoked behind the bleachers on the baseball field, near the current levee. Nip lived 12 miles away, in the Woodridge area,

*Bobby Spencer performing at St. Anne's County Fair, 1952. Kids helping with trick are (L-R): Delores Simpson, Lindsay "Buzz" Dorrier, Carol Rudolph. Spencer was a regular feature at the fair for several years. Photo by Russell Moon.*

and recalls walking to town to go to the dentist. This is a true story.

Chub Walsh remembers an even less expensive lunch: hot dog, Coke, and an ice cream cone, scooped up right by the door, at Lee's, for 15 cents. Lee always told the school kids as they left, "God bless you." Many students came in from the surrounding countryside, Walsh says; he had cousins at Green Mountain who walked three miles to catch the schoolbus. Some would do their family grocery shopping during lunch hour or take produce grown in home gardens to sell to a grocery store. "Not everybody had a car." Walsh quit high school one day in 1948 and the next was in the Navy.

Gene Harding credits the high school with making the community, giving it a sense of cohesion, and the loss of it, in 1967, with "the end of the town" and all the thriving locally-owned businesses. Saturday evenings, after workers had been paid, "I can remember it was like walking down Broadway. You'd have to step off the sidewalk into the road to get around, that's how thick it was with people. You'd wait in line at night" to get into Bruce's for a fountain soda.

Gene, too, remembers young people smoking. "But not on school grounds. Billy Pitts, at six years old, would stop at the fence around the school [where the library is now] and knock out his pipe on the gatepost, refilling it for the trip home." True story?

*Bobby Spencer performs magic at the Scottsville Library's Summer Program, 1978 (in the now-burned down Library on Bird St.)*
*Photo courtesy Bobby Spencer.*

## The Old Days

Bill Mason further describes the era by saying there would be no one left on the streets if there was a home baseball game on Sunday and that on the grounds near the diamond was still a blacksmith shop, where people using horses and buggies came for service. He remembers rollerskating up and down the sidewalks at night, taking a break and sitting on the recently reopened corner entrance of Dorrier's general store. As an older teen, Bill played golf on the four-hole course established at the rubber plant, along with a public tennis court, and touch football games on the grass there. He, Dave Catlett, and Don Combs, after their Saturday morning sports, would go to Roy Hamner's shop in the now-empty area next to the old post office, where Roy would be doing mechanical repairs. The boys, perching on John Deere tractors sold by the Meltons and eating nickel peanuts and drinking Coke from the machines, would listen every week with him to the "top-notch UVA football" games on the radio.

Bill remembers even earlier games at the other end of town, East Main Street, where the C&O railroad maintained what was

*Musician/Singer/Actor Robbie Limon, left, as Buddy Holly in "Singers and Songwriters" show with friend Bobby Spencer as emcee. Photo by Eleanor Kidd.*

called "The Park" between the depot and the tracks roughly in the area where James River Reeling and Rafting is now. The park was established at least by 1918, when his mother came to town, and was very popular. "Anybody who lived on the east end of town played there—a dozen or 15 people at a time for baseball, touch football, and mostly hide-and-seek, kick-the-can. My parents must have had nerves of steel," Mason now recounts, to let him play so close to the tracks and hide under the railroad cars, but the area was kept very nicely with hedges well trimmed. "We had more fun there," Mason remembers, fondly recalling the "East End Gang," including Sarah Porter's grandson Abraham Coles, Arthur and Sonny Thacker, Maynard Stinson, Ralph McGuire, and the Bryant brothers.

Larry Stallings worked at Bruce's Drug Store one summer in the '40s, doing "general police work, managing," he says. "Town was busy, there was the movie, always something going on." Bruce's closed at 9pm, after people had had a chance to walk around and get a soda. The baseball games "were a big thing," too. Larry recalls that at the first one he attended Skinny Spradlin hit a ball across Main Street to the Harris house (across from the former post office). "That was a

*Kirkwood the Magician, left, practices with student and protege Ian Thurston Browning for "Artful Deception," Kirkwood's 65th Anniversary Magic Show.*

home run!" Larry returned to Scottsville High School after serving in the Navy, 1945-47. He says there were "several vets, and we were kind of lionized. Veterans had a little degree of prestige then."

By the mid-1950s, the Scottsville phonebook still needed to describe how to make a call without, since 1952, Central to help. "Hold the receiver to your ear" was one tip. Tom Allison was teaching agriculture at the high school, where there were only three upper grades. A photo of a girl in flannel-cuffed blue jeans inspired the comment "Is it a boy?!" in the yearbook. The students attended a Rally Day with other country high schools at UVA, competing in track and field, volleyball, dodgeball, and other events for a trophy.

Somewhere out on the road, Jack Kerouac would write in 1957, "Where we going, man? I don't know, but we gotta go." Help Kirkwood celebrate this long trip with his 65th anniversary in magic, Saturday, October 22nd, at Victory Hall Theatre, with two performances, including a host of guest magicians.

*Originally published October 2011*

# 36.

## Life, In Black and White

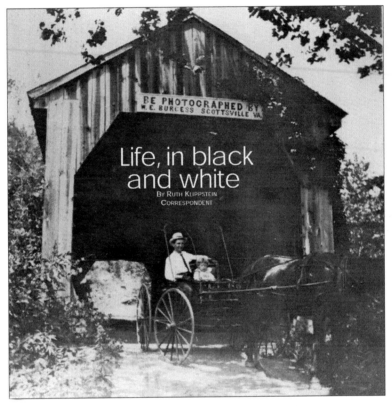

*William Burgess at the Temperance Bridge on the Hardware River.*

"We cannot offer you 'SPECIALS' in work," ran a June 29th, 1911 ad in the *Scottsville Enterprise* newspaper. But photographer William Burgess of Idylwood Studio promised "Our work is 'Special' all the time."

As photography was still beginning to make its broad—and continuing—effect on our world, one practitioner made it on a daily basis to Scottsville. William Edward Burgess, often know as Willie, and more recently called a "poet-historian with the camera," was born in 1871 at Locust Grove, his family's home on the Hardware River about six miles from Scottsville toward Fork Union. His father was Pleasant Madison Burgess, his mother Sarah (Sally) Clarke. There were eight children in all, two of the girls the first and second wives of Captain John Pitts of Scottsville.

**IDYLWOOD STUDIO**
W. E. BURGESS, Proprietor          SCOTTSVILLE, VIRGINIA
**High Grade Portraiture**
Sittings By Appointment

*Advertising from a Burgess calendar advertising his business; children include, center, Irene Dorrier Schneider's father Edward.*

This information and these Burgess family photographs come from Irene Dorrier Schneider, whose father, Scottsvillian Edward Dorrier "always referred to Burgess as 'Uncle Willie.' "Burgess was," Irene thinks, "somewhat eccentric, certainly nice-looking, and very focused on his work."

Irene spread her trove of photographs on a table and referred often to family genealogy she's amassed. "The Pitts, Dorriers, and Burgesses were all interrelated in different ways," she says. Someone once observed, "You have a tangled family!" Irene describes the Burgesses as "farmers, but fairly well-to-do." The children "travelled daily by horse and buggy to a one-room schoolhouse at Central

Plains," according to L. H. Halliburton in a December 1974 article he wrote with Bob Spencer for the Fork Union Military Academy *Saber*. Willie, she gathers, "was spoiled." Irene says that one daughter, deaf since childhood, was later sent to art school in Pennsylvania. This was Irene's grandmother Laura Adelaide, who continued to paint in watercolors, later oils, all her life, including a picture Irene displays of Willie's house and studio, Idylwood—on Driver's Hill, between the current Albevanna Spring Road and Route 6, now burned.

Three of the Burgess siblings, Irene says, were artistic, but she does not know any family history suggesting why or how Willie picked up photography, though it is assumed he was self-taught and, as a teenager, probably learned from books. His work, however, was not the first in town, as Fannie Patteson, in her

*Willie Burgess with sons Lawrence and Harold, probably at Locust Grove.*

1934 manuscript, *Childhood Days in Scottsville, Virginia, 1860-1870*, says: "About 1869 came the Floating Gallery and was anchored near the bottom of our garden in a wide part of the canal called the basin. That was the first we knew of photography, and everyone far and near hastened for a sitting.... Before that time, Mr. Ellis was our dependence for 'likenesses,' which was easier to say than 'daguerreotype.'"

Willie, his brother Lawrence wrote in a letter, 1987, now in

Irene's possession, graduated from Massey Business College in Richmond, "with a degree in accounting, and was employed on graduation by the C&O railway in their Washington, DC office. During the westward expansion of the railroad…to Chicago he was stationed at various construction locations to monitor the activities of construction contractors. During this time, he was actively pursuing his avocation of amateur photography. On completion of the railroad expansion, about 1905, he returned to Scottsville and established a professional photography business, with part-time accounting employment with the Pitts and Morris Construction Company, contractors for the last railroad job on the line from Bremo Bluff to Palmyra to Gordonsville."

Burgess collected a variety of photography equipment, some of it "state of the art." The story is often written of the "special box" he built to "place in the swift waters at the edge of the Hardware River near his home" to wash chemicals from his prints. Halliburton credits Irene's father, Edward Dorrier, with describing this.

Apparently, Willie's son, William, would help with this work. The Scottsville Museum's webpage on Burgess notes that his prints retain their archival quality "more than 100 years later." Jack Hamner thinks that Burgess' Scottsville photos "were extremely instrumental in putting Scottsville on the map, promoting the area. People got to know about us at a time there weren't a lot of other means to circulate information."

"He's very collectible," says Bob Spencer, who counts this "pioneer of

*William Edward Burgess and wife Gentry*

247

*Interior of Burgess' studio at Idylwood*

photography" as kin. "There's a great interest still in his postcards." Burgess would show up at all events—the earliest photograph in the museum's Burgess collection is of Race Day, 1890, at Scottsville's James River Valley Fair. In 1911, he recorded the Gault camping party setting off, boys in knickers, women in broad-brimmed hats and middy blouses, for a week of tent living and outdoor activities near Schuyler. A circa 1898 print in Council Chambers at the Municipal Building shows a lamplighter on Valley Street, looking north along the dirt-packed road.

Bob Spencer says Willie would also come to family parties with his tripod and big box camera, flash powder ready to be ignited, and ask everyone to pose, sitting still for the long time required for each exposure. Burgess was, in fact, sometimes considered "a pest." John Randolph Phillips, in *Of Town and the River*, 1976, says, "In his sentimental, delightful, and sometimes exasperating way, Mr. Willie Burgess was one of Scottsville's characters, with a capital C."

Besides the 485,000 postcard views and 20,000 pictures he left at his death by heart attack on a photoshoot in Altavista, 1935, Burgess also left a published version of "at least two anthologies of his poetry, perhaps more."

As his brother Lawrence writes, "he was a vivid and sensitive personality." He became the operator of Victory Hall when it opened in 1920, owning the franchise to show movies there— silent films with live musical accompaniment and early talkies—and other cultural events. The housekeeper Burgess hired after his wife's death was Bertha Mayo, who later operated the player piano for Burgess' silent movies at Victory Hall.

*Feeding the little turkeys at Locust Grove*

Mayor A. Raymon Thacker, a family friend, became "a reluctant executor" of Burgess' estate at the request of Burgess' sister, Helen Pitts, selling the pictures widely to raise money for the family. Currently, a grandson lives in Lake Monticello and a great-grandson in Charlottesville.

Burgess' photographs offer us a vista into history: how Scottsville saw itself, what it held important, and details we can still reference in maintaining the integrity of the town's architecture. Hairstyles and clothing have changed, the covered bridges are gone, but we can still see, thanks to Burgess, attitudes and places from the past, images that are always with us.

*Originally published July 2011*

## 37.

# Almost Forty Years Later, It's Still "Skippy's"

*Floodwaters of hurricane Juan rose fast into Skippy's. Photo by David Schumaker, 1985, courtesy of Scottsville Library.*

The most well-remembered store in the Dorrier building at the corner of Valley and Main Street—after the closing of C. R. Dorrier and Company General Merchandise in 1958, as Ted Childress remembers it—was Skippy's Market. "Les Brown did a real good job there," Childress adds. "Oh, it's just Dorrier's and Skippy's," says Lucinda Wheeler succinctly.

The grand opening was August 7th, 1972. Les Brown had bought the store, according to a *Rural Virginian* article of that week, "two days before the [Hurricane Agnes] flood. He was able to save about half the merchandise and some equipment. Now the store has been completely stocked....[with] nationally known brands."

Of course, the floods weren't done with Scottsville or with Skippy's. Agnes had put 18 feet of water in town. Preparing for what was to be a much milder flood in October of 1972, Susie N. Blair wrote in the *Charlottesville Observer* that "people were taking no chances.... Housewives bought one more loaf of bread, praying the water would not reach Skippy's Market, the only grocery store in town since Hurricane Agnes." Mrs. Brown and daughter Connie cashiered at the store, and Frank Norris of Charlottesville managed the meat section. There were six employees in all in 1972. The store was open six days a week and sold gas from the pumps to the south of the building, where a farm supplies shed once stood. The business flourished as other grocery stores opened in Scottsville: the *IGA* in the shopping center in 1975, as well as Swiss Way with gourmet offerings and prepared foods.

B. G. Stinchfield recalls her father-in-law, an orthopedic surgeon in New York City, would come to Scottsville as often as he could. "As soon as he got in the door, he'd say, 'We have to go to Skippy's!' I think it reminded him of his childhood grocery stores." The homeschooled children of nearby Springtree Community, when taken to the library for an afternoon, would be given a dime to spend gleefully on candy. Any resident could get an ice cream cone for free on their birthday, Jason Woodson recalls.

The business was often called Skippy's by townspeople even after it closed more than ten years later. Lee Loving ran it for a short while, according to Mayor Raymon Thacker, and others recall seeing Joe Jordan and his wife Ramona there, then John and Hazel Meyers, Lucinda Wheeler remembers. The Meyer family bought it in 1981.

In November 1985, the waters of the Election Day flood from Hurricane Juan rose fast, breaking the display windows. The Skippy's sign on the corner was dangling mere feet from the roiling brown water. Skippy's had not been emptied before the flood, as some other businesses were, reported the *Daily Progress*. Canned goods on the lower shelves were dislodged; cleanup workers stood almost to their knees in ruined merchandise. It was "a mess," said the *Progress*. That paper also reported that dozens of once-frozen turkeys were found, floated down the road and into the Methodist church, tucked into the furnace room.

The November 8th, 1985 *Daily Progress* article on the flood began, "The caribou, deer and ram heads high on the walls at Skippy's Market in Scottsville were the only items John and Hazel Meyers could salvage from their corner grocery store.... Below the stuffed hunting prizes, their entire food stock was gritty with siltation left behind from the floodwaters....

"The James River...broke five large store windows at Skippy's, ripped out steel shelving and swept away a soda machine that hasn't been found since. 'I never felt so bad in my life,' Mrs. Meyers said. 'I just thank the Lord the building isn't washed away.'" Businesses in Scottsville closed for almost two months, the *Rural Virginian* reported. They ran a picture of Les Brown, identified as manager, restocking Skippy's on January 29th, 1986.

It must be after this that the windows along West Main were covered, the corner entrance closed, and "jagged rocks were cemented in place so that people couldn't sit there," as Bob Spencer describes. Robert Pollard tells it this way: the men who sat at the edge of the column and around the door—George, Luther, Cecil, and others—were panhandling, getting money from people going in to shop. "It was like your town shopping tax," he says, giving us what he calls "the story behind the story." In later photographs, the doors are shown blocked inside by stacked groceries, and, in about 1996, covered with a continuous bank of cafe curtains.

The next inundation was the Good Friday flood of April 1987, when water rose just above the intersection of Main and Valley Streets. Les Brown, quoted in the *Rural Virginian* that week, said he does not panic anymore when he hears flood warnings...."I've gotten used to it. The best thing to do is stay as calm as possible." Brown removed the perishable merchandise and estimated that, while the store had sustained $100,000 worth of damages in the '85 flood, this one would cost roughly $15,000 in lost sales if they could reopen soon.

Perhaps Les Brown's attitude was perennially sunny: several people have reported that "he whistled all the time." "When it was Skippy's," sums up Linda LaFontaine, "it was always business." Sue Woodson recalls that Mr. Bailey would pump the gas. A very pleasant man, he was quick to come out and check your oil and wash the windows. "It was a well-stocked store."

Robert Pollard managed Skippy's for about six months, he recalls, after working for K-Mart around 1973. His mother had also worked for Les Brown and the Meyers. He recalls helping her move merchandise upstairs before one of the floods. The building, as he tells it, didn't look like it was from the 1950s as it does now. Coming in the rear door, patrons would see a large enclosed freight elevator that was operated by a rope pulley. Next came a wide set of free-standing steps, eight to ten feet across, in the middle of the floor. Pollard remembers Van Johnson playing Santa Claus, coming down

*New owners of the Dorrier building (Skippy's) are Jeff and Michelle Sprouse. Their intentions are to open the original entrance shown in the photo above and they'll be meeting with the Architectural Review Board for approval. Photo courtesy Steven G. Meeks; C.R. Dorrier building with original entrance intact, no date–early 1970s.*

*Final decisions as to the new businesses which will occupy the building have not been announced.*

the steps and telling the child he'd take him back to the North Pole when he went. "And he never did!"

Pollard assumes the interior was remodeled after the 1969 flood, the wide steps taken out, and other stairs, now gone, to the second floor added to the east side of the brick wall dividing the halves of the floor. The original pressed tin ceiling is still in place...."Very rare," Pollard notes.

Remembering back even further, Robert Pollard describes not only the splitting of the businesses within the original C. R. Dorrier and Co. building but the several outbuildings to the south of it in what is now the parking lot towards the Farmers' Market. There was Reeve Nicholas' and Cecil Harmon's long, low shed for feed, hay and other farm supplies, as well as two smaller produce places. "I bought my first gun in that shed, a bolt-action .22 caliber Springfield. It was around 1963. I was 12 years old and had five dollars saved up. They wanted $20 for it, so I gave $5 down and said I'd pay the rest when I could get it. This was without my parents' permission, too."

Sherry and Bob Slavit bought the Dorrier building, and Sherry established the Riverbend Grocery and Delicatessen in 1994. She had successfully run a similar business on Barracks Road in Charlottesville. Her advertising listed roast beef or eleven other sandwiches for $2.99 and a "large selection of imported beer and wine."

From 2002 to 2006, there were several versions of the James River Country Store in the building, one run by Ali, now established further south on Route 20 in Buckingham County. "He really got it going again," remembers Cenie Re Sturm. "And he could leave because he was successful!" says Lucinda Wheeler.

Another version of the James River Country Store was managed by Miles Goger from Esmont, September 1999 to December 2004. He added the canopy over the gas tanks and awnings over the small windows, "hoping especially," he told the Architectural Review Board regarding the changes, "to appeal to women shoppers." Goger offered pizza by the slice, and his corner sign advertised a grill and deli. By 1988, the town business directory lists no business called James River Country Store.

Town clerk Amy Moyer supplied these dates from the Scottsville records: from December 15th, 2004 to December 31st, 2005, the James River Country Store was in the hands of Hyder and Sons, LLC; and from February 1st, 2006 to February 28th, 2007, Gregorvis, Inc. owned it. Bob Slavit of Buckingham County, owner of the 1911 building, recalls that after Miles Goger had the store, it was run by "an Indian man. He had been doing well but suffered a heart attack. His father, who didn't speak much English, filled in for him." The next managers failed through problems Bob remembers as involving the lottery and an employee.

Nathan Blessing opened Country Blessings on August 8th, 2008 with what he called a "fresh attitude" and a business plan inspired by his father's work in produce and honed at the Darden Business School. "I want [the property] to be part of the Scottsville community," he said in the *Rural Virginian* that September, "supporting the local economy by buying from Farmers' Market merchants, as well as stocking other locally-grown and produced foods."

"The floors," Nathan said of the building in a *Daily Progress* article, September 2009, "'have a kind of funhouse feel,' a reminder of the devastating floods...." Nathan expanded to prepared foods and established an eating area, offered WiFi, case discounts for wine and gift baskets. Now concentrating on his work in Haiti, Nathan is rueful about his business closing, remembering well his hopes and the many people who supported him. In 2006, a James River Country Store brochure described the Dorrier building as "directly above the center of the earth and below the noontime sun. At the corner of Routes 6 and 20 in historic Scottsville on the James lies man's answer to the eternal question: Where can I find good times, good friends and good foods?" We will hope such items will be quickly restocked in this venerable building.

*Originally published February 2011*

## 38.

# At the Crossroads of
# History and Commerce

Early Scottsville was orient- ed to its river. The James was the basis of social and commercial networks that linked neighboring communities like Columbia, Howardsville, Warren and Warminster, and reached—with eventual road links—from beyond the mountains at Staunton and the Shenandoah Valley to Richmond. But with the turn of the twentieth century, new technologies developed new paths and new ways.

At the corner of Main, where our original commercial center developed, and Valley Street, a fine big structure helped inaugurate the feeling Virginia Moore calls "New Century, New Hope." On the site of a former building, looking north up the road

This 1919 credit receipt from Dorrier's reflects a fascinating variety of items purchased over the period of one month. The list includes: gasoline, lemons, a cap, plow points, bacon, seeds for planting, bread, oranges, grapes. As someone once said, "If you can't get it in Scottsville, you probably don't need it." Courtesy of Jack Hamner.

(not yet paved) as much as at the river, it faced the future. The first car came to town in 1910. Scottsville's pact with the "new century" was sealed.

The Dorrier Building is again empty of its commercial business, giving us an opportunity to review its history. The Dorriers, Larry Stallings notes, were "always a prominent family around town." Shirley Dorrier lists the brothers as Walter, James, Charles (C. R., 1885-1966), and Benjamin. "They came with their parents and settled at their country place, a beautiful big brick house by the Hardware River—Mt. Pleasant Farm. Their father got his money by making and selling barrel hoops."

Shirley says the boys' mother died, as well as a young daughter, and they were raised by a nurse. The family had a talent for making money. "They saw the future," Shirley says, "and thought that for them, it was not necessarily in farming." They went into banking and business and explored for coal in West Virginia and for railroads to carry the coal. C. R. Dorrier did well selling railroad ties, an enterprise he carried on at C. R. Dorrier and Co. General Merchandise, the store he established at the building, built by his father, on the corner at 280 Valley Street. C. R. would run the store for 50 years.

Fred Schneider, architect, owner and restorer of the Old Tavern on Main Street and a member of Scottsville's Architectural Review Board, says that the National Register describes the building as a six-bay, two-story brick masonry structure in a Late Victorian style, constructed in 1912 (which is probably an error). This was a time, however, when many large structures were built: massive Grand Central Terminal, 1913, in New York City; many of Charlottesville's distinctive buildings along Main Street, now the Downtown Mall; and the McGuffey School. All of these were photographed by Rufus Holsinger in the second decade of the 1900s. The Dorrier building's exterior brick walls are laid in American bond, meaning there is a course of headers—the short side of the bricks—every eighth course, or row, a relatively easily laid type of masonry.

"Among the formal details that contribute to the building's refined appearance," Fred continues, "are a projecting wood cornice with repetitive ornamental blocks (modillions), supported by a brick cornice with stepped (or corbelled) brick brackets; two brick belt courses below the cornice and a checkerboard header band between the first and second floors; segmental-arched window heads; and brick raised corner blocks (quoins).... The wood windows at both first and second floors are two-over-two, double-hung sash windows. The building has a shallow pitched roof behind a stepped brick parapet. The rear of the building has a projecting one-story brick addition topped by a wood frame, roofed porch at the second floor."

"It was one of my favorite places," says Bob Spencer, whose mother, Louise Pitts Spencer, worked as C. R.'s secretary and bookkeeper for years.. Bob would check in daily after school. "It was a great store, like an old-fashioned country department store," he says, "with every corner housing a specialty section." Bob lists men's and women's clothing, millinery and yard goods, shoes, groceries and hardware among the goods that were sold there.

Louise Spencer's office, in addition to C. R.'s, was at the south side of the store, elevated three steps on a platform and heated by a coal stove. There was also a "huge safe," as Bob Spencer remembers it.

Mrs. Spencer was an important part of the operation, Bob notes. Richard L. Nicholas remembers that sometimes when they were busy on the floor, she would come to help the clerks. One of her jobs, among many, was to ensure that there was enough money on Fridays, so that the store could cash payroll checks from the rubber plant workers, in hopes of selling them supplies.

Bob describes C. R. as "a good businessman, on the Albemarle Board of Supervisors and School Board at various times. He was tall, rather personable, but somewhat reserved. You knew he was the boss." Bob particularly remembers a gesture C. R. repeated when completing a bit of business: he slapped his hands together and exclaimed, "Ah, that's good!" C. R. married John Lee Pitts' daughter, Clara Pitts, and had several sons, including Lindsay Gordon, Shirley Dorrier's husband.

Bob fondly recalls the two long front display windows of the store, usually containing clothing and other merchandise for sale. At Christmastime they were transformed into Toyland. The window along West Main Street housed an electric train that ran through a miniature town representing Scottsville. This was set up by Reeve Nicholas and Mayor Raymon Thacker's father, who ran the hardware section of the store. Along Valley Street, the windows showed toys and miscellaneous gifts.

In between the display windows was a unique feature of the building: a four-step corner entry with access to both streets, divided by a column set in cement, with an Ionic fillip at the top, a tiled floor on the little porch and oak wood double doors. On an undated Burgess postcard, the column appears black. The windows and porch were decoratively topped by a projecting cornice, echoing the one at the roofline.

The building also had less elaborate doors where they are now, south of the corner entrance and on the rear side of the building. Larry Stallings and others, when asked about this building, first describe the corner entrance. "The men used to perch there on the steps around the column, as well as in front of the bank and other businesses," Larry says. "They looked like old crows sitting there," says another. "It was terrible when they took it out," Cenie Re Sturm says. "I remember going in that entrance, seeing Pop Dorrier behind the counter. We always called him Pop."

Lang Mason remembers the corner entrance as the best of all the building's features. "In the 60s," he says, "I remember crossing Route 20 holding my grandmother's hand. She was wearing purple gloves, and we were going grocery shopping. It would all take longer than expected because we'd meet people to talk to. I just loved the doors. It gave the feeling of Scottsville central square, our Piccadilly Circus, including the set-back door at Bruce's Drug Store, the hotel, the gas station—the heart of the town to me."

The first ad the Scottsville library has on file for C. R. Dorrier's, "The Quality Store," is in the *Scottsville Enterprise*, June 29, 1911, offering a car-load of welded poultry fencing. Other farm supplies were offered, including fertilizer and Southern States feed, which was kept in "a huge, long warehouse," says Bob Spencer, south of the building towards the current Farmers' Market. This structure, Shirley Dorrier remembers, was later run as a feed store, where horses were sometimes sold by Garvin Harrison; it's where she constantly went to look for a pony he promised her. "I never got that pony!"

As twentieth century prosperity grew, other important Scottsville businesses lined the streets north: besides the U. S. Rubber Plant, there was The Hub, with clothing, Bruce's Drug Store, Parr's Furniture Store, and Moon's Service Station. These businesses sponsored ads in the Scottsville High School graduation program and in the *Scottsville News*, where a March 24th, 1921 Dorrier's ad stated emphatically, "We do not handle any imitation goods but the genuine article every time. Let us serve you." In May of 1935, Dorrier's offered men's work shirts for 49 cents and neckties for 25 cents and up. "You profit by buying here," was the slogan. Dorrier's, Jack Hamner recalls, had Scottsville phone number 1 in the 1930s and 40s.

Mayor Thacker adds that his father ran the hardware part of the store until 1950. Virgie Mayo, Brenda Maxey remembers, was an employee there, and in 1967, for a year or less, her brother Kenny Davis ran Kenny's Superette in the front half. She believes Lindsay Herndon took over the grocery section when her brother left. Dowe Watson became the proprietor of the store, says Monty Duncan. "There were several in and out of there while I was gone," he says, "but everybody who was in there did well. Business used to boom."

Gene Harding describes the businesses splitting, divided by a wall with a door. Reeve Nicholas, long-time mayor of Scottsville, ran the hardware store at the rear, with employee Cecil Harmon; and Bob Coleman established the Coleman Jefferson Shop in the front. Coleman, according to his son Robert Coleman, Jr., left the Dorrier building around 1967, when Robert Jr. was nine. He set up a separate store in the old Masonic building at the corner of East Main and Valley Streets. This location had previously been the post office up until its move to West Main Street in 1964.

Robert Coleman remembers Reeve Nicholas running a grocery store in the south part of the Dorrier building, and a hand-drawn elevator to storage on the second floor. "The building was a nice place to be. I would always marvel at the hardwood floors. Those," he notes sadly, "had to be replaced after the flood damage of Hurricane Camille." Robert's father put down a sweeping compound every night. "And most of the time I was the one doing the sweeping in the mornings." Mostly, Robert remembers having fun there with his father and his sister.

Richard Nicholas tells of his half-brother Reeve going early to start the coal fire in the winter: "That store was cold! We used to buy groceries there all the time. We walked in on the corner, stepped up into the building. There was a wide doorway between general groceries and the hardware section. Folks always lived upstairs." Lucinda Wheeler recalls Reeve Nicholas' wife, Ampie. "The store had everything, and I still have two oil lamps I bought from Ample Nicholas. Yes, I remember the store and the pot-bellied stove. It was a country place."

Gene Harding tells a story of the Depression era at C. R. Dorrier's and Co. He says there were four employees, and C. R. saw that finances dictated that he needed to lay one of them off. He didn't want to pick the man to go, so he called them together, explained the situation, and went out of the room, leaving them to choose who would lose his job. When they called C. R. in, they laid out their plan: cut back to three salaries, but spread the money among the four workers. "You wouldn't find that today," Gene says.

*Originally published January 2011*

# 39.

# Local Family Says,
# "We Are Perfectly Delighted with Jerusalem"

A mong the treasures gathered in the Scottsville Museum when it opened in 1970 were James Barclay's letters from the period of his missionary work in Jerusalem. The eight letters were given by museum board member Susie Blair. Always known as "Miss Susie," daughter of dentist Dr. Joseph P. Blair and Susan Powers of Scottsville, she was a graduate of Hollins College, where she studied Drama, and later became a distinguished professor of English. Miss Susie directed Christmas pageants at the Scottsville Baptist Church, and put the "finishing touches" on the Scottsville Bicentennial Pageant, according to Bob Spencer.

These eight letters, covering 1850-1874, give us an idea of the broad geographic area covered by the name Scottsville, or Scott's Ferry, as one of them is addressed. Travel in this period, except for the emerging railroad, was by horse, river, or on foot. Nevertheless, Barclay's father lived near present-day Crossroads, and his mother, Sarah Coleman Turner, moved to a farm after her husband's death "on the road from Scottsville to Staunton, between North Garden and Batesville," according to the museum's website. She later married Captain John Harris of Viewmont, located on Route 20. All these were within the neighborhood of Scottsville, a region held together by complex family ties, as well as those of commerce, politics and religion.

Dr. Barclay's work in Jerusalem is the subject of a paper recently presented by Scottsville's Professor Emerita, Evelyn Edson, PVCC, at a conference in Jerusalem called "Visual Constructs of Jerusalem." Edson's paper, titled "An American Missionary's Maps of Jerusalem: Past, Present and Future," tells how Barclay, born in 1807 to a well-connected Central Virginia family, spent much of his time in Jerusalem exploring and mapping, searching for the exact location of biblical places, as well as trying to convert Jews to his own religion, Disciples of Christ.

Barclay's life story will be told elsewhere. Here, we remember that around 1846, he helped found and build the Scottsville Disciples Church, which now houses the Scottsville Museum. Barclay constructed an altar and pews for the church, and also served as its first minister. He married Julia Ann Sowers of Staunton, and with a medical degree from Pennsylvania University, he had opened a drugstore in Charlottesville in the early 1830s.

James and Julia had three children, and when he became a member of the Disciples of Christ Church and received permission and support to work abroad as a missionary, the whole family packed and set off, in what Julia characterized as "tiptoe anxiety to embark," on a deeply spiritual project that might mean they would see their family and friends in Scottsville "no more in this world." [Grateful thanks to Evelyn Edson for her long, diligent work transcribing these letters. She notes that Barclay's handwriting was good, Julia's less so, and many words odd to us made her work difficult.]

When the Barclays finally arrived in Jerusalem after "a truly horrendous voyage through the English Channel, Bay of Biscay and the Mediterranean," Barclay found missionary work very trying: "There was a death penalty for wooing Muslims from their faith, while Jews who converted were ostracized from the community.... His medical skills were more appreciated than his preaching," Edson says. The Barclays rented eight or nine different homes in an effort to find affordable lodgings that were comfortable and healthful. During the malaria seasons, they often moved to high ground after the two younger children almost died. Edson praises their "plucky" attitude in a number of difficult situations.

In the second letter owned by the museum, sent from Julia to the Staples sisters in Scottsville on the 27th of February, 1851, she says, "[We] have commenced housekeeping in quite a pleasant house for this part of the world." This was near the Damascus Gate in Jerusalem. "As you are aware that there are no slaves in this part of the world [the 1840 U.S. Census lists Barclay as owning 11 slaves], you will not be surprised when I tell you that we have no servant yet.... Dr. Barclay hired a man (the people here have white Arab men for their servants). I soon found that he would not suit me, so I dismissed him and found I could do my work very well, as we have commenced housekeeping in a very plain way

"Our bread is brought to us every morning by the baker, or milk by a country girl, and a Jew does our washing in an excellent style so that when we take into consideration the quantity of fresh and

*Shown here are the west front of the Barclay House, now the archives and office of the Scottsville Museum, and the Scottsville Museum, former Disciples of Christ Church. James Barclay was the first Disciples of Christ church missionary in the Holy Land. Photos by Ruth Klippstein.*

dried fruit afforded by the bazaar, of which we are very fond, really but little cooking is necessary. I hope, however, in the course of a few days to get a genteel girl to live permanently in our family, who will relieve me of all trouble in the culinary department."

"We have by far," she continues, "the finest oranges you ever saw in your life (all the year round) and at the low rate of 15 or 20 for one piaster or nearly 5 cents. Figs

*According to the magazine Eretz Israel, "in Israel, James Turner Barclay is known as the man who discovered Barclay's Gate, one of the ancient gates to the Temple Mount (see page 36). True archaeology buffs know that he also discovered Zedekiah's Cave, the vast cavern near the Damascus Gate that has fascinated Freemasons, treasure hunters, and thrill seekers (See Eretz 108, page 48)." Photo courtesy of the Scottsville Museum, Scottsville, VA.*

you can buy more than a quart for a piaster, and when fresh they are much cheaper. Lemons are rather higher, pomegranates are more than twice as dear as oranges and not so good to our foreign barbarian taste. Dried apricots are delicious and rather cheaper than dried peaches in Scottsville. Watermelons have just gone out of season in market, but we see some rinds in the streets occasionally. Besides fresh potatoes, radishes, turnips, onions, carrots, beets, lettuce, etc., they have many outlandish vegetables that I don't know the name of.... Peas in our garden are nearly ready to bloom (last year they were ripe at this time), can you beat that? The market abounds in the finest cauliflowers and cabbages I ever saw in my life—half piaster, about two and a half cents a head."

In the next letter, James Barclay writes to the Staples family in April 1851, complaining at length of both "the onorous [sic] Turkish postage" and the lack of return letters from Scottsville. Turner encourages these members of his Disciples of Christ congregation to come to Jerusalem to help with the mission work. "The Turkish women, however, sometimes express a little contempt for us by word and act (once even by spitting at us!)" But Barclay feels he has made some headway in conversion and describes baptisms he conducted in "a beautiful pool of pellucid water as broad as your dining room and several times as long." Another reservoir he describes by comparing its dimensions to that of "Edward Moon's property, the old Tavern" on East Main Street.

Barclay concludes with some domestic notes: "They have odd times and ways of eating meals and attending worship way down East here!" In response, he had to adjust his own schedule and could not hold church services until one o'clock and "occasionally again at dark." However, he notes, "we are perfectly delighted with Jerusalem, our happy home."

The next letter in this sequence is dated June 24th, 1852, from Julia (with a postscript from her husband) to Olivia Staples. It is long, and it was to be hand-delivered in the States by one of their many visitors. "Well," it begins, "we live in a large stone house which, with its iron-grated windows, heavy buttresses and massive walls, looks for all the world like a prison. There are two large courts and two wells of water. The top is flat except where the domes over the different rooms rise up. These domes give the rooms a beautiful appearance within, by their fantastic finish. The houses in Jerusalem are all built of stone, and such arches and crypts and vaults as you see everywhere here I venture to say you never saw anywhere else in all your life. We are so lucky as to have glass in nearly all our windows, except two, though there is not a pane of glass in ninety-nine-hundredths of the houses in Jerusalem nor do the good people generally see fire the whole year round, and yet they wear neither shoes nor stockings as a general thing but only wooden clogs.... Our bedsteads are all iron, and our beds either wool or cotton. Our seats are mostly divans, but we have a few chairs that are quite good. But Dr. B. is the maker of several of them, as he is of all the divans and most all of our furniture."

"Some things went very hard with us at first, I must confess, but we now look with the greatest complacency upon many things which at first were rather revolting," Julia says. She concludes, "As for creature comforts, I don't deem these as essential to happiness as I once did."

Letter five is dated July 23rd, 1852, again to Olivia Staples from Julia, and again with a long complaint about not hearing from her. "Since Dr. B.'s last sickness, we are willing to live in a cave if it were necessary for health. We found it absolutely necessary to leave the city and retreat to the country; and we are now staying in an old ruin on Mt. Olivet and have had excellent health since we left the infected air of Jerusalem."

A year later, July 8th, 1853, James Barclay writes to the Staples; this is to be the last account to Scottsville from Jerusalem. Perhaps a bit homesick, Barclay says he fancies himself "carried...back to old Vaginy," remembering "delightful events of bygone days—" "We have had some hard kicks and cuffs this year, principally from the priests and consuls, but out of the hands of them all the Lord has delivered us. We have had no sickness for some time but such as yielded readily to a dose or two of medicine, and yet our health is quite enfeebled, or should I say, our constitutions. The Crimean War is looming. The Turks have withdrawn their encircling troops, and Bedouins break out in tribal conflict around Jerusalem. The sound of gunfire is omnipresent."

The Barclays moved on to "civilized and refined" Malta, where Julia wrote, July 1854, to Scottsville. The family is relieved to see carriages and to drink soda water. "Sarah [who turned 17] is in ecstasies...." Julia looks forward to Scottsville to "see our dear dog again, a dog almost semi-human, possessed of such warming and endearing ways...."

The last letter in the cache is from New Jersey, 1874. In it, Barclay notes that the promised visit to Scottsville is, in fact, not to happen. He is working for the U.S. Mint and having bureaucratic troubles with them. Barclay is never much in Scottsville after his initial trip to

Jerusalem. He returns to the Middle East from 1857 to 1865, when his niece Oriana Moon joins him in his medical mission, as we have written earlier. He published *The City of the Great King* in 1858, and Sarah published *Hadji in Syria, or Three Years in Jerusalem* the same year. Barclay died at his son's plantation in Alabama in 1874.

The history of the Barclay house next to the church, now the museum, is confused and often spotty. Barclay may have lived in it, but perhaps not. The house was definitely owned by his mother in 1838; it is said she willed it to him. It stands, with the museum, on the National Register of Historic Places, as a part of the record of Scottsville and its broader world.

*Originally published January 2011*

# 40.

# More Horse Talk

In Manhattan, when the livery stable district was dismantled, Broadway's "Great White Way" emerged—an entertainment district "equally bright at midnight and noon, and loud with the horns of the new horseless taxicabs," according to writer Anne Matthews in *Wild Nights: Nature Returns to the City*, 2001.

Livery stables—there were three in Scottsville—were places where time was slower, where you could board or rent a horse, arrange for hauling and pickup, or just hang around and talk. When cars made them obsolete, many things in town changed. Let's consider the prevalence of horses in the early years of Scottsville's twentieth century and their culture today.

Garvin Harrison ran a barbershop on Valley Street, where Sports and More is now, Larry Stallings tells us, but he was mainly a horse trader. He had a barn behind C. R. Dorrier's General Store, the current site of Country Blessings, where he stabled animals he bought on trips through Pennsylvania and Tennessee. According to Stallings, "[Garvin] would drop his razor and go sell horses or machinery he had," if someone showed an interest.

Chub Walsh says there was a blacksmith's shop there as well, where Mr. Oliver and his son came from Buckingham to work on Saturdays. Chub says he "hung out there all day at the barn. It was a neat place." He recalls up to three horses and ponies, sometimes mules. Chub used to keep horses at his own farm but "can't really say I miss it, though I always enjoyed riding."

One of the children dreamily looking at the ponies was Shirley Dorrier. "I was always going down there," she reminisces, "to pick out a pony and tell my parents which one I wanted." Shirley never got her pony "because we didn't have a field to keep it in." But she considered Garvin Harrison a friend, and Shirley got to ride at W. S. Dorrier's, off Route 20. The Dorrier girls had ponies, and she would ride bareback. C. R. Dorrier had a pony and cart and would take children "on very fast rides—too fast for comfort, in fact," down the hill on Page Street, starting near Belle Haven.

Shirley married C. R. Dorrier's son Gordon. They went on to have a pony and three horses at their home, Endfield. Their daughter

*Nydrie Stud, on 2,000 acres, with brick barn and stables was a classic setting setting for breeding horses. Photo by Philip Beauline of landmark Nydrie Stud, Esmont, used by Jim Bonner, agent, when farm was offered for sale in Albemarle Magazine, October, 2005.*

Claire loved riding and competed in shows on the Paulett property, near the corner of 20 and 6. These were Tri-County Riding Club shows, before the club built its own ring.

Edna Anderson comes from a family that cares for horses. She recalls that when her mother first lived in the area, across the James River, she took her horse and buggy by ferry daily to school, stabling it at the Farmers' Exchange, now called the Canal Warehouse. There were men there to feed and care for the horses.

During World War II, when gas was rationed, Edna's mother gave a picnic for all the local teachers. The family lived four miles out of town, so the teachers borrowed horses and a wagon, and Garvin Harrison drove everyone there.

Horses were used for work in a variety of ways. Nadine Melton related her family's Scottsville history to Louise Holt as part of a Southside Fellowship project at age 86 in 1988. Nadine said her father was a wheelwright, "building wheels and putting wagons and buggies together—in the old timey way." He was also a farmer and grew sorghum that the horses helped process. At the mill, the "horse had a big pole hitched to it with the singletree and the horse—just like hooked to a wagon...carried that pole around and around in a circle." The juice was squeezed out into pans and cooked into molasses. "People don't do it anymore—too much work," said Nadine, who died in 1997.

Emma Rice, who lived in the Antioch Church area about five miles from Scottsville, remembers "driving a horse and wagon to school in Scottsville." How long the ride would have been! I heard Emma tell that story years ago, and it is recorded in "History of Antioch Baptist Church, 1858-1983".

Besides farm work, horses helped to log in the Scottsville woods. Troy Tapscott recalls that his father, Harvey had horses for years, to carefully skid out downed trees, but then kept them on "just to look at. He'd have 11 or 12."

Nydrie Stud, "one of the most successful farms in the country," according to the *Albemarle Monthly* of August 1980, was a "classic setting for breeding horses" in Esmont. On 2,000 acres, with a brick barn and stables, the operation was developed by Daniel Van Clief, whose parents had moved here from Buffalo, New York in the 1920s. In 1992, then general manager, Court Van Clief, Daniel's son, noted that Nydrie was "as small as it had ever been: eight mares, never more than 20." A "thoroughbred nursery," according to Court. The farm sold yearlings in Kentucky and Saratoga, New York. Their animals figure in the pedigrees of 1947 Kentucky Derby winner Jet Pilot and 1964 winner Northern Dancer.

Frank Bolling of Esmont was the "'groom of longest standing at Nydrie,'" according to a December 1979 *Albemarle Monthly* magazine article by Maryann MacConochie. Bolling said he learned about horses from his father, who had Jack and Fanny. They pulled a two-horse plow, one horse in the furrow, one on the unopened soil. "It didn't take them long to catch on to what you wanted to do," he told me. His father taught him that "with horses, you don't work the hours, you work the job."

Bolling recently said how much he enjoyed the work at Nydrie for 32 years, though it was "confining. Someone always had to be there." He liked cleaning the horses' teeth and sandpapering their hooves as they were prepared for the sales.

Scottsville resident Barbara Lane remembers that her father was farm manager at Nydrie when Jack Carpenter was in charge of the horses. "Though I'm scared to death of animals," she recalls, the horses were beautiful, and the atmosphere at the farm "peaceful and quiet"—"it was great, such a nice place to live."

A current horse operation in Scottsville, off Route 6, is Fairhunt Farm, run by Susan Skolnick-Lozano. It is "oriented toward young riders and quite a bit of foxhunting," according to the website. They participate at the Farmington Hunt Club. Susan's 2008 book, *Riding At Fairhunt: For Love, Life, and Therapy*, tells the story of her daughter's critical car accident and the years of recovery from traumatic brain damage through riding and driving horses. Susan's daughter, Rebekah, had been a rider since age seven, was a horse trainer in Albemarle County, responded to the proper horse after the accident, and is now "moving ahead, where no one expected us to go."

Susan champions the many lessons horses can teach young people and the personal growth they can engender. The local 4-H group,

Horseshoe Bend Riders, meets twice a month. "The members learn," leader Tamara Mann says, "that horses are a big responsibility. Riding builds confidence. Some of the kids have come a long way." Their monthly shows are at the farm of Leslie Davis, who's run Scottsville Saddlery for five years. "We have a fun show once a year," Leslie says, but the young riders also work for points in the Virginia Horse Show Association so that they can compete elsewhere in the state. Leslie teaches one of the area's few Western riding classes.

The Tri-County Riding Club, north off of Route 20, no longer holds horse shows, as it did in the 1950s, but remains an active social club. Originally, there were breakfast rides over the countryside, ending at an estate like Nydrie or Redlands, with grits and Bloody Marys. "We could have a good time and then ride back home. That was when you could ride a horse on Route 20," charter member Shirley Dorrier recalls.

Though cars have moved horses off the roads, our many horses still need care and attention. Once, Scottsville rural postman W. D. "Doc" Moon would respond to a note in the mailbox to come in and see a horse. Now, veterinarians are highly trained and busy. Scottsville's Stan Rudacil, a farrier since 1966, specializes in big horses. "Most farriers don't like to work them," he says, "but I have been doing it for Colonial Williamsburg for 15 years, for the Budweiser Clydesdales at Busch Gardens for six years, and for the Bundoran Belgians [in Albemarle County] for five.... We teach these horses to hold their feet up, and we get a better job that way."

Stan also teaches driving teams of horses and once hitched and drove a 40-horse team in Wisconsin. He notes that you need two assistants to help with all those reins. The horse population in the area, Stan says, is ten times what it was in 1970. "The growth of interest in horses parallels the growth of income." Stan finds children a "joy to teach" and has met a wide variety of friends through his work. "A lot of horse people now feel their horses are a backup if gas goes away," he says.

Horses are an iconic part of the Scottsville Fourth of July parade, just as much now as 100 years ago. Red Clements always has a horse and buggy in the celebration and also provides them (one formerly owned by Loretta Lynn) for weddings. Red's father trained horses, and Red has had them all his life. "They will do anything," he cautions, though he keeps "real gentle, good horses, ready to go" for his work.

Now, as in times past, as Susan Skolnick-Lozano writes, "Girls four to fourteen think of horses in romantic terms." At the library, they still take out stacks of horse stories. Young Peyton Lewis recently read *Black Beauty*. She rides a neighbor's horse, Peaches, and says she'll ride him all her life. "It makes me feel bouncy. I feel best on a horse," says Peyton.

As an antidote to romanticism, we can return to Frank Bolling, the Nydrie groom, who said, "Some horses are born intelligent, some you have to teach. Sometimes you can dress one so he looks better than he really is. They're just like people."

*Originally published January 2010*

## 41.

# A Real Variety Store

"My mother can tell you about a five-and-dime in Scottsville," says our town police officer, Ron Morris. That statement was reason enough for me to go to Charlottesville and visit with Neva Morris to get the story.

Neva is now 80 and was born with the surname Staton near Carter's Bridge. "There were a lot of Statons in Scottsville!" She remembers a very different Scottsville, when Dr. Stinson and Dr. Harris practiced, Mr. Branham had a service station on Valley Street, and Victory Hall showed a full schedule of first-run movies. Her father helped build Route 20, around 1900, driving a team of mules. Earlier relatives owned land on Main Street, across from the canal warehouse, and were boatmen on the James.

Neva and other children from Carter's Bridge went as youngsters to a small school in their neighborhood with three grades taught

*The Beal building is easy to spot in this c. 1898 photograph by W.E. Burgess, and fortunately is not among the "lost Scottsville" architecture. Used for many purposes in the past, the historically important building, currently under renovation, has great potential for future use in town. Photo courtesy of the Scottsville Museum, Raymon Thacker Collection.*

by Elizabeth Marshall. Later, they and others from as far north as Wood's Store were picked up by bus and driven to the Scottsville school. Neva would leave home at about 7:30 in the morning. The bus would travel at 30 miles an hour, and not all the roads were paved. "It was quite a long trip!"

At school, the students ate their bagged lunches and were free to walk in town. This is how Neva encountered Beal's, the variety store on the corner of Valley and Bird Street. "Beal's didn't mind if schoolkids came in. If I had a couple of pennies, I had to spend them!"

The Beal Building was constructed circa 1840 during what Virginia Moore calls the "golden era" of Scottsville's development. As an independent and thriving commercial center, Scottsville needed business and professional space, and this long brick building provided both. On the ground floor was the Beal mercantile business, and the Masons of Lodge 45 met for 29 years, until 1914, on the second floor. Under the slate roof, with its distinctive stepped parapet projections on either end, lawyer and U.S. senator Thomas Staples Martin kept his office, as later did lawyer Frank Moon. Martin was an impressive native son, who practiced 25 years in Scottsville and was an influential senator and advisor to President Wilson during World War I.

The Beal family is well-documented in Scottsville, and we are indebted to Jesse Grove for his account of them on the Scottsville Museum website. The town lot, number 148, where their commercial building is located, was donated by Peyton Harrison in 1841 to the Presbyterian church. The church was in place by 1832, and Joseph Russell Beal came from Richmond and took a 60-year lease on the land "in front of the church"—that is, downhill, facing Valley Street.

The Beal Building was erected, and Joseph's son Jackson started a mercantile business there with his brother Billy. Jackson became mayor of Scottsville, serving more than 20 years, and held court as Justice of the Peace on the second floor of the building. He tried "minor misdemeanors and imposed fines."

Jackson, junior, one of seven surviving siblings, had a brother named Wiley Powhatan, his middle name a gift of their mother,

Mary Emma Bledsoe of Fluvanna, who claimed family ties to Chief Powhatan. After Jack married, he left Scottsville for work with the Lane Construction Company and returned after the birth of his daughters. He opened the Beal Furniture Store, selling caskets as well, in the Beal Building.

Homer Thacker worked for Jack, and then his brother Raymon joined the staff. Raymon remembers that Jack sold his funeral business in 1929, and shortly after that the furniture business as well. In 1933, Jack and his wife Agnes opened the James River Market in the corner building across Bird Street.

Mayor Thacker says, "Now, that was the Depression. I remember working for 10 cents an hour. A dollar a day was a good salary." He was able, with a bank loan secured by William Burgess, to start the Thacker Brothers Funeral Home with Homer. "It worked out perfectly fine."

Wiley Beal continued with the variety store business, using the Beal Building. He married in 1929, and Raymon Thacker calls Wiley and Violet "two nice people." Wiley was also in construction, and Violet was treasurer for the town, as well as bookkeeper for Dr. Stinson. "Life in Scottsville," says Raymon Thacker, "is like a patchwork quilt."

Mayor Thacker recalls that Wiley Beal "ran a very nice business for a good while" in the 1940s and 50s. Beal's ad runs in the 1955 "Scotty," the Scottsville High School yearbook: "W. P. Beal and Co., Hardware – Sherman Williams Paint – Toys – Glassware. Phone 3867." Lud Nicholas remembers the old-fashioned cash register and "normal stuff like in Woolworth's—knick-knacks, everything was there." Raymon Thacker describes it as "not exactly a five-and-dime, but it had all kinds of things, cheaply priced—practical things."

"There are not a lot of memories left of them," Thacker considers. There are conflicting memories, facts we may never sort out. But Neva Morris is very clear about her experience at Beal's. She still has a two-inch metal brooch in the shape of a lion, very shiny to this day, that she recalls buying there. "I probably paid a nickel for it," she says. There were household goods, toys, "all kinds of little stuff," all laid out on tables.

Margaret Napier worked at Beal's while she was in high school, about 15 or 16 years old, on Saturday evenings, 1 to 9 P.M. She lived at Dr. Stinson's Valmont Dairy, where her father was employed, and she would walk into town or get a ride there somehow. "We always worked," she says, to help the family. While employed at Beal's, she made $1.72—"a whole lot of money to me at the time." She recalls selling clothes, canned goods, cosmetics, "all kinds of stuff." "It was a nice store. You could get most anything. It was the only five-and-dime in town, so we were busy all the time." Margaret especially recalls the candy they sold by the pound—chocolate, peanut candy, old-fashioned sorts, and the candy near the window that "smelled so good when you walked in." People came to buy candy before attending the evening movie at Victory Hall. "It was good times," she reminisces.

Her sentiment is echoed by Marguerite Hughes, who worked at Beal's between high school graduation and her marriage. Saturday evenings, Mrs. Beal's maid would bring sandwiches for all the staff to eat for supper, mostly tuna and egg salad. She remembers about five or six people working at a time in half-day shifts.

Edna Nees remembers Beal's for its "little odds and ends." She thinks it had more clothing earlier in time. Later, it became the place she'd go for household items, Easter baskets, and all kind of miscellany. She recalls the "delicious candy, measured out with weights, and the popcorn." Edna and Margaret Napier, who grew up in nearby Fluvanna, are sisters.

Ted Childress bought the Beal Building in 1970. He had previously run the Scottsville Florist with his wife Bootsie on the north corner of Bird and Valley, as well as the dry cleaners with his father. While he was cleaning out the upstairs of the Beal Building, Ted found lots of bottles, whiskey and wine. Ted recalls that Wiley had a "very good selection" of merchandise and was very accommodating with customers. "Most local people shopped there," he says. On Friday evenings, it was "so crowded, there wasn't even room on the sidewalks. Scottsville changed to a different place on Friday and Saturday evenings. The town really boomed."

Ted tells about a vault Wiley and Violet Beal installed in the rear of the building, a massive two-door safe that was eight feet by six feet. It hadn't been opened in 30-40 years, Ted guessed, when he took possession and found it sinking into the wooden floor. He contacted the Smithsonian Institution, who sent some men to Scottsville. They verified the date on the brass plate, 1860, and said they'd take just that and the brass hinges. Ted declined their offer, having hoped they would remove the vault and patch the wall. Instead, he kept the brass work himself and winched the vault over on its face, the wooden floor removed below it, and covered it with concrete. The vault, in fact, is part of the floor of the building now. Inside were papers—invoices, bills, and the like—not the gold and jewels some had surmised.

After Ted Childress ran the Scottsville Furniture Store, he sold the building to Walter Neighbors of Maryland, who is renovating it. Neighbors recently donated a window sash from the Beal Building, incised with Milton Dunn's initials, to the Scottsville Museum. As William Faulkner has written, "The past is never dead; it's not even so past."

*Originally published May 2009*

# 42.

# An Honored Life

Lottie Moon, Southern Baptist missionary to China from 1873 to 1912, was a "legend in her own time," according to the International Missionary Board of the Southern Baptist Convention. Born December 12th, 1840, at her family's plantation Viewmont, between Charlottesville and Scottsville, she is honored today with the Lottie Moon Christmas Offering, which annually raises an average $20 million in support of the church's foreign missions.

Lottie Moon will be the focal point of a projected History Room at the Scottsville Baptist Church, planning to observe its 170th anniversary in 2010, writes church historian Robert Spencer. Enhancing the project is a recent gift to the church of a private collection of Lottie Moon memorabilia and ephemera presented by Jill Johnson Harwood.

Ms. Harwood, of Jamestown, North Carolina, "has roots in the Scottsville church and community as daughter of the late Gilbert L. and Frances (Nelms) Johnson and granddaughter of the late Charles B. and Ruth (Allen) Johnson…. She has been assembling this collection," Spencer continues, "from the time she was a youth in the Girls' Auxiliary division of the Baptist Woman's Missionary Union, and everything pertaining to Lottie Moon's life and ministry has been a passion and hobby for her."

Ms. Harwood taught the Girls' Auxiliary, now called Girls in Action, for over 25 years. She says she "always enjoyed the plays our GAs would act out." She visualized the journey of Lottie Moon to her students with objects she began collecting—a Chinese jacket, a ceramic version of a boot, and furniture of the type Lottie Moon would have used. Most importantly, she began researching her family genealogy and learned that one of her ancestors, Susan Moon, was a cousin of Lottie's. Her interest and commitment grew.

Ms. Harwood's collection will join the Victorian black horsehair sofa and chairs from Viewmont, "lovingly transported," writes Virginia Moore in *Scottsville on the James*, to the new brick church the Moons had helped build. In years prior to 1840, "regular Sunday services had been held at Viewmont...." Anna Maria Barclay Moon, Lottie's mother, had convinced her Presbyterian husband Edward to become a Baptist.

The Moons had money and position in Albemarle society. They owned 50 slaves and more than 1,300 acres fronting what is now Route 20, south of Carter's Bridge. In the February 2006 Local History column, we explored the path chosen by Lottie's older sister, Oriana, who "dared to set a new precedent in education" and persevered to become a doctor. She and her doctor husband, John

Charlotte "Lottie" Digges Moon, was born at Viewmont in Albemarle County, Virginia, on December 12, 1840. She was the dughter of Edward and Anna (Barclay) Moon, wealthy landowners and a Scottsville merchant. Lottie Moon received her education as a teacher at the Virginia Female Seminary and Albemarle Female Institute and accepted an appointment as a Baptist missionary to China in 1873. She was absolutely devoted to the Chinese people for nearly forty years. During a 1911-1912 famine, Lotttie Moon shared her own meager money and food with everyone around her, severely affecting her health. Weighing only 50 pounds, Lottie Moon died on December 24, 1912, from severe malnutrition. (The Robert Spencer Collection,Scottsville Museum)

Andrews, worked in Confederate hospitals in Richmond and, after the war, established the First Sanatorium of Southside Albemarle at Old Hall, Harrison Street in Scottsville.

Lottie also pursued more education than most females of her day. Originally intending to be a teacher, she went to the Virginia Female Seminary at Botetourt Springs, which later became Hollins College, and Albemarle Female Institute. Lottie was accomplished in her studies and excelled in Latin and English composition. She was known as a practical joker with a "devil-may-care attitude," according to Catherine B. Allen in *The New Lottie Moon Story* (available at the Scottsville library). It was not until her eighteenth year that she was moved by the evangelistic fervor of the times. In December 1858, she "made her profession of faith in Jesus Christ" during a meeting of the Charlottesville First Baptist Church.

*Jill Johnson Harwood and some of her lifetime collection on the life of her most admired Lottie Moon. Photo courtesy Scottsville Baptist Church.*

Beginning in 1866, Lottie Moon taught at the Danville Female Academy, where, Allen says, "she began to fall under the spell of faraway China," inspired by reports of a returned missionary. Life at Viewmont was straitened due to general economic conditions in the South after the war. Lottie continued teaching to help pay bills, moving to Cartersville, Georgia in 1871. However, she heard in 1872 that her younger sister Edmonia "had, without warning, gone to China to serve as a Southern Baptist missionary" (Allen). Though, traditionally, Southern Baptists did not send single females into the field, other denominations did, having special success reaching women otherwise shut away from their influence. Change had begun.

Lottie Moon left for China in 1873, at age 32. She joined Edmonia and other missionaries in Tengchow, a large northern port city. Here, Lottie first experienced the Manchu culture—the pigtailed men in robes, women with bound feet, travel by donkey and "coolie-carried" sedan chair, a new etiquette, and eventually the 1894-95 Sino-Japanese war. She began to learn Mandarin. Here is an excerpt from her undated papers:

"'We are going on a picnic' was the announcement. A picnic! Truly it had a pleasant sound, but would it be right to lose a day from study of the language? A little explanation served to clear up matters. The ladies of the mission proposed to visit some of the country villages for the purpose of imparting religious instructions, and as they would take their dinners and spend the day, they styled the expedition a picnic. There would be no harm in accepting such an invitation as this, since mingling with the people is one of the best methods of acquiring the language" (from the Mission Board website).

But Lottie was soon to leave China, in 1875, with her ailing sister. They retired to Viewmont for rest and medical attention. By 1877, Lottie was eager to return, declaring in a November 24th letter, "I feel very natural to be here again, I do so love the East and eastern life.... I honestly believe I love China the best, and actually, which is stranger still, like the Chinese best."

Strange, we assume, because Lottie Moon was not easily taken into Chinese society. She baked tea cookies to give the children, who at first would not eat them. Gradually, her perseverance won people over, and she was able to visit homes, talk about her religion, and finally, establish a school for Chinese women and eventually six schools for girls and one for boys. In her 39-year missionary service, she always pushed to do more. Lottie adopted local clothing, and it is said that her short stature helped ensure her popularity. Her strength, vitality, and faith were her hallmarks.

In a 1905 letter, Lottie wrote, "My life is too full for much longing.... No one in Virginia really needs me." Her self-sacrifice extended to giving away her food during the famine in 1912, which led to her mental faculties, as another missionary wrote, becoming "seriously impaired." She was put on a freighter for the trip home but died December 24th, 1912, near Kobe, Japan. A memorial service was held in Richmond the next month, and her ashes were buried in Crewe, where she had last lived with her brother Isaac and his family.

Now Scottsville celebrates Lottie Moon's connection to the area through the Scottsville Baptist Church and their proposed History Room, with thanks to the collection of Jill Harwood. As Robert Spencer writes, Lottie Moon is "an iconic personality, a remarkable woman whom Scottsville is proud to claim for her cameo role in its storied, rich history."

*Originally published April 2009*

# 43.

# Never To Be Forgotten

shby Mayo's life in Scottsville has left a number of traces, but detailed memories of our postmaster, who served from 1932 to 1958, are fading. A visit to the archives of the state library in Richmond reveals his "papers, 1918-1919." But what about the man himself? We are indebted to those who shared their memories of him.

Mayor Raymon Thacker recalls a "nice person," born in Fluvanna County, July 1894, whose father was called "Ep." "As a young man around Scottsville he participated in a lot of activities." There are photographs documenting Mayo's membership on the Scottsville community baseball team and the Methodist Young Men's Sunday School class under Mrs. Sprague. Harold Parr, Homer Thacker, and Guy Moon are also shown with this group.

He "loved to fish," Thacker remembers, and would come home with 15-20 fish on his stringer. Mac McNamara used to fish with Mayo and calls him "a great guy." They'd take homemade wooden jon boats from Scottsville to the Hardware River,, then drag the boats up on shore.

One summer, when Mac was in graduate school, there was a two-boat trip "on one of the hottest days in July" down to Columbia. It took 12 hours, and Mac, the "Yankee," got very sunburned. Mayo was always delighted by these spontaneous trips, ready to turn the post office over to an assistant and "leave on a whim." Bob Spencer recalls that Mayo's sister, later Mrs. Ben Herndon, was an active fisherwoman, and he used to see her walking through town with her pole and bucket.

Mac's wife is Kathleen McNamara, whose mother Katherine

Pitts taught in Scottsville with Ashby's wife, Pauline Mayo. She recalls the excellent lunches Mrs. Mayo would pack for the fishermen, causing her mother to try to reciprocate. Mrs. Mayo's memory resounds with her strictness and her music. In charge of sixth grade, she brooked no nonsense, and her students, like Edna Anderson, still recall her reprimands. "She was very strict!" She always had a sixth-grade flute choir that performed for special events; Bob Spencer still has his flute. Mrs. Mayo conducted singers for civic occasions and sang herself at weddings. She offered "Ave Maria" for Kathleen and Mac on the porch at Belle Haven and sang "Indian Love Call" at Jacqueline and Jesse Grove's ceremony. The Mayos had no children.

Ashby is noted for his interest in gambling in general and poker in particular. He was "a great player," according to Jesse Grove, and played "with a gang every week at the old flour mill" on Main Street. Peggy Boatwright recalls that Mayo's interest in gambling extended to auctions, which he liked to frequent. At one that she still remembers—"It was years ago"—Mayo bid and rebid until he had secured a dish for his wife for $92: "a lot in those days. Everyone was 'wow!'" Peggy's husband S. J. played in the poker group, which continues today, with Ashby Mayo and recalls how much he liked the game.

Mayo is remembered as a member of the Scottsville Volunteer Fire Company and was a very active supporter of the Fireman's Bazaar, according to Bob Spencer. Bobby describes the roulette-style game Mayo always ran, where patrons bet money on numbers and colors, and Mayo spun the wheel. This fundraiser was in the Canal Warehouse, covering all three floors, every autumn. Edna Anderson thinks Mayo was also a member of the Lion's Club and remembers Mr. and Mrs. Mayo, who "enjoyed dancing" at the Fireman's Balls. Bob Spencer says that the Mayos liked movies at Victory Hall, where he took tickets as a teenager and had to answer Mrs. Mayo's repeated question, "Have you done your homework, Bobby?"

The Mayo home, which they had built from a Sears Roebuck kit, was on Bird Street across the corner from the library. The design, Dutch Colonial Revival, was ordered from the catalog, and the preformed elements were sent by rail.

Mayo, after high school, was employed as a clerk at the Scottsville

Post Office, when it was housed in the Masonic Building, where Coleman's is now, and Samuel Gault was postmaster. Shirley Dorrier thinks Mayo "had a big image to follow" in Gault, who was widely

*(L to R) U.S. Postmaster Samuel R. Gault and his assistant, Ashby Mayo, stand in front of the Scottsville Post Office located in the Masonic Building on Main Street. The Masonic Building was built in 1914 and hosted the town's post office on the bottom floor until 1964 when the post office moved to its current location on West Main Street. Sam Gault served as Scottsville's postmaster from 1893 to 1932; he was succeeded by Ashby Mayo, who retired as postmaster in 1958. Photo courtesy of Scottsville Museum.*

popular and outgoing. A more reserved person, Mayo nevertheless ran "a friendly post office." "If you needed a personal postmaster," Shirley says, "you had one in Ashby Mayo." Bob Spencer concurs that he did an excellent job, and Mayor Thacker says, "Everybody liked him. That's the best you can say about anybody."

Mattie Leigh Golladay Wilkie, according to her sister Eloise McKenry—both now at Morningside Assisted Living in Charlottesville—worked for Samuel Gault as a very young girl. Her family lived across the street from the post office, on the second floor of the Traveler's Rest Hotel, and she'd come in about 6 A.M. and begin sorting the mail to find her family's letters. This became a regular job when Mattie Leigh was around 13 years old, with Gault giving her about $1.20 a week. It's assumed this was from his own pocket. She later took the postal service exam, and when Mayo succeeded Gault upon the latter's death, she continued to work for him. She recalls him as businesslike and good with the public. Elaine Johnson, who visits the Golladay sisters, elicited these reminiscences.

Bob Spencer, as a young boy, used to get his family's mail daily. He "haunted the post office" when he began ordering equipment for his magic tricks, and he remembers the sound of Ashby Mayo calling out patrons' names as their packages were sorted onto steel racks. The mail was delivered to the post office four times a day by train. Bob says the packages were Mayo's special department, his "gruff voice" identifying the lucky recipients. Ragland Daniel was another postal employee, as well as the men who delivered on the rural routes.

Mayo "did a wonderful job as postmaster," Bobby says. When Bob left town for college, his mother began retrieving the mail, and Ashby gave her a "better box" than number 48, one that was down very low so that Bobby could open it as a child. This "very private person," according to Peggy Boatwright, was known in retirement for driving around the countryside "as people did then," Mac McNamara tells. "He'd slam on the brakes, jump out, and pick up any piece of metal he'd find" to take to a junkyard in Charlottesville. "We called him the junkman."

Ashby Mayo's papers in the state library include postcards, now worn soft and almost illegible, from his draft board, 1916-18. He received his 1-A status, "qualified for military service and subject to call," on March 26th, 1918, signed by John Minor in Charlottesville. He attended truck training school there, May-July 1918, and sailed from New Jersey on the Empress of Asia with Company A, Regiment 323, Division 8 on August 1st. From Liverpool, he went to Le Havre and the Eastern Sector.

Mayo rose from private to corporal. He first saw action in the St. Die defense, September-October 1918, and at that point had engaged in the Meuse offensive, which started August 30th, 1918. Then, 90 years ago last November, the war was over and the armistice signed. Mayo and his company walked 150 miles back to their base. Disabled by fallen arches, he stayed in two different base hospitals in France. He finally sailed home to the port of Hoboken and was discharged from Hampton, Virginia.

In a questionnaire Mayo filled out for the armed services, he noted that he had no further trouble with his arches and was able to return to his postal clerk job, from which he would retire in 1967. Mayo wrote that he felt "honored to know that I could serve in the defense of my country." He considered, in a serious vein, that camp life was "educational and building of one's physical condition and ability" and, less seriously, that corned beef wreaked havoc with the men, making "the wild cats of 8 Division wild." The effects of his overseas experience? "Long to be remembered." He learned that "prayers were answered in the hours of danger" and that the fighting was defined by "cruelty and bravery."

Author Mona Simpson, thinking about people in service during this era, says "most of us will, because of our gratitude and guilt, forever want to know how they felt." We know one last thing about Ashby Mayo. As he summed up the effect of all his experience in 1918, he wrote, in elegant Palmer script, "War is Hell."

*Originally published May 2009*

## 44.

# "Shave and a Haircut, Two Bits"

*1976 photo by Masha Glenn to illustrate her "Architectural Survey of Scottsville" for a UVA class. She dates the building to 1880-1890, describes it as "one room and starway wide, two rooms deep and two stories in height." Housed Charlie Robertson's barbershop. Available for study at Scottsville Library.*

"Off and on through the years, there's been a number of barber-shops" in Scottsville, Mayor Raymon Thacker reminisces. His memory goes back to Charlie Robertson's, on the second floor of the building where Dr. Blair had his dentist practice in a frame building—now gone—east of Coleman's on Main Street.

Accompanying the barber was Harry Walker, who had a shoe shine stand and "had learned how to flip those cloths, so he could make music with them."

Thacker next remembers Bob Steger's barbershop in the location now the apartments on Main Street. Dr. Stinson built this structure after a circa 1924 fire gutted the area. At one point, the Miller grocery store was on the ground floor, later run by John Davis, and the second floor was apartments. Steger and his son Raymond were the barbers there until the family relocated to Texas in 1929.

Thacker next lists the barbershop in the lobby of Carleton House, the hotel on the southwest side of Valley Street at Main. Larry Barnett, who now has his real estate office here, notes that the building was erected in 1832 and first used as the Eagle Tavern and Hotel. During the Civil War, there was a 100-bed hospital upstairs.

Garvin Harrison ran a subsequent barbershop in part of this space, the second one north of the corner and no longer a hotel, now housing Evolve Hair Design. Harrison added a balcony, according to Mayor Thacker, as a beauty salon for women. Garvin, who had "a bunch of barbers who worked for him," gave Bob Spencer his first haircut "when my curls were taken off." Spencer was "not too happy" with his first barbering experience. Later, Bob remembers so well, his father would take him regularly for a haircut, and he'd sit on a little platform that fitted across the chair, with handles he could hold.

Sam Spencer recalls that Harry Walker worked at Harrison's and "could handle the shine rag so deftly as to entice a tune from it." Two other barbers, Bill Duncan and Sidney Tapscott, worked there—Thacker recalls F. A. Cole in the late 1930s and 40s—and "over the years, several beauticians, among them Ethel Wilson Grandstaff, Gertrude D. Moore, and Audrey Gentry had the beauty shop" there. Sam says "a long flight of stairs with little protection for the ladies' modesty led to the open balcony area exposed to the loud, often risque speech of the barbershop below." Later, says Larry Stallings, a curtain was added to screen those going upstairs from "prying eyes."

Garvin was, Sam notes, "primarily a trader." He bought used farm equipment in Pennsylvania, brought it to Scottsville to repair and paint, and sold it from the vicinity of the current farmers' market, where there was a barn and open sheds for the horses he later sold. Shirley Dorrier recalls looking often and longingly at ponies she hoped her father would buy her. Larry Stallings reports that, when someone came to the barbershop for the machinery, Harrison—always seen with a cigar—would immediately put down his scissors and take him to the lot. "He always had something going," Sam declares.

The barbershop, Stallings says, had a comfortable, collegial atmosphere. There was a barber pole outside and a leather strop by each chair, where the barber sharpened his straight razor. When he was young and his father took him for haircuts, "the clippers tickled my neck so much it was painful, but I couldn't laugh." In fact, Stallings thinks, the barbers "didn't pay much attention to boys." It was later that he would get the full treatment: neck shaved, lotion applied, and collar brushed off. No fancy styling, but a good 25-cent haircut and 15-cent shave. S. J. Boatwright recalls Bill Duncan giving him his first professional haircut when he was in first grade. Like others, his family cut his hair before that time.

Harrison had a prominently situated checkerboard, and Sam Spencer says passersby could see, through the large picture window in front, the checker games frequently in progress between the barbers and their clients. "Local champ was Willie Boyd Catlett, father of David Catlett. Bill Duncan was number 2 champ, and Sidney Tapscott number 3."

Sam recalls a most remarkable story set at Harrison's barbershop. He tells it this way: "On the shop wall was a tall coat and hat rack with a deep fold seat that was used to store supplies. One of the local boys shot his pistol into a bowl of soup being consumed by a local customer at Lee's Restaurant. The bowl and soup went in every direction and the shooter went to Harrison's barbershop, where he hid the pistol in the hat rack. A search by the town sergeant followed."

Bill Duncan's son Monty Duncan says that Garvin Harrison decided to sell his shop after he developed health problems. The Dorrier brothers of Buckingham bought it in 1956, according to a *Spirit of Scottsville* newspaper feature published in February 1983. John Dorrier, who had a shop in Charlottesville, first worked with Harrison and was later joined by his elder brother Earl. John, who was deaf, is described by his sister-in-law Gladys Banton as an excellent barber who put you back in the chair if he didn't think the cut was perfect. "You were his customer for life," she says, and weren't to go to any of his brothers. Andrew Dorrier worked at the shop only occasionally, perhaps Saturdays, and Paul, Gladys' husband, the youngest, later had shops in Fork Union and Sprouse's Corner.

The Dorriers kept the checkerboard set up, and, according to Chub Walsh, "people would hang around." "It was a meeting place," says Earl's widow, Marveline. "They had fun." Marveline remembers two men who came each morning and stayed all day, delivering their children to school and waiting to pick them up. The men would "sit and talk, laugh and tell jokes," she says.

Earl never cut women's hair, according to Marveline Dorrier. Chub says men could get their shoes shined by Harry Walker, have a shave, haircut, and facial massage, and get their hair singed. This was a process of burning off the newly cut end of the hair, "so it wouldn't look like you just had a haircut," Chester Baker says. "It was supposed to keep you from getting bald," Chub adds—but doesn't.

Dorrier's was "always the main barbershop," Chub says. As a child, he'd get his hair cut on Saturday by Bill Duncan. Bill always called it "a Saturday haircut." Later he had his hair cut by Cash Mundy, who worked for Harrison, then Dorrier's.

Walsh, as well as Bob Spencer, reports that Dorrier's had a shower at the rear of the building, probably much used by the railroad crews and traveling men. Dorrier's, Bob says, sold some hair tonics and creams. He remembers the fascination of watching customers, virtually lying down in the reclined barber chairs, being lathered and carefully shaved by a straight-edge razor. "It was great," he recalls, to be sprinkled with cologne and have your hair combed just so, with a 50-cent cut.

The women going upstairs, either through the barbershop or later, after a remodeling, via outside stairs in the rear, had their own delights. Cenie Re Moon Sturm recalls a vent in a wall—after the balcony—that allowed them, standing on a bench, to peek down into the shop below, listen to the men, and "hear them laughing."

In the mid-1950s, Bill Duncan bought the east side Valley Street shop, where Stacy Sheer now cuts hair. He and Garvin Harrison had been not only business associates but good friends, according to his son Monty. Bill "didn't always see eye to eye" with the Dorriers, so he set up on his own shop. Monty says he "had to go to the barbershop and sit in the chair" to get his own hair cut. "I had to be on excellent behavior. I couldn't complain or speak. But I hated it. I hated to have my hair cut." Bill Duncan became ill and died in 1959.

Gladys Dorrier Banton says her husband Paul's barbering became unprofitable when most men started commuting to other towns for work, "and long hair came in." Scottsville barbershops became unisex. Kevin Armstrong opened the old Dorrier space as Scottsville Family Hair Cuts with a tanning bed, as well as cuts and perms. "Call to set up an appointment," says the ad, something that never happened in the barbershop. One of Kevin's "regulars," Wally Woodphin, according to an *Observer* article, October 1994, opened the shop at 8 A.M., made coffee, turned on the radio, and got ready for the day's clientele, many of whom still enjoyed just sitting and talking. When they got in the chair, Kevin told the reporter, they'd say, "Start cutting, and keep on until you run out of hair." Earl taught Kevin, who'd studied cosmetology, how to use the electric clippers and came in on Mondays for a period to cut the hair of the older

*W.E. Burgess postcard of men at the July Fourth parade, circa 1925. The barber Bob Steger, white shirt and boater, is marked near center of group on grounds at the north side of the current Scottsville Apartments. Courtesy of A. Raymon Thacker.*

men, the farmers, "who didn't want to go to a beauty shop," according to Marveline.

Now Stephanie Chisholm runs Evolve in that space, with white walls, track lighting, colorful curtains, and paint. But there are still chairs to wait in and magazines to read. Larry Barnett uncovered the distinctive leaded glass panel above the window and restored the tin ceiling. The balcony was removed in a 1990s renovation. Earl's granddaughter, Allison Dorrier Toney, worked for Stephanie for about eight months as a stylist. "My husband would have been so happy to know he had a granddaughter in the same building," Marveline says.

Stacy Sheer, at Run-In With Shears, has been cutting hair in Scottsville since she first got a job with Kevin Armstrong. She bought and renovated the Rescue Squad office in a building across the street, recently Minor's Diner, and then moved away from town. Seeing no one to do men's hair in Scottsville, she returned. With room for a second chair, she added Charlottesville barber Rodney Harris, experienced in varieties of "ethnic hair," something Stacy is learning. "It's nice to cross cultural barriers," Stacy says of hiring what she believes is the first black barber in town. She appreciates the new potential in refurbished Scottsville and hopes businesses will flourish.

That's how the Dorriers reported feeling in 1983, when their shop was 27 years old and had gone through several disastrous floods. "I feel," Earl told the newspaper, "like I've been through the worst that could happen, and I'll stick with it to the end... We should all begin tidying up our town and looking forward to meeting the challenges of the future of Scottsville"—a future that includes, apparently, women in the barbershops and men in the beauty salons.

*Originally published September 2008*

# 45.

# July Fourth: A Scottsville Tradition

Scottsville's July Fourth has long been a special summer holiday for town and family celebrations. The 1914 photograph showing grand marshal Sam Gault, postmaster, leading the marchers on horseback, with the Scottsville Band, Junior Order of American Mechanics, and the local Women's Christian Temperance Union is an iconic image of Southern summertime. The band was large, with lots of brass, white trousers, blue blazers, and captain's hats. Flags waved, floats were decorated, and women watched from the sidewalks in long white dresses.

Mayor Raymon Thacker remembers that between 1914 and the early 1940s, various groups would organize a July Fourth parade, including the Veterans of Foreign Wars, Chamber of Commerce, and the town. In 1935, the Scottsville Museum website notes, the *Scottsville News* reported "Nothing Doing" that year: "All signs point to a safe and sane and extremely quiet Fourth in Scottsville today. So far as is known, no celebration of any kind is planned...."

At that time, town baseball was popular, as well as homemade lemonade and ice cream. Virginia cookbooks dating to 1860 have recipes for chicken fricassee, iced calf's foot jelly, drop and beaten biscuits, cherry pudding, and cakes with 12 eggs. Summer activities reported by T. Ellison Bruce in his "Letters of Courtship" to Mary Estes Brown, 1911-1915 (available in the Local History Corner at the Library), include picnics, "porch parties," dances, and tent revival meetings. In July 1915, there was a minstrel show and, another year, an operetta with a lawn party, but he does not mention a parade.

In 1936, Thacker recalls, he and Harold Parr, a Scottsville

businessman, organized the Scottsville Fire Department. Until then, the Scottsville Fire Battalion fought fires with two hoses pulled on wheels. In the 1920s, a block of south Main burned down when the Charlottesville company, called to assist, could not thread their hoses to Scottsville's hydrants. Around 1942, Mayor Thacker says, the department took on the community activity of organizing the parade yearly.

Well-established by 1958, the town celebration included a horse-drawn buggy carrying Bob Spencer dressed as a clown, a 1922 Ford, Miss VFW Gayle Stargell on the back of a VW bug convertible, and a greased pig contest. Mayor W. R. Pitts and Master of Ceremonies C. F. R. Moon, Jr., in an Uncle Sam costume, reviewed the parade from a platform at the baseball diamond, now Dorrier Park.

Scottsville re-inaugurated the July Fourth parade as the Scottsville Festival in 1974. As then-owner of the Canal Warehouse Frances Joseph wrote in the *Spirit of Scottsville* newspaper, June 29th, 1983: "The town [in 1974] was still recovering from the disastrous flood of June 1972 [Hurricane Agnes]... Scottsville has seen many changes... but looks more prosperous than at the time of the first Festival."

*July Fourth in Scottsville, 1914. Photo courtesy Scottsville Museum.*

The festival of the 1970s and 80s offered a variety of activities. Frances Joseph remembered folk music at the Canal Warehouse and a bluegrass quartet at the museum. Art was displayed, crafts sold, and the museum mounted folk art and antique toy exhibitions. In 1975, the newly opened shopping center raised money for the festival by making the "World's Largest Salad," tossed in a plastic wading pool with ingredients measured by the bushel. The public brought their own bowls and forks.

In 1983, Ruth Self, who had a vintage clothing shop on Main Street, gave an extensive historical fashion show on the museum steps. A main attraction of the festival, then and now, has been the flea market, sometimes held at the canal warehouse, sometimes run by Doris Jones at the old school. The market, Joseph wrote, "gets bigger and better every year." The parade and fireworks, however, have always been the headliners of the holiday. In 1983, the Veterans of Foreign Wars, Post 8169, sponsored the parade. Frances Joseph noted they had sponsored parades in Scottsville "for around 30 years." Fireworks were paid for by donations from community businesses and organized by Duane Karr. In 1983, a record crowd estimated at 8,000 attended.

In 1984, the Scottsville Volunteer Fire Department offered a barbecue, and there were two country music shows, as well as parade awards, including "couple present married the longest" and a trophy for "Best Appearing Band or Drum and Bugle Corp." Patriotic feelings fueled the mid-1970s festivals leading up to the Bicentennial. A flier lists 1974 activities, July 4th-6th, including the VFW parade, craft demonstration and show, museum musicale, town walking tour, needlework exhibit, and folk music concert on the evening of the Fourth, ending with the fireworks sponsored by the Scottsville Chamber of Commerce.

A folded program, paid for by over 30 Scottsville businesses, with a cover showing a packet boat on the canal, lists 1975 events: after the parade, a speech by the state attorney general, Virginia Log Chopping Championships, "open to anyone," children's games run by the Rescue Squad, and the historical pageant ($1 for adults, 50 cents for children) on the Uniroyal plant grounds—now Hyosung.

This was, Bob Spencer says, a "dress rehearsal" for 1976. At the urging of various interests in town, he had quit teaching summer school to take on this production, written by John Randolph Phillips, called "Of Town and the River." There were sound effects, costumes, many scene changes, and a large cast. As reprised 10 years later, the pageant was highlighted by the Yankees riding in on horses to set fire, harmlessly but loudly, to a trash can.

In 1975 and 1976, the local Springtree Community offered a café in the Canal Warehouse to serve lunch—"old-fashioned food at old-fashioned prices." In 1975, the price of a plate lunch was 75 cents. This turned out to be a bit too old-fashioned and was raised "a bit" the next year. The menu included cheese pie, an egg salad sandwich, turkey and rice salad, macaroni salad, potato salad, tossed green salad, bread, and lemonade or iced tea. The community's children helped make and serve the food, and all profits went to the library.

By 1990, ads encouraging viewers to "Celebrate July 4th in Historic Scottsville" included the parade and barbecue, sidewalk sales, and the indoor-outdoor antique show and flea market. The Scottsville Volunteer Fire Department and Chamber of Commerce were sponsoring the parade then, with John Collins the parade marshal,

*Scottsville Band, approximately 1919. Photo by W.E. Burgess, courtesy A. Raymon Thacker Collection.*

and 15 trophies were given in various categories to entrants. In 1992, local storyteller Kathy Coleman offered "local legends and lore" at the museum in the afternoon, and the Scottsville Baptist Church presented a concert of adult and children's choirs in the evening.

The Scottsville Volunteer Fire Department was the sole sponsor by 1993 and added a carnival July 1st through the 3rd. There was music Friday and Saturday nights and fireworks, as well as activities and "events too numerous to list" on the flier. In 1994, the parade began at 6 P.M. on July 4th. There was a ceremony at the end, swearing in the new Town Council members, with presentation of certificates by the Governor of Virginia, George Allen. Then the carnival reopened, and fireworks went off at 9:30. Tim Karr was in charge of the parade.

One treat of the July Fourth parade has been the throwing of candy to onlookers from the floats. Christine Coleman "couldn't wait," as a Brownie Scout, to throw candy in 1995, the Daily Progress reported, so she started handing it out before the parade. Another main characteristic of the parade has been noise: lots of sirens, motorcycles, reenactors' guns, firetrucks and rescue vehicles, delighting many youngsters.

In 1995, St. Anne's Parish of the Episcopal Church sponsored clowns, music, face painting, a pet show, crafts fair, and funnel cakes, and the parade was held at 6 P.M. In 1996, the parade was held once more in the morning. Governor Allen swore in Scottsville's first new mayor in 30 years, Robert K. Spencer, and helped the town honor outgoing mayor Raymon Thacker. Thacker was declared Mayor Emeritus and was presented with a silver plaque. "You'll always be Mayor Thacker," the Progress reported Allen told him. Emily Couric rode in the parade that year, in a car. Allen, as usual, was astride his horse.

The fireworks were postponed by rain in 1998. In 1999, there were about 150 entries in the parade, Tim Karr reported, and David Cupp presented "My Friend Mr. Jefferson" at the Municipal Building. In 2001, the Rural Virginian said Scottsville was "the liveliest place in Central Virginia" on the Fourth. The Lions offered free sight and hearing checks in an equipped trailer at the Shopping Center, and bands played all afternoon in Dorrier Park, as well as in the evening, when Rhythm on the River presented the Scott Ward Band and the Hogwaller Ramblers.

It's been flag-waving, candy-throwing, yard sales, and bluegrass since then, with lots of crowds and difficulty parking. ("You're on your own," Tim Karr told the newspaper.) The firework displays are wonderful, and the sense of the town celebration being a "slice of Americana," as Emily Couric called the event, is strong. Scottsville: home of the brave, especially on the Fourth of July.

*Originally published July 2008*

## 46.

# Scottsville Fire Department

Fire destroyed a house in the historic district on January 28th, the home of Shea Farrar and Mariah Tolton. No one was in the recently remodeled building at the time. A poignant *Daily Progress* photograph shows Bobby Spencer watching the blaze. His grandparents, William and Bettie Pitts, had owned the 98-year-old structure. A second fire that week, during the night, completely gutted a newer brick house on Kidd's Dairy Road in nearby Fluvanna County. Again, no one was home at the time. Two vehicles were also destroyed.

The Scottsville Volunteer Fire Department has responded to such fires and other emergencies in Scottsville and the area since 1905, when the first bucket brigade was established. In 1916, fire hydrants and mains were installed, and the volunteer firefighters raised enough money to buy two hose reel carts pulled by six or eight men each. The first equipped fire truck was purchased after many fundraising events, including a "womanless" beauty pageant in 1942.

Modern technology and training, with support from the community, enhance the fire company's capacities, but the memory of fire in Scottsville lingers. Hay rolls and brush fields burn seasonally. The 1994 fires in the municipal building and Uniroyal plant were contained. The historic house, River View, under restoration by Tim and Sandra Small, suffered damage in 1989. Scottsville's most vivid images of fire come from two major conflagrations, in February 1976, that threatened to burn down blocks of the town.

The newspaper pictures are still frightening. Flames and smoke burst from the windows of the 1909 Traveler's Rest Hotel, near the corner of Routes 6 and 20, outlining trees, casting reflections in the wet streets. Firefighters run as walls collapse. A propane tank explodes. Just as frightening are reports of the worry about the cause of the fires, and the worry that more would happen. A *Washington Star* article reported store owners sleeping "in back rooms armed with shotguns." The *Daily Progress* reported that a Scottsville firefighter said, "This is just as bad as when the Yankees went through here."

*This firefighter takes a breather after snuffing out the fire on Jan. 28. Photo by John Bowers.*

The first fire, February 26th, 1976, broke out about 1:30 a.m. in the Traveler's Rest Hotel, which had been converted to apartments, and was discovered by the only resident of the building. As the fire company arrived, the fire spread to Turner's Exxon station. Both buildings collapsed, and flames shot 200 feet into the air. Only one fire hydrant near the structures was functioning. In fact, only three of 22 in town were operating, according to an article in the *Daily Progress*. The fire chief, Grover Mowbry, said they could have saved the hotel with adequate water. "I'm mad—really mad," the *Progress* reports Mayor Raymon Thacker saying. He believed the Albemarle County Service Authority, which owned the water system, was to blame for the problem, to which they had been alerted the previous year.

The second fire, February 28th, 1976, engulfed the entire block between South Main and Valley Street. Starting at Paulett's Hardware Store, which was destroyed around 10:45 p.m., it spread to the adjacent Methodist church, which was severely damaged. Firefighters went immediately to the river for water with an estimated 300 firemen and 75 to 100 tankers assisting in the effort. "We're even with the river now," the *Star* reported Mayor Thacker stating.

The earlier fire, at the time, was thought possibly to have been accidental. Arson was suspected in the second. The sheriff's office conducted several lie detector tests, though no final assignment of blame was officially made. Town officials worked with county authorities to upgrade the hydrant system. A ramp was constructed to the James River, so fire trucks would have safer access. Paulett's Hardware was rebuilt on Route 20, the Exxon station was rebuilt where it stood, and the Methodist church met briefly in St. John's Episcopal Church until it could use its own annex and rebuild the sanctuary.

The wall along the north side of the Methodist church's parking lot, draped in greenery, is a standing reminder of the disastrous fires. Volunteer firefighters, community members, friends, and neighbors all rose to those occasions. Today, Shea Farrar, Mariah Tolton, and their two children are offered help and support. As Mayor Thacker said in the spring of 1976, "We certainly have hopes of bouncing back."

*Originally published March 2003*

# 47.

# The Beals of Scottsville

Old Hall, across from St. John's Episcopal Church on Bird Street, was the seat of the Beal family from 1850 to 1952. This is an impressive fact by contemporary, peripatetic standards. The house itself is still impressive. Stand by the corner of Bird and Harrison, and feel the simple, weighty grace of it. Our history is still alive.

Jesse Grove, husband of the late Jacqueline Beal Grove, graciously gave an afternoon to talk of the family he's known so long. Through the windows of his house, we could see the white fence and tall pines around Old Hall as he told the often-recited history, always emphasizing that the Beals were "all characters, very outgoing and fun-loving," adding that "they were great storytellers."

The Beals established themselves in Pennsylvania and were probably Quakers, coming from Scotland in the early 18th century, Mr. Grove believes. They came to Scottsville from Eastern Virginia, where some of the family had migrated. Joseph Russell Beal and his brother William Samuel were merchants and acquired a 60-year lease on a lot at the corner of Valley and Bird Streets in 1851 for the princely sum of $65 per year. They built a large brick building that became known, as the family operated stores there over the next 100 years, as the Beal Building. Period dioramic photographs show the building, horse and buggy waiting on the dirt street, with barrels and cases of merchandise on the sidewalk and the name BEAL in large block letters between the windows on the second floor.

"The building across Bird Street," Mr. Grove said, "was also a hotel operated by William Beal after the Civil War. During the three days 'the Yankees were in Scottsville,' General Sheridan's Chief of

Cavalry, Wesley Merritt, used Old Hall as a headquarters. The Beal family lived in the basement."

Old Hall was built by Benjamin Magruder, a lawyer who worked with Thomas Jefferson, in 1830. It was used as a hospital from 1879 to 1883, staffed by doctors John Andrews and Orianna Moon Andrews. There have been very few alterations or additions. The author of the 1937 Works Progress Administration manuscript "Survey of Albemarle County Homes" states, "I would rather not undertake to describe 'Old Hall'—it is the hardest one to do justice to that I have struck."

This is a feeling you might still experience yourself. The house is set back on surrounding lawns, shaded by tall trees and softened by massed boxwoods. Classic magnolias and Southern garden ornaments decorate the lawn. A slate roof tops the house, with chimneys at either gable end of the main wing, and a shorter chimney at a back alcove. The windows 9 over 6 on the main floor and 6 over 6 above are shuttered, with simple white-painted wooden lintels, sills, and iron fittings. The door is framed in single panes of glass, including a rectangular transom, and the entry portico seems truly welcoming. Above it is a balustrade of white, carved spindle work typical of the period.

Old Hall is built in a two-story T-shape of brick, laid on the front wall in Flemish bond—that is, with the short and long faces of the bricks alternating in each row. Other walls are in English

*Jackson Beal, Sr. with granddaughter.*

bond, with courses of the long and short sides of the bricks showing. The WPA author survey continues, "As one approaches the porch with its flight of steps and fluted columns supporting a cross-member with ornate work that is put on with wooden pegs, one is in a small way prepared for the treat that is to follow." These Federal-style details, with Doric frieze and cornice, are balanced and restrained.

The entry hall, the WPA writer noted, "is of unusual beauty." Simple and of excellent proportions, it is divided by a Greek-style arch and has a graceful stairway of mahogany rails and newel posts on the right side that turns to form a balcony before ascending to the second floor. The walls were sparkling white, never done in anything but "old-fashioned whitewash," according to Louise Beal, the family member then living at Old Hall. The living room is on the left, entered by a double cross door. A wide chimney extends into the room, and the fireplace and mantel are, the WPA author notes, an "outstanding example of beauty," supported by fluted columns and ornamented with deeply carved wood designs.

"As we sat in this old room, appropriately furnished with old pieces, one felt the quiet and 'homey' atmosphere of the Old South."

The Beal family helped populate the South. Jackson Beal, Sr. married Mary Emma Bledsoe in 1886 in a big wedding at the Methodist church, followed by a reception with a dance at Old Hall. Their eight children were born in the family home. Jesse Grove tells the story of six of them, including Louise, who lived on at Old Hall and ran her father's insurance business; William, a "well-known character" in Scottsville; Wiley, a merchant who married Violet Walls, sister of Robert Walls, who later owned Old Hall; and Jackson, Jr. This Jackson was Jacqueline Grove's father. He bought the house diagonally across from Old Hall, on the corner of Bird and Harrison Streets. In 1921, he started the funeral business later taken over by the Thacker brothers, who worked for him. Jackson's wife, Agnes, ran the James River Market, across from the Beal Building on Bird Street, from 1935 to 1967.

Louise Beal, who sat with the WPA writer after showing him from the basement to the top floor rooms, from the old nursery to the back porch, participated with the rest of her family in local politics.

There is one last picture of her in Virginia Moore's *Scottsville on the James* (1969), standing "as usual in front of the polling place (the fireman's hall), ringing a bell and passing out hard candies" during an election. "Her famous bell," Jesse Grove says.

There were four William Beals in Scottsville's history, including one who bought "Chicken Roost," just beyond the Fluvanna border along current Route 6, and planned to make his millions mining silica there—a plan that failed to materialize.

Jesse Grove remembers hearing many Beal stories and has the many genealogical papers, deeds, newspaper clippings, and a very well-thumbed *Scottsville on the James* that his wife Jacqueline saved and used. Memories of Jacqueline herself—active, inquisitive, passionately involved in the community and the ongoing lives of all of us—bubble to the surface. A quiet afternoon spent with Jesse is full of those boisterous, living memories.

*The Jackson Beal Sr. family on the lawn at Old Hall.*

*Originally published April 2003*

# 48.

# Scottsville on the James—
# Life on the Water

"Beginning in 1840, Scottsville flourished as the chief port above Richmond for freight and passenger boats on the James River and Kanawha Canal. The town played a vital role in the opening up of the west," states the historical marker near the bridge in Scottsville. It's instructive and enjoyable to envision this older flourishing Scottsville.

Cities and civilizations have always followed water, before the internal combustion engine or even horses took us over land. Think of the Tigris and Euphrates, think of Lewis and Clark on the Missouri and Columbia. Scottsville was a natural, if eventually dangerous, place to put up buildings, businesses, and a courthouse where all could gather. It is believed that Monacan Indians first settled on our big horseshoe bend.

Then Europeans came up the James and stopped here. Edward Scott, a Goochland sheriff and burgess, patented five-hundred-and-fifty acres of land on the northwest curve of the river in 1732. It could be assumed that the native population, as well as newcomers, saw the dual advantage of fertile lowlands for agriculture and high ground for dwellings. The James, Rivanna, and other rivers would have been traveled in dugout canoes in the earliest times, both for personal transportation and for freight.

As the settlements of whites grew, their economy encompassed tobacco and wheat, and their need for transport grew. Scott's Landing, Columbia, and Howardsville became busy places, with many hogsheads of produce passing through daily. In 1749, a tobacco farmer from the Tye

River area, Robert Rose, devised the Rose tobacco canoe, two dugouts lashed side by side, 60 feet long and capable of carrying nine large barrels laid across the gunwales. These craft were copied widely and used successfully—at least downriver as far as the falls above Richmond—during the last part of the 18th century. Thomas Jefferson was instrumental in encouraging river transport in Albemarle and was proud of his efforts to improve the Rivanna with dams and sluices for better navigation. What was needed, to move more agricultural crops, was even better craft.

A major flood in May 1771 destroyed or damaged many dugouts. There was a great loss of life, too. Since there were fewer and fewer of the large trees needed for the dugouts, the batteau was born—"a unique Virginia invention," according to Minnie Lee McGehee and William C. Trout III in their book published by the Fluvanna County Historical Society in 2001, *Mr. Jefferson's River: The Rivanna*. The credit goes to Benjamin and Anthony Rucker of Amherst County, who later patented the design of these large, shallow-draft freighters. Thomas Jefferson wrote in his account book for April 29th, 1775, that he watched his neighbor launch the new "battoe."

What the craft looked like was a matter of conjecture until construction for an office building at the base of Capitol Hill in Richmond uncovered the silted ruins of five batteaux in the Great Basin of the James River and Kanawha Canal. Eventually, remains of 48 batteaux would be found.

Also called a tobacco or market boat, these craft took their name from the French word for boat, bateau, and follow lines of the Nova Scotia dory, which is descended from French fishing boats. The Virginia Canals and Navigation Society has researched and chosen the current American spelling, batteau. The craft is keel-less, to slip sideways across river currents or around rocks when necessary, and flat-bottomed. It can float in a foot of water. Pointed at both ends and steered with one or two sweeps, 12 to 15 feet long, fixed to the decking, the batteaux are generally 50 to 60 feet long, six to eight feet wide, and two feet deep. French fur trappers used a similar but heavier craft in Canada. Ruckers' batteau was widely popular and was soon used as far west as the Ohio River.

The batteaux usually carried a three-man crew, often free blacks or slaves. Going with the current downriver, two were needed to fend off the rocks with long poles, while the third steered with the sweep in the back. They were reported to go from Lynchburg to Richmond, fully loaded, in three to five days. Upstream was harder. Often the crew set planks over the gunwales to avoid cargo on the floor of the batteaux and walked along these planks after setting their poles into the riverbed. Sometimes the crew had to get into the water to haul the craft by hand and with ropes. The trip from Richmond to Lynchburg would average ten days. Imagine what it was in low water!

But onwards the batteaux went, proud and strong crew camping at night, cooking along the riverbank or on a dirt or ceramic hearth in the boat. Virginia Moore, in *Virginia is a State of Mind*, says, "rowers' rations consisted of sixty pounds of bacon and two bushels of meal apiece per trip, with whatever trimmings they could filch from water, bag, barrel, or keg." They carried a large portion of the 30 million pounds of tobacco shipped out from Richmond in 1775. The introduction of the batteaux, in fact, caused the tobacco trade in Virginia to increase by 40 percent. The batteaux also carried coal by 1800, as well as pig iron, lime and marble, firewood and barrel staves, hemp for rope, beeswax, grain, and its value-added product, whiskey. On the return trips to upland Virginia, the batteaux transported trade goods, manufactured luxuries, and staples such as molasses, sugar, coffee, salt, and rum.

This "old time boating on the James," as David Brown quotes a nostalgic riverman in his *Batteaux* (published with his evocative photographs in 1988), enhanced the economy of Virginia as the state grew westward and made Scottsville a boomtown full of taverns and the bustling, grand canal warehouse. In 1830 alone, batteaux in Scottsville were loaded with 25,000 barrels of flour, 600 hogshead of tobacco, and 50,000 bushels of wheat—as well as other produce from the surrounding area—for shipping to Richmond. The boatmen were often romanticized in literature and journalism. But it was a grueling life and a difficult means of transport, dependent on weather and independent shippers, coming to a halt in extreme low water and thereby stranding farmers and planters with crops harvested and ready for market. Progress demanded a new technology.

Taming the rocky James, as well as the Rivanna, had begun with dry, stone-constructed wing dams, encouraging the formation of calm, shallow pools and sluices, channels providing deeper water for the laden batteaux. There were constant calls from citizens for clearing rocks, snags, and other obstructions from the navigable sections of the rivers. The turning basin in Richmond improved the ability of batteaux to maneuver and lowered the cost of shipping. The next step, envisioned of course by Thomas Jefferson, was the canal.

The James River and Kanawha Canal was part of an economic development that was to bring agricultural products from the Ohio Valley and points east to shipping centers along the coast. It could even, eventually, unite Virginia and New Orleans. The company

*In 1748, Rev. Robert Rose's carpenter, Richard Ripley, constructed a double dugout canoe for the purpose of carrying tobacco from Rose Isle (Roseland, Nelson Co., Virginia) to market in Richmond, Virginia. In May 1749, The James River overflowed its banks and the double dugout canoe was lost at Seven Island (between the mouths of Hardware and Slate Rivers, downstream from Scottsville, Virginia). In 2002, Howard Williams created a replica of the Double Dugout Tobacco Canoe with 3 large "hogshead" barrels. It was launched at Scottsville, VA during the drought and anchored in the James River for the winter. In February 2003, the James River flooded its banks to 23' at Scottsville, VA. The Double Dugout Tobacco Canoe floated away. Can you find it? Howard Williams, P.O. Box 123, Covesville, VA 22931. Story and picture are by Diane Easley.*

began this herculean task after re-incorporation as the Second James River Company in 1820. Old locks and canals were to be rebuilt, with new ones promised upriver to Covington, where a road would proceed around the falls of the Kanawha, and then the river would be cleared of obstructions to Ohio.

Progress always has a price, and for the James River Co., the price was far more than expected. Development ceased in 1828, with 27 miles of canal from Richmond to Maidens and seven-and-a-half miles through the Blue Ridge to Balcony Falls. But the dream didn't die, and in 1832, a company was established to carry on west: the James River and Kanawha Canal Company. They proposed to start the work at Scottsville.

Despite complaints, elaborated by Virginia Moore in *Scottsville on the James*, and sounding quite contemporary in concern for citizen-government relationships, the project began with the turning basin, now the heart of Canal Basin Square. Many Irish workers—and later, African Americans—were hired to dig the basin and canal. In July 1840, James River water filled the first section of the canal. Work proceeded, and by December, traffic up and down the towpath went to Lynchburg.

Batteaux operated on the canal, pulled by mule or horse, and continued to carry freight. Packet boats took mail and passengers, and a new era of romance began in 1851. While some travelers complained of crowding, others loved the packet boat journey. At locks along the way, crowds gathered to cheer. Virginia Moore says, "For twelve years, the packet boat horn was the most exciting sound in . . . Buckingham, Fluvanna, [and] Albemarle . . . Counties: trah-nahn-nnnnn. You could hear it far up in the hills. These packets . . . were . . . the arch enemies and ultimate destroyers of the old, merry, bowling stagecoaches. . . ."

Photographs show these boats, 60 to 90 feet long, hauled by lines hitched to horses or mules, with crew and passengers often carried atop the boats' superstructure. Below was a cabin acting as a dining room and sleeping quarters, with a kitchen behind. Many found the ride calm and soothing, and the scenery beautiful. Frequent calls of "low bridge"—there were 135 such in all—obliged them to duck carefully. Locks raised and lowered the boats along their way. These packet boats, despite the ire they raised in "old time" batteaumen, were remembered fondly by most people along the river.

The packet boat trip from Scottsville to Richmond left daily, at 11 a.m., arriving in Richmond the next day at 8 p.m., or vice versa. One regularly scheduled packet was called the Farmer, Captain G. Wythe Munford, and one was the Plough-Boy. The Richmond Business Directory, undated, advertises that "persons traveling on these Packet can get all their meals on Board." There were 13 stops between Scottsville and Richmond. The cost of a ticket was $5.27. Trips also left daily for Lynchburg. In the Scottsville Library's Local History Corner is a small copy of Colton's Traveler and Tourist's Route Book (1850), listing the canal traffic from Maine to Illinois, as well as stage and rail lines. Our town is listed there as Scott's Ferry and stands next to Warren and Warminster, now nonexistent as towns, lost to modern traffic. Scottsville itself, in 1850, was little suspecting that the railroads soon would become the most effective, inexpensive way to transport goods and people after the Union troops in the Civil War broke up the canal, upon which, as Virginia Moore puts it, "Scottsville's goose was cooked."

Today, Scottsville can look forward to continued visits from travelers and tourists, coming in cars from all points, and to living here comfortably ourselves. Our products and manufactured goods are sent by truck, for the most part, but we enjoy the renewal given us by the Batteau Festival, begun in 1986 by Joe Ayers of Columbia, who first spearheaded the recreation of a batteau, and to the pleasures of our new park, the Canal Basin Square.

*Originally published June 2003*

# 49.

# Scottsville "Blows Off the Lid"

Prohibition, the "noble experiment," as President Herbert Hoover called it, changed American life during its enforcement, 1920-1933, and—arguably—continues to change it through current times as well. The attempt to legislate "healthier people, safer cities, and more efficient society" failed. Instead, the era is remembered as the Jazz Age, characterized by flappers and speakeasies, organized crime, and bootleg gin.

Virginia Moore notes that, during this period, "Scottsville blew off the lid on Saturday nights....The town policeman . . . had his hands full." While homemade ice cream parties and a booming economy make more idyllic small town stories, this other side of civic life, adjusting to the government's first attempt to limit personal liberties with the full weight of the Constitution, should offer us a more nuanced picture of our little town. Most of these stories are still hidden.

Alcohol consumption and civic life, in fact, seem to go hand in hand. By 1748, just after it was organized in that famous February 1745 meeting near Scottsville, Albemarle County had issued licenses for "over ten" taverns, inns, or ordinaries where alcohol could be sold. There were two taverns "at the courthouse" and one "opposite the courthouse." Thomas Jefferson, in his farm book, made note of the distillery in nearby Milton. Closer to Scottsville, there was a distillery in Warren, established in 1796, owned by Samuel Shelton. Edna Anderson says she wrote a high school report on the distillery, tied to extensive farming in the area and great hopes for Warren's growth and importance. She no longer has the paper.

The Whiskey Rebellion in Pennsylvania, 1794, gauged the depth of popular dissatisfaction with paying taxes on alcohol. Many people in the region made their own, utilizing grain or fruit they grew. "Papa used to make it all the time," Earl Hamner has one of his spinster sisters in *The Homecoming* tell Clay-Boy. "It gives us something to do in our old age . . . and it makes people happy...."

When the Works Progress Administration (WPA) surveyed buildings in Virginia in 1936, they heard from "older citizens" in Scottsville about a one-and-a-half story brick building, 20 feet square, between Main Street and the canal area at the east end of town. It had been vacant for years, was torn down in 1933 but re-membered as a store Peter Fields Jefferson ran. (Fields is the name used in R. E. Hannum's report. The Scottsville Museum website tells us that Thomas' nephew, Peter Fields—a name from the maternal side of the family—Jefferson bought Mt. Walla in 1822.)

The report, available on the Library of Virginia website, continues: "It is said that Mr. Jefferson sold whiskey here, but had a peculiar way of dispensing it. He kept it in a room separate from the store. When a customer wanted his jug filled, Mr. Jefferson would enter the other room and close the door, slip a panel and reach his hand out

*Dispensary building, with Town Council chambers upstairs, Main Street Scottsville, circa 1914. Legal alcohol could be bought only in stamped bottles there. (Photo used by Rebecca Jane Bruce in her "Letter of Courtship" with no further information.)*

for the jug, fill it and pass it through the hole to the purchaser. He was never seen during the transaction and often stated that, 'No one ever saw me sell a drop of liquor.'"

People in Scottsville remember a time when there were as many as ten saloons. Raymon Thacker says, "I was a little teeny fellow when I became aware that whiskey was sold in bar rooms," one at the corner of Valley and Main, one at the far end of East Main. To control the sale of alcohol—and reap some profit from it—Virginia enacted dispensary laws around 1900-1911. In Farmville in April 1901, all saloons were closed by this law, and legal alcohol could be bought only in stamped bottles at the dispensary. We assume the same was true for Scottsville.

Our dispensary building was a two-story brick structure in what is partly the open space and partly the police office at the southeast corner of Valley and Main. The mayor's office and council chambers were upstairs. It had been a school from 1876-1906, Raymon Thacker remembers; later it was used as a meat market. Uncle Billy Beal worked in the dispensary, as recalled by Jesse Grove in the Scottsville Museum newsletter #16. In about 1927 or 1928, Thacker says, Dr. Harris successfully petitioned the town council to allow him to buy the building. He tore it down "brick by brick" to build his own house on another site.

On the matter of profit to the Commonwealth, the *New York Times* reported in late 1900 that after six months of sales, the dispensary business in Franklin returned one quarter of its sales, $150, to Virginia. This would be at least $3,000 in today's economy. This trial run helped open all the state to the dispensary law.

But during this time, there was a vigorous movement for Prohibition in Virginia. The effort can be traced at least from the 1840s. During World War I, when the men were away, Thacker says, "the women took the chance to get the Volstead Act passed." This October 1919 legislation closed loopholes in the 18th Amendment, ratified in January 1919, which prohibited only the manufacture, sale, and transportation of beverage alcohol. The Volstead Act defined "intoxicating liquor" as "over one-half of one percent alcohol," banning "medicinal beer" but allowing a half-pint of rum, brandy, or whiskey to be sold by doctor's prescription to an individual every ten days.

Jonathan Pitts, Civil War veteran and Scottsville resident, is remembered by Thomas Cleveland Sadler in his 1971 typescript, "Memories of Bygone Days," in the Local History Corner of the Scottsville library. Pitts, in his weakened later days, said to his grandson Laurie Pitts, "The [Temperance] Movement was started by a bunch of fanatic women. I am nearly 100 years old. I don't remember taking my first drink. I have drank all of my life, but when I die, some of these women will say, 'Poor old man John Pitts killed himself drinking.'"

Sadler continues with a story about Walter Shultz, "who came from a good family....He lived a mile from Scottsville and would go into town, and almost always he would get drunk. They would lock him up and put a fine on him until every cent that he had was gone. They told him that if he got drunk in town anymore, they would have to lock him up but would not put anymore fines on him." And Shultz thanked the officers for this attempt to help him, as he "couldn't resist temptation."

Sadler, who lived near Antioch Church, knew the many characters of this small community. John Tompkins, who lived farther away in Fluvanna County, "was a good worker on Tuesday, Wednesday, Thursday, and Friday of each week, but on Saturday he went to Scottsville. He would walk about seven miles each way unless someone would give him a ride. He would buy a half-gallon jug of corn whiskey, which you could get then for 75 cents.... He would come back home with the jug in a bag over his shoulder . . . and he would say, 'None but the wealthy can afford it,' and proceed to drink all weekend."

"A number of people sold whiskey around town," Raymon Thacker recalls. "There were bootleggers all around Schuyler, Esmont, and some in Scottsville." Bob Spencer adds, "There were some surprising bootleggers in Scottsville." Bill Walker, when he married Patricia Munger, near Antioch, was often taken by her uncle to visit "an old lady who was making plum brandy." He says the sheriff knew she did it but that she "just made enough to get by on," and nobody bothered her. Most of these Prohibition Era stories aren't told publicly now. Connie Geary, co-president of the Scottsville Museum, reports that some have been written up for the museum's oral history project but are sealed until the deaths of the people involved.

Dr. Paul McFarlane, a Scottsville physician and amateur architect, who was interviewed at age 86 in 1987 by Charlie Fry, told of the Masonic lodge having parties during Prohibition with plenty of "punch or cocktails or something like that.... [All the parties] were alcoholic." He reports that there were no speakeasies in town, "but there was delivery, home delivery."

McFarlane tells about a man who'd take orders for quarts at the University of Virginia on Thursday nights when he was studying medicine there, and "a little retail business" run by the Staples near Keene. Once, McFarlane stitched up the forehead of a man who got into a fight in Scottsville. He charged him only three dollars based on how poor the family looked. Dr. Stinson later told him he'd missed a good chance to make money—the man was "the biggest bootlegger around."

McFarlane said he allowed one man to hide his pistol in the doctor's office while he walked Scottsville's streets. This bootlegger told him he would periodically report one of his own stills to the agents, who then broke it up. The bootlegger would rebuild with contributions from the other bootleggers, and the agents would get publicity in the paper. "Oh, you have to do that once in a while."

*Originally published April 2008*

*Part II (next article) originally published May 2008*

# 50.

# The "Whiskey Question": Part II

Long before Prohibition, the "whiskey question" was much on the mind of T. E. Bruce, Scottsville's pharmacist and later mayor, as he patiently wooed the temperance-minded Mary Browne, a Scottsville schoolteacher.

Their often-daily writings are collected as "Letters of Courtship, Mary Estes Browne and Thomas Ellison Bruce, 1911-1915," edited by their daughter Rebecca Jane Bruce, Shirley Dorrier's sister, and available in the Local History Corner of the Scottsville library.

In this collection, Tom describes his growing aversion to the Dispensary. This institution on the corner of Valley and Main was established by Virginia around 1900 to sell alcohol in stamped bottles and return revenue to the Commonwealth.

July 22nd, 1914, Tom writes to "My dear Miss Browne" that "Charles Dorrier [owner of a large general merchandise store in Scottsville] and I circulated the Dispensary petition last week, and got nearly every voter in town to sign a call for an election on September 18. Then if the petition goes through all right, and I have no reason to doubt but that it will, it's good bye Old Dispensary."

Later that month, Mary writes from her parents' home in Palmyra—she commuted this long distance only on weekends and holidays—that she was making paper flowers for a W.C.T.U. (Women's Christian Temperance Union) float for Scottsville's upcoming Cotton Carnival.

But closing down the Dispensary was not to be so easy. The petition was returned by a Charlottesville judge on a technicality, and Bruce reported that "Captain Pitts does not appear to be as enthusiastic as he was some time back." However, Tom heard a stirring temperance speech in August 1914 and became "red-hot" for closing dispensaries statewide, as well as the "great immoral institution" in Scottsville. "[The Dispensary] is just too embarrassing.... I believe if Scottsville people could go away from home and realize how other people look on us, it would not be a necessity to have a vote on the question.... I made a new rule in the drug store yesterday—No more drinks sold on Sunday. I've wanted to do it for some time and moved ahead yesterday to close the store up tight for everything except medicines. I may lose a few customers, but I certainly feel much better about it." The Dispensary was eventually closed around 1927.

Shirley Dorrier, asked about her father's zeal, says that it was Mary, her mother, who was most influential in his stand. She recalls that Bruce's drug store was, during Prohibition, licensed by Dr. Stinson to sell liquor by his prescription, and that in fact Tom Bruce was known for selling the liquor less than discriminately.

Jack Hamner, local history enthusiast and board member for the Scottsville Museum, recently purchased two of Dr. Stinson's prescription record books in an estate sale. Covering the periods from July 1923 to September 1924 and November 1924 to November 1925, the books list identical "medicines": a half-pint of whiskey. "Use as directed," each one reads, or with eggs and milk, to cover ailments listed from colds to "sarcoma," heart disease, measles, and pneumonia.

One woman, in the space of six months, got four pints and went from bronchitis to acute bronchitis to chronic bronchitis; she was still sick the following year. The American Medical Association had disassociated itself from such "folk medicine" in 1916, noting that the efficacy of alcohol in illness was not supported by any study.

Although most of Stinson's prescriptions go to Scottsville area people, including Esmont, Warren, Shores, and Antioch, some of the patients are from Palmyra, Lynchburg, Richmond, and Culpeper. Stinson had to apply yearly, in triplicate, for permission to prescribe liquor. None of the prescriptions could be refilled. The licensed pharmacist could fill "emergency prescriptions," but he and the doctor had to follow regulations to make a subsequent regular prescription for the record. Violations of this process led to a $500 to $1,000 fine, with possible jail time.

After 1920's 18th Amendment to the Constitution enacted Prohibition, and the Volstead Act defined what was meant by "intoxication liquor," people who wanted liquor "continued to obtain it illegally through the misuse of druggists' prescriptions, importation from Canada and the West Indies, local distilling, and re-distillation of industrial alcohol," one historian writes.

Another says, "Prohibition managed, in virtually every respect, to achieve the precise opposite of what its adherents claimed to want, serving mostly to prove the law of unintended consequences. Mainly, Prohibition made alcohol more popular than ever and gave organized crime a foothold in the United States that it has never relinquished."

While I learned no tales to tell about the manufacture of white liquor in Scottsville today, it is easy now to read about raids on stills by a variety of interested officials in Virginia, especially in rural Franklin County, "moonshine capital of the world." Four large stills, run by a "prominent businessman," were broken up there in January 2008 after a large crackdown in the 1990s had seemed to slow the trade.

Doris Ripley Overcash reports that she used to hear people say they were going to make a run to get moonshine, but she thinks they went to Powhatan County. "If they made it around here, they kept it from me." Chub Walsh says, "There was white lightning around, but I don't know where it was made. There used to be a lot of things going on in Scottsville." He and others remember "little signals"—maybe wash hung in a certain way on the line, indicating that liquor was available at a moonshiner's house.

Minnie Reynolds, in her typescript "Hand in Hand Together" (Local History Corner), gives a recipe for whiskey she collected from an older patient when she was director at the Blue Ridge Nursing Home: "Use barrels or boxes. Put in cornmeal and mix . . . cook it . . . then put in sprouted dried ground corn. Let it sit until the meal goes to the bottom. Put it in the still and boil it. It is delicious."

Jack Hamner recalls a story that his "granddaddy went to re-possess a car" for the Scottsville dealership he owned. With a friend, he drove to Langhorne Road, off Route 6 and across from Shirland Farm. As the two slammed their car doors, armed men rose out of the woods across the road and surrounded them, thinking they were revenuers. Alec Wilkinson, writing in *Moonshine* about illegal white liquor distillation in North Carolina, 1985, reports, "Still people used to say that if they ever got a shot at an agent, he might get better, but he'd never get well."

There are other ways to put fear into a moonshiner. Bill Mason remembers a story reported in a local paper about a Nelson County man tending his still in the hills the night Hurricane Camille deluged the region in disastrous rain and flooding. The moonshiner swore to God, "If you get me off this mountain, I'll never make a jug of whiskey again!"

Other moonshiners have had less dramatic times. Leroy Herndon, who farms locally, says, "Everybody back then was making moonshine. It was the number one industry in the area." One of his cousins, who lived near Antioch Road, "made the best." But Leroy's uncle was always looking for the product, cutting into profits. So the cousin would hide half-gallons of his liquor in holes carefully cut into the pasture, covered back up with neat divots of broom straw. The uncle surveyed the pastures on his knees. The cousin also lowered jugs on rope down into hollow maple trees along the Hardware River. His uncle "tore up every pair of pants he had shinnying up all the trees looking for liquor." These are stories, Leroy cautions, people used to tell sitting on the porch on a Sunday afternoon. Kids like himself would be listening to all manner of "lies." "You didn't know what's the truth and what's a story."

The Commonwealth of Virginia has one of the last words in this tale. Prohibition over, as mandated by the 21st Amendment on Dec. 5th, 1933, we became one of 18 "control states" and have operated under the Department of Alcohol Beverage Control since 1934. This agency says its job is "to enhance the quality of life for Virginia citizens by balancing service, revenue, and control in the distribution, sale, and consumption of alcoholic beverages." In the last five years, the ABC estimates, it has contributed "over a billion dollars to the Commonwealth." Since 1936, the ABC has had funds to act against bootlegging and moonshining.

This assures us there is still someone out there tending an operation, well-hidden in the woods, behind fake tombstones, in a barn or even underground, making white liquor and selling it. Probably it is still "delicious."

# INDEX

## A

Abortions, 56, 172

Adcock, Eddie, 138, **142-148,** 196

Adcock, Martha, 147, 196

Albemarle County courthouse site, 193

Albemarle County Service Authority, see Water

Albemarle High School, 151, 186

Alberene stone, 101

Albevanna Springs, 16, 176, 181-182, 216

Algoma (house), log 73

Allen, George, Governor of Virginia, 196, 300

Allison, Tom (1915-2000), SHS principal, 133-134, 243, 187

Ancell, William H., 205

Anderson, D. Wiley (1864-1940), architect, 13, 17, 166-167, **176-183,** 216

Anderson, Captain John Bledsoe, (1819-1911), 11, 177

Anderson, Edna, 23, 271, 286, 315

Anderson, Haden (1920-2012), 130-131

Anderson, Mollie, 17

Andrews, John, 281-282, 306

Apothecary, 93

Architectural Review Board, Scottsville, 126, 190

Ayers, Joe, 314

## B

Baker, Chester, Chevrolet dealership, 76, 293

Baker, Frances, restaurant owner, 76-77

Banks, Scottsville branch, National Bank, 103
Fidelity Bank, 85

Barbershops, 269, **290-295**

Barclay, James T., Disciples of Christ Church, 94, 163, **262-268**

Barclay, Julia Sowers, **262-268**

Barnett, Larry, 291, 295

Barns, Lloyd, 219

Baseball, Scottsville team, **67-74,** 240, 242, 285-96

Batteau, 310; batteau mural, 143, 197